Goodwill Green Acres
1010 Green Acres Rd. A
Eugene, Or. 97408
(541) 343-4332

7/19/2023 11:34:46 AM   Shonna

Wares .Misc	$1.99
Item discount 50%	($1.00)
Wares .Misc	$1.99
Item discount 50%	($1.00)
Men .Misc	$14.99
Item discount 75%	($11.24)
Books\Media .Misc	$3.99
Item discount 75%	($2.99)
Books\Media .Misc	
8 @ $3.99ea.	$31.92
Books\Media .Misc	$3.99
Item discount 75%	($2.99)
Round Up Donation	$0.05

TOTAL   **$39.70**
Visa $39.70
Item count: 14
Trans:40452   Terminal:050017009-019002

THE LIFE & LEGEND OF
BRAS-COUPÉ

*The Fugitive Slave
Who Fought the Law,
Ruled the Swamp,
Danced at Congo Square,
Invented Jazz, and
Died for Love*

BRYAN WAGNER

Louisiana State University Press
Baton Rouge

Published by Louisiana State University Press
Copyright © 2019 by Louisiana State University Press
All rights reserved
Manufactured in the United States of America
First printing

DESIGNER: Michelle A. Neustrom
TYPEFACE: MillerText
PRINTER AND BINDER: Sheridan Books, Inc.

LIBRARY OF CONGRESS CATALOGING-IN-PUBLICATION DATA

Names: Wagner, Bryan, author.
Title: The life and legend of Bras-Coupe : the fugitive slave who fought the law, ruled
    the swamp, danced at Congo Square, invented jazz, and died for love / Bryan Wagner.
Description: Baton Rouge : Louisiana State University Press, [2019] | Includes bibli-
    ographical references and index.
Identifiers: LCCN 2018036953 | ISBN 978-0-8071-7025-0 (cloth : alk. paper)
Subjects: LCSH: Bras-Coupé, –1837. | Fugitive slaves—Louisiana—Biography.
Classification: LCC E450 .W135 2019 | DDC 306.3/62092 [B] —dc23
LC record available at https://lccn.loc.gov/2018036953

CONTENTS

ACKNOWLEDGMENTS

This edition would not have been possible without the support of archivists and librarians in Louisiana. I thank Christina Bryant and Irene Wainwright at the New Orleans Public Library; Rebecca Smith at the Historic New Orleans Collection; Bruce Raeburn, Lynn Abbott, and Alaina Hébert at the Hogan Jazz Archive at Tulane University; Chianta Dorsey at the Amistad Research Center at Tulane University; Florence Jumonville at the Earl K. Long Library at the University of New Orleans; Kathie Bordelon at the Frazar Memorial Library at McNeese State University; Sally Reeves and Siva Blake at the Notarial Archives of Orleans Parish Civil District Court; and Patricia Nugent at Loyola University Library.

Sarah Jessica Johnson generously provided her translation of Louis-Armand Garreau's "Bras Coupé" for inclusion in this volume. Garreau's short story was discovered and printed in its first modern French edition by Éditions Tintamarre of Centenary College in Shreveport, Louisiana. I thank Dana Kress and Fabrice Leroy for their work on this indispensable book series. This edition has also benefited from Kevin Watson's research on Bras Coupé, which is on deposit at the Historic New Orleans Collection.

Material in the introduction to this critical edition has been revised based on suggestions from friends and colleagues. For their generous engagement, I thank Jason Berry, Stephen Best, Kelvin Black, Ray Buffalo, Nahum Chandler, Kwami Coleman, Jeroen Dewulf, Richmond Eustis, Freddi Evans, Jeremy Glick, Gwendolyn Midlo Hall, Saidiya Hartman, Jared Hickman, T. R. Johnson, Ben Lee, Maurice Lee, Eric Lott, Kim Magowan, David Marriott, Jack Matthews, Deborah McDowell, Fred Moten, Sam Otter, Giuliana Perrone, Lloyd Pratt, Kent Puckett, Megan Pugh, Michael Ralph, Joseph Roach, Matt Sakakeeny, Scott Saul, Ned Sublette, Christopher Tomlins, and Edlie

Wong. For their patience and support during the editorial process, I thank Rand Dotson, Judy Loeven, Neal Novak, and Derik Shelor.

I thank Mary Lee Eggart for her careful mapmaking and Richard Campanella for his expert assistance in pinning down locations. For research and production support, I thank Romeissa Belmeliani, Summer Collins, Charlotte Conner, Jim Conner, Dexter Hough-Snee, Linda Kinstler, Geordie Milne, Brian Pavlich, Alexandra Quinn, and Mia Villanueva. For their interest and support, I thank James Bryan Wagner, James Caillier, and Lambert Boissiere. For their own efforts to tell the story of Bras-Coupé, I offer appreciation and respect to the artists Langston Allston, Henry Lipkis, and Demond Melancon. For bringing Bras-Coupé into the lively debate over memorialization and public memory in New Orleans, I thank Bryan Lee, Sue Mobley, and their brilliant collaborators on the Paper Monuments project.

Research for this volume was generously supported by the UC Consortium for Black Studies in California, the Hellman Family Foundation, and the New Orleans Center for the Gulf South at Tulane University. I thank audiences at Boston University, Dartmouth College, Hunter College, Tulane University, and the University of California at Irvine, whose questions and provocations have helped me to explain the story of Bras-Coupé.

The introduction to this edition includes material adapted from my first book, *Disturbing the Peace: Black Culture and the Police Power after Slavery*, which appears courtesy of Harvard University Press. The English translation of Louis-Armand Garreau's "Bras Coupé" first appeared in *Transition* No. 117 (2015) and is reprinted here courtesy of Sarah Jessica Johnson and Indiana University Press. The excerpt from Vernon Loggins's *Where the World Ends* appears courtesy of Louisiana State University Press. Permission to reprint the *Koanga* libretto by Frederick Delius, © Copyright 1935, 1974, and 1980 by the Delius Trust, is granted by Boosey & Hawkes. Inc. Permission to excerpt Herbert Asbury's *The French Quarter*, copyright © 1936 by Alfred A. Knopf, a division of Penguin Random House LLC, copyright renewed 1964 by Edith Evans Asbury, is granted by Alfred A. Knopf, an imprint of the Knopf Doubleday Publishing Group, a division of Penguin Random House LLC (all rights reserved). Permission to reprint J. Andrew Gaulden's "Tiger of the Bayous," which first appeard in *Negro Digest* 5 (1946), is granted by Mae and Mark Gaulden. Permission to excerpt Robert Penn Warren's *Band of Angels* is granted by the William Morris Agency, copyright © 1955. Permission to excerpt Sidney Bechet's *Treat It Gentle: An Autobiography,* copyright © 1960 by Twayne Publishers and Cassell & Company, Ltd., is granted by Hill and Wang, a division of Farrar, Straus and Giroux. Permission to reprint William Gottlieb's photograph of Sidney Bechet is granted by Getty Images. Municipal records on Bras-Coupé appear courtesy of the City Archives, Louisiana Division, New Orleans Public Library. Obvious typographical mistakes in the primary source materials reproduced in this edition have been corrected without notation.

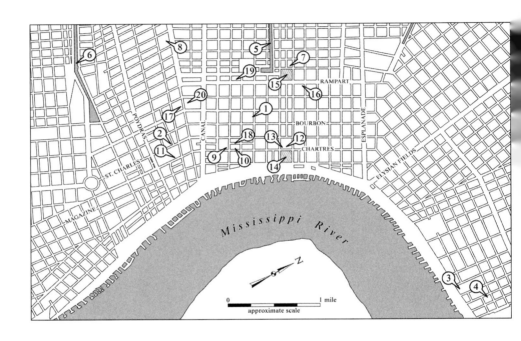

RAMPART

BOURBON

CHARTRES

ESPLANADE

ELYSIAN FIELDS

POYDRAS

CANAL

ST. CHARLES

MAGAZINE

Mississippi River

N

0   1 mile
approximate scale

The Vieux Carré

(1) 112 St. Louis Street. The primary residence of William DeBuys during the time when Bras-Coupé was his slave and when Bras-Coupé was at large in the city. (2) St. Charles and Union Streets. The location of the cotton press owned by William DeBuys. (3) Levee between Piety and Desire Streets. The location of the sawmill owned by William DeBuys. (4) 42 Elmire Street. The primary residence of William DeBuys starting in 1838. (5) Carondelet Canal, where Bras-Coupé is supposed to have robbed and pillaged and where Elsie is drowned by her master in Louis-Armand Garreau's "Bras Coupé." (6) New Basin Canal, where Bras-Coupé is supposed to have robbed and pillaged. (7) Orleans Parish Prison, opened in 1837 when Bras-Coupé was still at large. The construction of this prison was one of the main initiatives of Mayor Denis Prieur. (8) Charity Hospital, fifth building, in service from 1832 to 1936. Several sources, including Garreau's story, suggest that this was where Bras-Coupé's arm was amputated. (9) 41 Bienville Street. The office of the *Louisiana Advertiser*, one of the newspapers arguing for demilitarization and disarming of the New Orleans Police Department. (10) 110 Chartres Street. The office of the *New Orleans Bee*, a bilingual newspaper that reported on Bras-Coupé and the maroon settlements in the cypress swamp. (11) 72 Camp Street. The office of the *New Orleans Picayune*, founded January 1837, another newspaper that reported on Bras-Coupé. (12) St. Louis Cathedral, seat of the Catholic archdiocese and a church site since 1718. (13) The Cabildo, which operated as city hall until the 1850s, included the office of Mayor Denis Prieur and the New Orleans Police Department. Francisco Garcia transported Bras-Coupé's body to the Cabildo in July 1837 to collect his reward from the mayor. (14) Place d'Armes, now Jackson Square, where Bras-Coupé was hung in effigy. (15) Congo Square, a public commons where slaves gathered on Sundays to dance, drum, sing, socialize, and sell wares. Bras-Coupé became associated with Congo Square in 1880, after Cable identified him as one of its most famous performers. (16) 331 Rampart Street. Louis-Armand Garreau's home during his first residence in New Orleans in the early 1840s. Garreau ran a school for boys on the corner, and his wife operated a school for girls in the adjoining building. From 1945 to 1956, this building was J & M Recording Studio, where Cosimo Matassa recorded Fats Domino, Little Richard, Lloyd Price, and many other pioneering rhythm-and-blues musicians. (17) 190 Common Street. This was the office of William C. Black and Company, Cotton Factors, and where George Washington Cable claimed he heard the story of Bras-Coupé. (18) Exchange Alley, between Conti and Bienville Streets. Lafcadio Hearn claimed that it was here at Alexander Dimitry's bookstore that Cable heard the story of Bras-Coupé. (19) 88 Rampart Street. Louis Moreau Gottschalk's residence from 1831 to 1833. (20) Mechanics Institute. Robert Penn Warren places Bras-Coupé here in July 1866 at a constitutional convention attacked by a white supremacist mob.

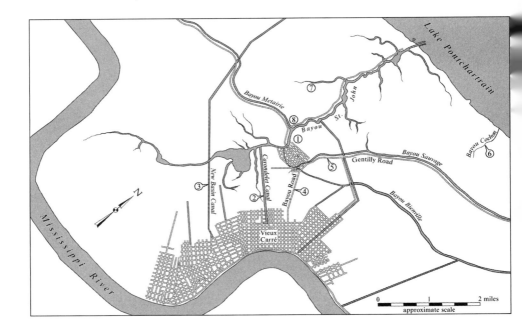

New Orleans and its Surroundings

(1) Estimated location near the guard station by Bayou St. John where Bras-Coupé was shot in the arm and arrested by an auxiliary police patrol in January 1836. (2) Caronde-let Canal, where Bras-Coupé was supposed to have robbed and pillaged and where Elsie was drowned by her master in Louis-Armand Garreau's "Bras Coupé." (3) New Basin Canal, where Bras-Coupé was supposed to have robbed and pillaged. (4) Bayou Road, where Bras-Coupé was supposed to have robbed and pillaged. (5) Gentilly Road, where Bras-Coupé was supposed to have robbed and pillaged. (6) Bayou Cochon, where Bras-Coupé and another maroon named James were alleged to have committed a murder in June 1836. Bras-Coupé was outlawed following this event. (7) Estimated location on Louis Allard's property where Bras-Coupé was shot by police officers in April 1836. Bras-Coupé escaped after he was left for dead by the officers. (8) Estimated location of the cabin where Bras-Coupé was killed by Francisco Garcia.

The Life and Legend of Bras-Coupé

Introduction

Bras-Coupé was one of the most notorious outlaws in the history of New Orleans. After escaping from his master, General William DeBuys, Bras-Coupé became a leader of the maroons who lived in the cypress swamp outside the city. Although he was still called by his old name, Squire, the outlaw became famous as Bras-Coupé ("severed arm" in French) after a limb was amputated following an injury he received from the police. For years, Bras-Coupé and his gang raided stores and taverns on the outskirts of New Orleans. These criminal exploits were widely publicized in newspapers, on wanted posters, and in policy debates among city officials, who held that Bras-Coupé was a threat to public safety, demonstrating the need for well-armed police. In June 1836, Mayor Denis Prieur announced a $250 reward for Bras-Coupé, dead or alive. One year later, Bras-Coupé was betrayed by an accomplice and murdered. His mangled corpse was displayed for several days on the Place d'Armes (now Jackson Square), across from the Cabildo. This gruesome display was supposed to serve as a warning to the city's slave population.[1]

Since the 1830s, Bras-Coupé has been a prominent figure in the folklore of New Orleans. Sometimes he is treated as a villain, and other times he is imagined as a hero, fighting against the rich and powerful like Robin Hood, or more immediately, fighting against slavery like Nanny, Makandal, Boukman, Three-Fingered Jack, and other maroons. Examples from the oral tradition about Bras-Coupé have appeared in newspapers, memoirs, city histories, tourist guides, and ethnographic collections. In the oral tradition, Bras-Coupé was given superpowers. He could breathe fire. He could teleport. His skin, it was said, could not be punctured by bullets. His gaze could turn you to stone. It was suggested, moreover, that Bras-Coupé was an African prince before he was kidnapped and brought to Louisiana. He was the most famous performer at Congo Square, playing a central role in the preservation of African music and dance. Sidney Bechet, one of the most important reed players in the musical history of New Orleans, even proposes in his autobiography, *Treat It Gentle*, that it was Bras-Coupé who invented jazz.[2]

The purpose of this critical edition is to collect and introduce the most important versions of the Bras-Coupé legend from the major phase of its development between the 1830s and the 1960s. Beginning with contemporary newspaper reports, this edition follows the legend as it is adapted in a surprising range of works, including Louis-Armand Garreau's short story "Bras Coupé" (1856); George Washington Cable's novel *The Grandissimes* (1880); Louis Moreau Gottschalk's memoir *Notes of a Pianist* (1881); Frederick Delius's opera *Koanga* (1896); Herbert Asbury's history *The French Quarter* (1936); Lyle Saxon, Edward Dreyer, and Robert Tallant's folklore anthology, *Gumbo Ya-Ya* (1945); and Robert Penn Warren's historical romance, *Band of Angels* (1955), a work that was subsequently made into a film starring Sidney Poitier as Bras-Coupé and Clark Gable as his brooding master.

Drawing evidence from newspapers, conveyance reports, census documents, city directories, police records, treasurer's books and ledgers, public proclamations from the mayor's office, city council minutes, and family histories, this introduction begins by explaining everything we now know about Squire, the historical person who would become legendary—at first locally and then nationally and internationally—as Bras-Coupé. Before he escaped from slavery to the cypress swamp, Bras-Coupé—still known as Squire—was owned by General William DeBuys, the scion of a "good old typical Creole family," the head of which was thought to have been "present with Bienville at the laying out of the city of New Orleans."[3] DeBuys was a leader in the Bataillon d'Orleans in the War of 1812. He served later in life as city postmaster and as Speaker of the House in the Louisiana state legislature before mounting an unsuccessful campaign for governor. When Squire was still his slave, William DeBuys lived at 112 Saint Louis Street (between Bourbon and Dauphine streets in the French Quarter), although soon after he moved to a newly constructed residence at 42 Elmire Street (now Gallier Street) between Greatmen and Casacalvo Streets (now Dauphine and Royal streets in Bywater). The new home on Elmire Street was blocks away from a levee-fronting sawmill owned by DeBuys. Along with a cotton press in the Faubourg St. Marie, the sawmill was one of DeBuys's major investments in the city. DeBuys also owned a large estate in Grand Isle with several houses, docks, stables, thousands of orange trees, and prodigious fields of Sea Island Cotton. He was renowned as a "great fisherman and hunter," and it is a matter of record that DeBuys regularly brought Squire, his favorite slave, on hunting trips. DeBuys gave Squire guns, taught him to shoot, and allowed him to travel freely.[4]

Squire eventually began to leave DeBuys for days and even weeks at a time, a practice known as *petit marronage*, meaning a temporary escape, as opposed to *grand marronage*, which referred to slaves who fled from their masters with no intent to return. During these trips, Squire strengthened his personal connection to the maroon communities in the cypress swamp, whose members included exiles and pariahs of many races—fugitive slaves and free persons of color, Choctaw and Houma Indians, as well as various other refugees, bandits, and wanted criminals. This was a common practice at the time. Many slaves, like Squire, traveled openly into the swamp on the pretense that they were going hunting or fishing. The watchmen at the city gates were supposed to check for passes or the badges that slaves were obliged to wear on their shirts, but in truth this almost never happened. It was easy enough to walk from the city center along the Carondelet Canal, which connected to Bayou St. John, or along Bayou Road and out through Bayou Sauvage, which formed a passable topographic ridge, eventually known as the Gentilly Road, extending all the way to the eastern marshes and the Rigolets. From this main ridge, the maroon settlements that flourished between Bayou Sauvage and Lake Pontchartrain (to the north) and along Bayou Bienvenue and Lake Borgne (to the south) were easy enough to access through smaller passages and waterways, provided you knew where you were going or had a willing and knowledgeable guide. In 1827, a slave woman, who had returned to New Orleans after sixteen years, described one maroon settlement surrounded on all sides by "swamps resembling quick sands" that would "swallow up" any "inexperienced" person who entered their "vortex." She explained that the maroons had "discovered the means of passing through this morass" and built houses on the "small tracts of firm ground" in the swamp, known as "trembling prairies," where they lived in relative peace while raising hogs and poultry and planting "corn, sweet potatoes, and other vegetables."[5]

This traffic between slaves in the city and maroons in the swamp was a matter of concern to authorities who were alarmed by the quick trips made by *petits marrons* like Squire. The *New Orleans Bee,* a bilingual and conservative creole newspaper, condemned the "practice of negroes" carrying "fire arms" into the swamp "under the pretence of killing game." These negroes, the *Bee* suggested, were in continuous contact with the "runaway slaves who are known to infest the swamps in the rear of the city." Hunting was a "plausible pretext for absenting themselves" from the city, but the *Bee* held that the main purpose of these trips was to "supply their comrades with . . . provisions." "The interior of the swamp," the *Bee* added, "is . . . a scene of bloodshed and murder. Dead bodies are not infrequently found in its recesses. These are doubtless the victims of the heartless miscreants that make the swamp their home . . . [who] could neither commit these atrocities nor continue many days in their haunts, if they were not furnished with arms and ammunition" by sympathetic slaves, such as Squire, who were themselves more than likely to turn maroon, once and for all, in their own time.[6]

The maroons in the swamp were socially, politically, and economically intertwined with the population of the city. In the terms coined by Sylviane Diouf, they were borderland maroons, meaning they were adjacent and connected to the city, rather than hinterland maroons, whose settlements were remote and relatively autonomous. An active trade brought manufactured goods (including rifles, metal tools, and clothing) from the city into the swamp as well as building materials (cypress logs), food (roots, fruits, vegetables, herbs, fish, and game), and crafts (reed baskets and wooden bowls) from the swamp into the city. This commerce included smuggled and stolen goods. As marginal actors in the city's economy, maroons played an important role in fencing the illicit merchandise that arrived through the port. There was also a longstanding tradition of hiring maroons for piecework, paying them in cash as well as in bartered goods, a practice that was common in the lumber mills downriver from the city, where maroons would stay to work a day cutting boards after selling their pine and cypress logs. We cannot say for sure, but we can imagine that DeBuys's sawmill on the river between Piety and Desire could have been a place where Squire would have established a personal relationship with maroons.[7]

Squire appears to have made a permanent break with General William DeBuys in 1835. After traveling to the swamp, first with permission, hunting for game, and then absenting himself for longer periods without consent, Squire finally escaped for good and joined the maroons, only to emerge as one of their most fearsome leaders, surviving long enough to become one of the most notorious bandits in the history of New Orleans. For Squire, however, everything changed on January 21, 1836, when a police patrol discovered him in a cabin located on one of the tributaries of Bayou St. John. Resisting arrest, Squire was shot in the arm by a deputized officer, identified elsewhere as Monsieur Fleitas from St. Bernard Parish. Here is a translation of the arrest record:

> Squire, a negro belonging to Mr. DeBuys, was brought to the Post by the Civil Patrol of the Bayou St. John, consisting of Mister Coquet, B. Flaitasse, P. Massia, Auguste Brungier & Philippe Lambert, who arrested him in a cabin near the woods; but since the negro did not want to turn himself in, and since either he or his friend had fired at the Patrol, the Patrol fired as well, seriously injuring said negro. A gun was deposited at the Post and the negro placed in the police jail at two o'clock.

After the injury became infected, Squire's arm was amputated at Charity Hospital in Faubourg St. Marie. Lying prostrate after the operation, enfeebled by an attack of dysentery, Squire was left unguarded. Taking advantage of this lapse in surveillance, Squire leapt through an open window and escaped back to the swamp, an event that launched the major phase of his criminal career.[8]

Following his spectacular escape from the hospital, Squire became both celebrated and reviled throughout New Orleans as Bras-Coupé, the Brigand of the Swamp, thereafter known by an epithet ("Severed Arm") inspired by a wound he suffered from the police. From January to June 1836, Bras-Coupé and his gang of outlaws continued pillaging along Bayou Road and the New Basin Canal, then under construction, becoming increasingly bold over time, even raiding shops near the DeBuys family residence in the First Municipality. All of a sudden, it seemed like Bras-Coupé was everywhere, as crimes that he may or may not have committed were attributed to him. On June 6, 1836, the *New Orleans Bee,* describing a murder attributed to Bras-Coupé and his gang, took the opportunity to demand an all-out war against the maroons. Complaining that the "cypress swamp is now almost full of runaway negroes" and that "robberies are almost daily committed by these runagates," the *Bee* urged Mayor Prieur to bring the full force of his office, including the "police under his authority," to wipe out the maroon settlements. Less than a month later, Prieur followed up on these demands, confirming the decision

The original arrest record reporting Bras-Coupé's injury at the hands of a deputized officer. The injury led to the amputation of his arm. New Orleans City Guard, Reports of the Captain of the Guard 1826–1836, 21–22 Janvier 1836, City Archives, Louisiana Division, New Orleans Public Library, New Orleans, Louisiana. Published courtesy of the New Orleans Public Library.

of the court recorder in the Third Municipality, by outlawing Bras-Coupé, along with one of his comrades, a maroon named James. It was observed that Squire was "un negre marron . . . appartenant à M. DeBuys" (a negro maroon belonging to Mr. DeBuys) who was "coupables de plusieurs déprédations" (guilty of many crimes), including a "muerte horrible" (horrible murder) on Bayou Cochon. Prieur posted a $250 reward for Bras-Coupé, the same for James, and $50 for other members of their gang. The mayor also authorized the establishment of special police units, including newly deputized citizens, "pour les envoyer a la poursuite des marrons qui infestent les bois dans la troisième municipalité" (to prosecute maroons that infest the woods in the Third Municipality).[9]

The city's propaganda campaign against Bras-Coupé was shaped by specific events happening during the eighteenth months—January 21, 1836 to July 18, 1837—when the fugitive was at large in the swamp. This was a time when the city was exceptionally unstable, both economically, as unemployment exploded and banks failed due to an international financial crisis that hit New Orleans with particular force, and also politically, as the government tried to implement an ill-conceived plan to partition the city into three municipalities, a plan that was put into effect in March 1836, two months after Bras-Coupé leapt through his hospital window. This instability caused widespread anxiety that in turn intensified the moral panic about Bras-Coupé.[10]

In these years, there was also intense controversy about the composition of the city's police department, a controversy that reached its climax during the manhunt for Bras-Coupé. This controversy began in 1830 when a homicide committed by a police officer in the course of duty prompted the city council to pass a law disbanding the department. Mayor Prieur vetoed the legislation, but for years to come the reformers would continue to press their case. Newspapers such as the *Louisiana Advertiser* published editorials protesting against the police's right to deadly force, describing the department as a "remnant of barbarism" in a "land of liberty." Above all, the reformers wanted to take the guns from the police. The campaign lasted for years, triggering policy changes, including a new regulation that said that three warnings had to be given before violence could become an option. In January 1836—the same week Bras-Coupé lost his arm and escaped Charity Hospital—the city council proposed an ordinance removing all weapons from the police except their spontoons, a slightly larger version of what we now call nightsticks. Prieur opposed the measure, but it was adopted over his objections. Implementation proved awkward, for the change came as the city was being partitioned, but in the main, the reformers got their wish. The police lost their guns.[11]

In the wake of this new legislation, Prieur remained one of the most vocal defenders of the city guard's right to deadly force. "Let us ameliorate it, improve it, but let us not change it," Prieur wrote about the department, responding to the fifth article in the council's reform proposal in January 1836, which dictated that a police officer should be outfitted with a "spontoon" and a "rattle" but nothing more. Prieur saw this as nonsense. Prieur believed the proper model for the department was not the constable-watch systems on the northeastern seaboard, where watchmen were armed with small clubs, but the Charleston police, whose officers were "armed as soldiers" and drilled with even greater precision than their counterparts in New Orleans. Charleston was the better model for New Orleans, Prieur explained, due to the "similarity" between "their social system and ours." The self-evident similarity to which Prieur referred, of course, was slavery.[12]

In the months after the city guard lost their guns, Bras-Coupé became a centerpiece for the propaganda campaign in support of the police's right to deadly force. In a city as violent as New Orleans, with a sizable population of transient river workers, it would have been easy to refer to many familiar situations where it would be good for the police to have guns, but Prieur and other supporters of the city guard decided to invoke a more traditional rationale. When they argued that the police needed heavy weapons to protect the city, the threat they summoned was from slavery, and in the months after the passage of the reform measure, the threat posed by slavery was best exemplified by Bras-Coupé. Responding to the reformers, the police began to publicize their campaign against Bras-Coupé, with wanted posters and advertisments announcing the reward for his capture, dead or alive. Newspapers aligned with the city guard detailed Bras-Coupé's crimes, demanding the police be given sufficient resources to combat the fugitive and his gang. Who will defend you from Bras-Coupé, they suggested, if not the police? How will the police defend you if they are stripped of their ability to act by all available means? Singled out from the swamp, made larger than life, Bras-Coupé was named as an exemplary threat, the type of threat to which the reformers had no answer.[13]

The proclamation of outlawry for Squire and James, signed by the recorder of the Third Municipality, later to be approved by Denis Prieur. Ordinances and Resolutions, Third Municipality, vol. 1, Résolution du 2 Juillet 1836, City Archives, Louisiana Division, New Orleans Public Library, New Orleans, Louisiana. Published courtesy of the New Orleans Public Library.

During the police manhunt, Bras-Coupé remained a topic of "constant discussion in the city." Prieur and his allies dramatized their argument about Bras-Coupé with wanted posters and newspaper editorials, but their most effective means of communication was the proclamation of outlawry and the associated reward. Rumors swirled about the amount of the reward. Some said the reward was $1,000, $2,000, or as much as $6,000 (or "6000 piasters," the term that was used in the city at the time for United States dollars). No less than the missing arm, the rumored reward posted by Mayor Prieur became a key aspect of the legend, focusing the story of the police manhunt and indicating the gravity of the public threat posed by Bras-Coupé.[14]

Bras-Coupé remained at large and unscathed until April 1837. One likely reason for his success in eluding the police is that he seems to have shifted his base of operations in the months after he was outlawed. When he published his proclamation on Bras-Coupé, Prieur ordered the police to focus their attention on the woods beyond the Third Municipality by Bayou Sauvage and Bayou Bienvenue where Bras-Coupé had most recently been active. Subsequent reports indicate that Bras-Coupé moved westward to Bayou St. John. It was there that the fugitive was discovered the following April by two police officers, on an unenclosed tract belonging to Louis Allard, likely on the land that is now City Park. Bras-Coupé fired a gun at one of the officers, missing him. The officer fired back, hitting Bras-Coupé in the torso. Bras-Coupé fled the scene but soon collapsed. The officers left him for dead, planning to dispatch a patrol to collect his corpse, but the body was gone when the patrol arrived. Bras-Coupé was not dead after all.[15]

Bras-Coupé's criminal career slowed down after this near-fatal encounter. He appears to have remained in the vicinity of Bayou St. John, nursing his wounds. Finally, he was killed on July 18, 1837, by Francisco Garcia. Garcia claimed that he was fishing on the Petite Rivière near the base of Bayou St. John when Bras-Coupé fired a rifle at him, nearly hitting his boat. In his statement to the mayor's office, Garcia said that he pursued Bras-Coupé and struck him three times with a crowbar, killing him. Garcia wrapped up the body and brought it to the Cabildo, where he demanded his reward. Garcia was reportedly outraged that the reward was only $250 and not the $2,000 he expected to receive. At the time, many believed Garcia's encounter with Bras-Coupé was no coincidence. It was rumored that Garcia was an acquaintance, and perhaps even a member of Bras-Coupé's gang, and that he decided to betray Bras-Coupé after learning about the outsized reward that the mayor had supposedly offered. The payment of the reward is confirmed in the city treasurer's records and in the financial ledger of the Third Municipality, which record $250 paid on July 20 as a "dépense extraordinaire" (extraordinary expense) to "F. Garcia" for "l'arrestation du nègre Squire" (the arrest of the negro Squire).[16]

After Squire was brought to the Cabildo, Prieur ordered that his corpse should be put on display in the Place d'Armes as a warning to the city's slave population. "That thousands and thousands rushed to that historic square to take a look at the ghastly remains," Henry Castellanos remembers, "is a matter of notoriety." Castellanos adds: "No Mardi Gras procession, no special pageant that I know . . . ever attracted such surging crowds as were witnessed under that broiling, solstitial sun. Men, women, children; whites and blacks, freedmen and slaves; professional men and laborers in their working blouses, all seemed to have gathered there to satisfy their morbid curiosity." With his skull "crushed and mangled" by Francisco Garcia's crowbar and his torso lacerated with the "unhealed and gaping wounds . . . inflicted by the city guard" in the near-fatal encounter three months earlier by Bayou St. John, Bras-Coupé came to an ignominious end.[17]

While his corpse was still on display in front of the Cabildo, local newspapers published comprehensive obituaries reviewing Bras-Coupé's career. "The negro Squire," the *Bee* begins, "so celebrated for his brigandism, and who had obtained the appellation of *bras coupé* from the circumstance of his having lost one of his arms in resisting the patrol who attempted to arrest him, has at length paid the forfeiture of his accumulated crimes and enormities." The obituary in the *Bee* continues by supplying further details of Bras-Coupé's injury and escape; his violent crimes, including the alleged kidnapping and murder of an unnamed woman; the rumor of the inflated reward; and the circumstances of his death, from the fatal encounter with Francisco Garcia to the gruesome display of his body on the Place d'Armes. The obituary in the *Bee* was anticipated by a similar article in the *New Orleans Picayune*. "It will be remembered by all our citizens," the *Picayune* proposes, "that Squire was the negro who so long prowled about the marshes in the rear of the city. . . . The annals of the city furnish records of his cruelty, crime, and murder." The *Picayune's* death notice, which includes not only details of crime but a call for the police to scour the swamp and destroy the maroon settlements, eventually reached not only a local but also a national audience, as it was reprinted by a number of newspapers, in large cities and small towns, including the *New York Spectator, Boston Courier, Huntsville Democrat, Natchez Weekly Courier, Philadelphia Public Ledger, Cleveland Daily Herald, Jacksonville Republican, Long-Island Star, Vermont Phoenix*, and *Wisconsin Territorial Gazette*.[18]

Bras-Coupé's career was also covered in the northern abolitionist press. William Lloyd Garrison's antislavery newspaper, the *Liberator,* for example, published articles on Bras-Coupé in July 1836, when he was outlawed; in April 1837, when it was rumored he was caught by the police; and in August 1837, after he was killed by Francisco Garcia. The *Liberator* continued to invoke Bras-Coupé for years to come as an example of the lengths to which slaves were driven to win their freedom. Bras-Coupé was described in the same way—as a freedom fighter, not a villain—in other abolitionist publications, such as *The Friend of Man,* the newspaper published by the New York Anti-Slavery Society; in abolitionist annuals, including the 1839 edition of the *Anti-Slavery Almanac*; and in slave narratives, including Aaron's *The Light and Truth of Slavery* (1845). In September 1837, an abolitionist newspaper, *Human Rights,* based in New York City, reprinted the death notice that appeared in the *New Orleans Picayune. Human Rights* framed the reprinted article with a critical commentary, "A Hero in the Swamps of New Orleans," which replied point-for-point to the *Picayune.* In this commentary, *Human Rights* posed a series of rhetorical questions about Bras-Coupé:

> What white hero ever fought more bravely for liberty, or with better cause, than he whose story is given below?—Why is he not honored by those who honor chivalry? He may have been a "villain" and a "scoundrel" but what inducement did he have to be otherwise? What right have slaveholders to execrate him for doing what every one of them avows that he would do in the same case? What a state of society does this story exhibit! A whole city in terror at the fugitive tenants of a swamp! The authorities decreeing a triumph over, and the grand exhibition of the body of an outlaw! And how infatuated are those oppressors to hope that such exhibitions will cure their whip-galled vassals of the love of liberty!

The *Picayune,* in turn, reprinted the article from *Human Rights,* adding a reply: "What language is this for civilized white men?—What language for men calling themselves disciples of that Religion whose attributes are peace and brotherly love? We hate your black duplicity—we hate your papers, and we hate yourselves." The *Picayune's* response ends by daring the editor of *Human Rights* to "*come in person*" to New Orleans, summoning him, by implication, to a duel.[19]

Among abolitionists on both sides of the Atlantic Ocean, Bras-Coupé was understood as a romantic hero and as a tragic symbol of the wrongs of slavery. These are the common themes in the representation of Bras-Coupé in articles in abolitionist newspapers like *Human Rights* and the *Liberator* and also in antislavery literature. It is in this tragic mode that Bras-Coupé is first represented in fiction. The short story "Bras Coupé" (1856) was authored by Louis-Armand Garreau, an émigré journalist and educator who ran a school for boys in the 1840s, located across from Congo Square at the corner of Rampart and Dumaine Streets. Garreau wrote for newspapers in the city, including *Revue Louisianaise,* and edited a short-lived weekly, *Democritus,* which lasted for nine issues. After returning to France in 1850, Garreau published several Louisiana-based stories. "Bras Coupé" was published in *Les Cinq Centimes Illustrés,* a feuilleton newspaper based in Paris that was priced and designed to appeal to a mass audience. "Bras Coupé" was one of four short stories Garreau published in *Les Cinq Centimes Illustrés* between February and October 1856 as "Souvenirs D'Outre-mer" (Overseas Memories). "Bras Coupé" followed another story in the series, "Un Nègre Marron" (A Negro Maroon). Both stories feature fugitive slaves in conflict with a cruel master named "Monsieur D—," which is possibly a reference to General William DeBuys. Other names in Garreau's short story are altered as well. In the story, Squire is "Jim" before he is turned into "Bras Coupé." Francisco Garcia is named "Jacoppo Burmudez." In other respects, Garreau's story conforms to oral tradition, narrating the loss of the arm, the escape from the hospital, the police campaign in the cypress swamp, Garcia's betrayal, and the rumored reward. Garreau also represents the legend's setting with unusual and imaginative detail, taking us to the bank of the Carondelet Canal where Elsie is murdered, and to the grog shops on Bayou St. John where Elsie is accused of theft and Jim returns to pillage.[20]

Like several other adaptations in literature, Garreau's short story deviates from the oral tradition by embedding Bras Coupé in a love story, in this case the story of Jim and Elsie, two slaves belonging to Monsieur D—. When Elsie, pregnant with Jim's child, is accused of stealing, Monsieur D— has her whipped. When Elsie threatens suicide, Monsieur D— drowns her in the Carondelet Canal. These events give the legend a different emotional gravity, propelling its tragedy through the murder of a loved one and unborn child. This change serves the story's antislavery message by strengthening identification with Bras Coupé. In the story, events represented in the newspapers as wanton criminality become psychologically motivated and morally justified as Bras Coupé seeks vengeance for a specific and heart-wrenching wrong done to his family.

Garreau's short story is also an early example of the international diffusion of the Bras Coupé legend. It is unlikely that Garreau would have been able to publish the story in Louisiana, given its antislavery message, and Garreau says as much in "Un Nègre Marron," the companion story, in which his narrator, a newly hired overseer shocked by Monsieur D—'s cruelty to his slaves, confides to the reader that "il est prudent à New Orleans de cacher certains sentiments philanthropiques et de ne pas faire une réputation d'abolitioniste" (in New Orleans it is prudent to hide certain philanthropic sentiments so as not to establish a reputation as an abolitionist).[21]

After Garreau's story, Bras-Coupé would not be represented again in literature for several decades. In the meantime, people in New Orleans continued to share stories about him. Sources confirm that Bras-Coupé remained one of the most popular characters in the city's oral tradition. He is described, for instance, in *The Historical Sketch-Book and Guide to New Orleans* (1885) as a "hero of the swamps" whose "sanguinary exploits" were widely known throughout the "whole of Louisiana." Herbert Asbury agrees that the legend of Bras-Coupé was told across the state, but he insists on its preeminence within the "folklore of the New Orleans Negroes." Henry Castellanos emphasizes that the legend was Janus-faced. Sometimes Bras-Coupé was imagined as "Robin Hood of the swamps," and other times he was treated as a monster whose name was "pronounced in hushed and subdued tones." An article from the *West Baton Rouge Sugar Planter*, for example, describes Bras-Coupé as a gothic fiend in the city's oral tradition. "Everybody knew," the article explains, "that Bras Coupe was . . . a great villain and had often been shot at by more courageous hunters, but always escaped without a wound, until, at last, it was commonly believed that he bore a charmed life being under the special care of the Evil One." The article recalls in particular the spine-chilling stories told to the city's youth. "Parents," the article continues, "would scare refractory small children into the most abject submission by simply threatening them with old Bras Coupe, while those of a larger growth could be frightened from any mischief they had in contemplation by suggesting a probable encounter with that demon of the swamps." The writer recalls as well times when he was "wandering in search of blackberries" in the woods or swimming in the "not over clean water" in the Carondelet Canal, and one of his companions would scream, "'Here he comes!'" causing everyone to scatter.[22]

In the oral tradition, the legend was pushed in the direction of fantasy. It was alleged, for example, that Bras-Coupé had supernatural powers. In some cases, these powers served an explanatory purpose in the plot. For instance, it was said that long before he escaped from his master, Squire was already practicing shooting with both hands, as he had a premonition that he would one day lose his right arm and "become Bras-Coupé." Other stories describe superpowers that enable Bras-Coupé to parry and escape from the police. "Strange rumours," Louis Moreau Gottschalk remembers, "were in circulation." Bras-Coupé would turn a corner only to disappear without warning. "If seen in one place," Castellanos writes, "he was soon to be met miles away, laughing at his would-be captors." On the trail of Bras-Coupé, police officers would suddenly disappear into a "cloud of mist." Hunters would shoot their rifles at Bras-Coupé only to watch their bullets flatten against his chest. Others reported bullets bouncing off the outlaw's body and careening "dangerously close to their own heads." Still others insinuated that Bras-Coupé was "fireproof" and "invulnerable" to wounds of all kinds. Everyone understood, moreover, never to look Bras-Coupé directly in the eyes, as his gaze could hypnotize you or turn you into stone.[23]

The most influential versions of the Bras-Coupé legend come from the decades in the late nineteenth century when folklorists such as George Washington Cable, Alexander Dimitry, Clara Gottschalk Petersen, Lafcadio Hearn, and Henry Krehbiel began to work in earnest transcribing creole stories, songs, and sayings passed down by slaves and their descendants in New Orleans. Many of these works concerned social life in the maroon encampments in the cypress swamp. Some reference the subsistence practices (gathering "wild berries" and "fishing for perch") and petty production (collecting and bartering "pokeberries" for "making ink" and "sassafras" for "making tea") that supported the maroons. Others are taunts hurled at the militia and the city guard by fugitive slaves ("Oh General Florido / It's true they cannot catch me!"). Still others are functional expressions that served a concrete purpose, such as a song that was used as a signal by traders gliding along the "forest-darkened bayous," calling for people to haul the proceeds from hunting and trapping for exchange at the boat. George Washington Cable translates this song: "Out from under the trees our boat moves into the open water—bring us large game and small game!" In his ethnographic essay "Creole Slave Songs" (1886), Cable also includes a song commemorating the maroon leader Saint Malo. The song was transcribed in St. Bernard Parish from an ex-slave named Madeleine by Alexander Dimitry, a government administrator, diplomat, historian, and linguist who ran a bookshop in Exchange Alley in the years before he died in 1883. The song is a dirge mourning the maroon's death at the hands of the Spanish colonial government: "For poor St. Malo in distress! / They chased, they hunted him with dogs, / They fired at him with a gun, / They hauled him from the cypress swamp." The song is a lamentation, but it is also a song of defiance that proceeds to celebrate Saint Malo's refusal to incriminate his colleagues or confess any crime. Executed in 1784 in the Place d'Armes, in front of the Cabildo, the same spot where Bras-Coupé would be hung in effigy fifty-three years later, Saint Malo would stand in the oral tradition as a prototype for Bras-Coupé, helping to set the archetypal pattern through which Bras-Coupé would be commemorated.[24]

Cable was actually researching Saint Malo when he stumbled upon Bras-Coupé. Reflecting on this discovery, Cable explains that when he was an aspiring author in the early 1870s he took "great pains" to speak with "old French-speaking negroes" who had once been slaves in the city, "not trusting to the historical correctness of what they told me, but receiving what they said for its value as tradition, superstition, or folklore." At the time, Cable was working as a bookkeeper in the counting room at William C. Black and Company on Common Street. One day when he was at work, he asked the "little old fellow" who worked as a porter in the counting room whether he knew about Saint Malo. "My old darkey informant," Cable writes, "had heard of Saint Malo but his mind constantly returned to the far more powerful impression left by the memory of Bras-Coupé." Amazed by what he heard from the porter, Cable decided to "make a story" about the legendary outlaw. Cable struggled to write and publish the story. Rejected twice by *Scribner's Monthly,* once by *Appletons' Journal,* and once by the *Atlantic,* Cable's version of the legend would not see print until it was turned into the "foundation" for *The Grandissimes,* a historical novel published serially in *Scribner's* in 1879 and 1880. Integrating the legend into his novel, Cable transformed its plot, changing forever how Bras-Coupé would be remembered. Many subsequent versions of the legend, such as Frederick Delius's opera, *Koanga* (1897), are based directly on the novel, while others, including the influential version in Herbert Asbury's *The French Quarter* (1936), combine aspects from the vernacular tradition with innovations introduced by Cable.[25]

In some respects, Cable stays true to the oral tradition. He keeps the outlaw's name as Bras-Coupé and preserves the narrative of his escape to the swamp. Other details from the oral tradition are insinuated in *The Grandissimes*. These include the projection of the Grandissime and De Grapion family to the founding of New Orleans, potentially a winking acknowledgment of the DeBuys family mythology, and also the rumors of the outlaw's supernatural powers, which in the novel are condensed into a voodoo "curse" that Bras-Coupé places on his master's lands, causing the withering of his crops and sickness among his slaves. Cable, however, also breaks with oral tradition in at least five other ways, transfiguring the legend for subsequent generations.[26]

First, Cable backdates the legend. *The Grandissimes* is set during the first decade of the nineteenth century in the wake of the Louisiana Purchase. Bras-Coupé, however, dies eight years before this novel begins—moving his career backward in time from the 1830s to the 1790s.[27] In *The Grandissimes*, Bras-Coupé survives only in the oral tradition. His story is told in the novel several times by several different characters, though it is printed only once in a summary version. The memory of Bras-Coupé is also kept alive in the novel's present tense by fictional characters such as Palmyre Philosophe, who summons the fugitive as an avatar of slave revolution, cursing her enemies with a voodoo charm "in myrtle-wax, moulded and painted with some rude skill, of a negro's bloody arm cut off near the shoulder—a Bras-Coupé—with a dirk grasped in his hand."[28]

Cable knew that he was changing the legend by projecting Bras-Coupé backward in time, and he explained that this decision was motivated by the "natural revolt of feeling" he experienced on "becoming acquainted with the harsher provisions of the old Black Code of Louisiana," referring to slave laws in force while the territory was a colonial possession of France and Spain. Cable's protest against the Code Noir appears in *The Grandissimes* through the brutal punishment that Bras-Coupé receives for striking his master: he is branded, and his ears are shorn. Cable says he places Bras-Coupé in the 1790s to facilitate a critique of law, but it may be more accurate to say that he abstracts him from one legal context—the controversy over police violence in the United States—in order to insert him into a situation where the law at issue—the Code Noir—belongs not to the United States but to the French and Spanish empires. This change in setting transforms the legend, not least by obscuring its connection to a municipal campaign supporting the police's right to deadly force, but it also has further implications that become apparent when Cable's other interventions are taken into consideration.[29]

Cable makes a second change to the legend that is even more surprising: he reinstates Bras-Coupé's missing arm. In the novel, Bras-Coupé is never shot by the police, and his arm is never amputated. *The Grandissimes* is explicit that Bras-Coupé has "two goodly arms intact." This is a grave departure from oral tradition, which gives several explanations for the missing limb but never preserves the arm whole. As critics such as Robert O. Stephens have observed, readers were outraged by this change to the legend. "They considered . . . my version . . . was faulty," Cable confesses, "because I had . . . trifled" with this "precious verity of history." In the novel, Bras-Coupé is still known as Bras-Coupé, but he is never shot or dismembered. Instead, he names himself, looking not outward to the police but homeward to Africa. "His name," Cable writes, "was ——— ———, something in the Jaloff tongue, which he by and by condescended to render into Congo: Mioko-Koanga, in French Bras-Coupé, the Arm Cut Off." The outlaw's name, in the novel, refers not to an injury he received from the police. Instead, it is associated first with the idea that "his tribe, in losing him, had lost its strong right arm close off at the shoulder," and second, with the idea that his enslavement is analogous to the loss of a limb. The novel settles on the second possibility, proposing that Bras-Coupé chooses this name to make himself into a "type of all Slavery, turning into flesh and blood the truth that all Slavery is maiming." Reinstating the amputated arm, Cable turns a slave maimed (and thereby named) by the police into the unmaimed vehicle for the romantic expression of this universal truth.[30]

Cable makes a third change to the legend when he suggests that Bras-Coupé is an African prince newly arrived to America. In the extant documentation on the legend, Cable is the first person to make this suggestion, though he was inconsistent in describing the fugitive's ancestry, sometimes calling him Wolof and other times Arada—two peoples, it is worth noting, who lived thousands of miles apart, separated by language and culture. Bras-Coupé's characterization in the novel as a captive king—and by extension, as a noble savage—draws from literary conventions that developed in English antislavery writing in the seventeenth and eighteenth centuries. These con-

Albert Herter's representation of Bras-Coupé with two arms intact, from the 1899 edition of George Washington Cable's *The Grandissimes*. Albert Herter, "Bras-Coupé," in George Washington Cable, *The Grandissimes: A Story of Creole Life* (New York: Charles Scribner's Sons, 1899), 260.

ventions were inaugurated in Aphra Behn's *Oroonoko* (1688) and extended in stage melodramas like *Prince of Angola* (1788); long poems like *The Wrongs of Almoona, or The African's Revenge* (1788); and sentimental novels like *The Royal African* (1749), *Julia de Roubigné* (1777), and *Slavery, or the Times* (1792). During the nineteenth century this tradition extended to works written in the United States, such as William Cullen Bryant's "The African Chief" (1836), Henry Wadsworth Longfellow's "The Slave's Dream" (1842), and Herman Melville's "Benito Cereno" (1855). In the spirit of this tradition, Cable solicits sympathy for Bras-Coupé based upon his nobility. In the novel, it is the prince's honor, written into his "fine" features and "royal" stature, that transforms the dishonor of his slavery into a tragedy. Bras-Coupé's noble savagery also plays into the tragic love plot involving his unrequited passion for Palmyre, a device that recalls not only Garreau's short story but also an entire literary tradition stretching back to *Oroonoko*.[31]

The claim that Bras-Coupé was an African prince may have been invented by Cable, or it may have been invented in oral tradition and then adapted by Cable, it seems unlikely this claim is accurate, especially in the absence of corroborating evidence. In *The Grandissimes*, where the legend is set in the 1790s, the claim is at least plausible, as this was a decade when slave importation from Africa, especially from Kongo, spiked in reaction to the expansion of the region's sugar industry. This claim is less believable after the abolition of the transatlantic slave trade in 1807. Although pirates continued to import slaves directly from Africa, it is far more likely that Squire was born in Louisiana or else transported to Louisiana through the domestic slave trade, which remained active into the 1860s. In fact, there are versions of the legend that suggest that Squire came to Louisiana from Virginia, but available ship manifests and conveyance records are inconclusive. There are a number of slaves with the name "Squire" who arrived in New Orleans in the decades before 1836–37, but none of them is linked to William DeBuys or William Boswell, the notary who typically handled slave sales for the DeBuys family, making identification impossible.[32]

Cable makes a fourth change to the legend by erasing the battles between the maroons and the police in the cypress swamp. In the novel, Bras-Coupé is a loner. Literally, there are no people other than Bras-Coupé in the swamp, whose "inmost depths" are "clear but lifeless." The "endless colonnades of cypresses" and "motionless drapings of gray moss" are kept company by "owls and bats" and "flowers that no man had named," and their "stillness" is "disturbed" by no human other than Bras-Coupé. No longer a charismatic leader of the maroons in their war against the police, Cable turns Bras-Coupé into a recluse. In *The Grandissimes*, Bras-Coupé's valor on the battlefield occurs only in Africa, where he is a warrior prince. As Cable removes the maroons from the legend, he also erases the wanted posters, the outlawry proclamation, and newspaper headlines that originally focus the manhunt for Bras-Coupé, all of which are points of interest in other versions of the legend. In the novel, moreover, Bras-Coupé's corpse is never displayed on the Place d'Armes. The public exhibition that routinely brings the legend to its end is never referenced in the novel. Filtering out all evidence of the state's role in creating the legend, the novel also removes from its plot—with one notable exception—all references to the police.[33]

Cable makes a fifth change to the legend in representing the abrupt end to Bras-Coupé's sojourn in the swamp. In *The Grandissimes*, Bras-Coupé is captured not when he is betrayed by Francisco Garcia but instead when he is recognized while dancing at Congo Square. In the novel, Bras-Coupé leaves his solitude in the swamp to join the crowd in Congo Square, an open grassy field on Rampart Street adjacent to the Carondelet Canal, where slaves drummed, sang, danced, socialized, and sold their wares on Sunday afternoons. As slaves were generally not allowed to play drums or gather en masse elsewhere in the United States, Congo Square was a special place where traditional African music and dance were openly performed and connections were forged between slaves from throughout the diaspora. When Bras-Coupé arrives at Congo Square, he immediately takes center stage and performs a series of dazzling moves that catch the crowd's attention. He hurdles with "tinkling heels" over the head of his "bewildered partner," and everyone in the square "[howls] with rapture." According to Cable, Bras-Coupé is the "blackest of black men" in this performance. He epitomizes the "whole company of black lookers-on." Describing the action at the Congo Square, the novel waits for Bras-Coupé to push the scene to its saturation point: it is his entrance that sparks the experience of "unison." But when Bras-Coupé is about to soar in a "more astounding leap than his last," the police throw a lasso around him and bring him "crashing like a burnt tree, face upward upon the turf."[34]

As best we can tell, the strong association between Bras-Coupé and Congo Square began with *The Grandissimes*. No sources before the novel indicate

This iconic illustration is from Cable's ethnographic essay on Congo Square. The dancer in the foreground has sometimes been mistaken for Bras-Coupé. Edward Windsor Kemble, "The Bamboula," in George Washington Cable, "The Dance in Place Congo," *Century Magazine* 31 (1886): 525.

that Bras-Coupé was captured at Congo Square or that he was a celebrated performer there. Versions of the legend communicated by Garreau, who lived and worked across Rampart Street, and Gottschalk, whose childhood home was blocks away, never refer to Bras-Coupé in connection with Congo Square. Cable, furthermore, makes Congo Square indispensable to Bras-Coupé's characterization in *The Grandissimes*—it is where he reveals his sovereign power as prowess in the dance—but he does not mention Bras-Coupé in his nonfiction essay "The Dance in Place Congo" (1886), a decision that would seem to indicate that Cable saw Bras-Coupé's celebrity at Congo Square as appropriate to a novel but not to ethnography, as something fictional not to be mistaken for fact.[35]

One possible source for this scene has been suggested by Barbara Ladd, who argues that Bras-Coupé's capture at Congo Square is likely inspired by the legend of François Makandal, a maroon in San Domingue whose planned revolt was foiled in 1757 when he was betrayed by one of his collaborators and captured by the police at a public dance. Like Bras-Coupé, Makandal was a fugitive slave who escaped from his master into the wilderness to become a maroon leader, and like Bras-Coupé, Makandal was maimed when he lost his right hand—in his case, to the machinery in a sugar mill. We know, moreover, that Cable was reading widely in Caribbean history when he was writing *The Grandissimes,* compiling the secondary research that he would eventually incorporate into "The Dance in Place Congo," and we know his account of Congo Square, in the novel and in the essay, borrows descriptions from books about dances that were happening on Saint Domingue, including Médéric Louis Élie Moreau de Saint-Méry's *Description Topographique, Physique, Civile, Politique et Historique de la Partie Française de L'isle Saint-Domingue* (1797). It is quite plausible that Cable was inspired during this research process to move the scene of Bras-Coupé's capture from Bayou St. John to the more colorful and evocative setting of Congo Square, following the legend of Makandal.[36]

After *The Grandissimes* was published in 1880, there were some folklorists, including Lafcadio Hearn, who were quick to correct Cable's account. Hearn believed it was important to distinguish Cable's fiction from historical truth. Hearn wrote that Cable's version was "founded on facts" but that Cable also took "poet's license" by changing important aspects of the story, including the loss of the arm, the rumored reward, and the betrayal and murder by an associate. Despite Hearn's objections, the legend was forever transformed by the success of Cable's novel. Not long after it was published, local-color books published for tourists, like James S. Zacharie's *New Orleans Guide* (1885), were describing how Bras-Coupé was "lassoed in the midst of the Congo dances," citing events from the novel as if they were facts. In most cases, people did not retell the entire story from *The Grandissimes.* Instead, they took specific details, most often the claims that Bras-Coupé was a captive king and the most celebrated dancer at Congo Square, and integrated them into the familiar legend about the maroon who fought the police in the swamp.[37]

By the time that Herbert Asbury featured Bras-Coupé in his highly influential chapter on Congo Square in *The French Quarter* (1936), it was nearly impossible to separate Cable's novel from the oral tradition. Asbury discusses DeBuys, the escape to the swamp, the loss of the arm, Prieur's offering of the reward, the police campaign, Garcia's betrayal, and the gruesome display on the Place d'Armes, but the main idea in his chapter, which is used to frame these conventional characters and incidents, is the proposition that Bras-

Coupé was "one of the famous Bamboula dancers" at Congo Square. Asbury notes that Bras-Coupé was an "expert wielder of the beef bones," which were used to play the bamboula drums, and also "the first to attach little bells to his ankles instead of the customary bits of metal." Asbury's amalgamation of source materials is significant, given how many folklorists, musicologists, and historians have subsequently based their own accounts of Congo Square on his chapter from *The French Quarter,* as shown in classic works from a variety of disciplines, including Benjamin Botkin's *Treasury of Southern Folklore* (1949), Marshall Stearns's *The Story of Jazz* (1956), Lynne Emery's *Black Dance in the United States* (1972), and Middleton Harris and Toni Morrison's *The Black Book* (1974)—all of which quote paragraphs or entire pages from *The French Quarter,* taking Asbury at his word.[38]

As an example of Bras-Coupé's surprising and far-reaching influence in cultural history, consider Vernon Loggins's *Where the World Ends* (1958), an influential biography about Louis Moreau Gottschalk, the pianist whose immensely popular classical compositions adapted creole melodies and syncopation from folk traditions in Louisiana and the Caribbean. Loggins proposes that Gottschalk's most celebrated composition, *La Bamboula* (1849), was directly inspired by the music made by Bras-Coupé at Congo Square, asserting that, as a young boy, Gottschalk heard "big-voiced" Bras-Coupé hundreds of times, shouting "Dansez Bamboula!" while "leading the slaves in their revels on the Place Congo." There were hundreds of voices on Congo Square, Loggins suggests, but there was "only one" about which Gottschalk "could be sure," the voice of Bras-Coupé, the "best known of all the slaves of New Orleans." For Gottschalk, there was "no mistaking" Bras-Coupé when he thundered: "Dansez bamboula! Badoum, badoum!"[39]

Loggins's account was influential in its time, but it has since been debunked by other scholars. Frederick Starr explains that there is not a "shred of evidence" to support Loggins's account, which is riddled with mistakes, including the suggestion that the public dances at Congo Square happened on Saturdays not Sundays. Moreover, there is no evidence in Gottschalk's own writings to support Loggins's claim that Gottschalk was inspired by Bras-Coupé. Gottschalk writes about Bras-Coupé in his memoir, *Notes of a Pianist* (1881), and he also writes about Congo Square. However, he does not write about them in connection with one another. Gottschalk's description of Bras-Coupé matches the oral tradition from his time, portraying Bras-Coupé as a legendary maroon who fought the law and ruled the swamp, but it does not place Bras-Coupé at Congo Square, and it does not portray him as a musician or famous dancer. Gottschalk, in other words, is not the source for the claim that *La Bamboula* was inspired by Bras-Coupé. The most likely source for this claim is Asbury, who explains that Gottschalk had "based one of his best known compositions, La Bamboula, on what he heard . . . in Congo Square as a boy." Asbury does not link Gottschalk to Bras-Coupé, but he does say Bras-Coupé was one of the most famous performers at Congo Square, and Loggins may simply have been following Asbury in connecting the dots between Gottschalk and the legendary maroon.[40]

Bras-Coupé plays a similar role in early writing on jazz tradition. In the 1930s and 1940s, Bras-Coupé became a tacit point of reference for historians looking for evidence of how African musical practices—call and response, polyrhythm, and variable timbre—were transmitted to the generation that invented jazz. Studies such as Frederic Ramsey Jr. and Charles Smith's *Jazzmen* (1939), Robert Goffin's *Jazz: From the Congo to the Metropolitan* (1944), Rudi Blesh's *Shining Trumpets* (1946), and Marshall Stearns's *The Story of Jazz* (1958) look back to Congo Square to describe the transmission of tradition, suggesting the first generation of jazz musicians learned about African musical styles by watching the performances there. In some instances, this claim is expressed as an origin story about a young musician, often Buddy Bolden, who hears the drums at Congo Square and becomes inspired—an origin story, in other words, similar to the one that Loggins tells about Gottschalk. Like Loggins, these stories about jazz starting at Congo Square draw extensively, and in many cases exclusively, from Asbury's chapter, which is to say they draw their primary evidence from an account of Congo Square with Bras-Coupé at its center. Unlike Loggins, however, these works never actually name the legendary outlaw who stands in Asbury's chapter as an exemplar (in the dance), an expert (on the drums), and an innovator (in stringing bells around his ankles). Some refer to a famous dancer who could "leap higher and shout louder" than all the others, an oblique homage given without elaboration, and several quote the words that Asbury attributes to Bras-Coupé: "Badoum! Badoum!" In Loggins, these words are chanted by Bras-Coupé, inspiring everyone at Congo Square, including Gottschalk, but in jazz history, they stand as an unattributed quotation. Written out of this origin story, Bras-Coupé is folded back into an anonymous mass of folk performers. Left un-

25

named, the strange thing is that Bras-Coupé is nevertheless undeniably still there, an apocryphal yet inescapable presence overheard by Buddy Bolden and his contemporaries, encouraging the first wild strains of jazz.[41]

These works in jazz history set the stage for one of the most fascinating reflections on Bras-Coupé—Sidney Bechet's as-told-to autobiography *Treat It Gentle* (1960). The opening scenes at Congo Square in *Treat It Gentle* could be mistaken for excerpts from *Jazzmen* or *The Story of Jazz* except for one crucial difference. *Treat It Gentle* restores Bras-Coupé to the center of the scene. If jazz historians approached this scene from the imaginary perspective of racial or generational outsiders who salvaged something from these performances, Bechet insists that jazz was invented right at Congo Square. Moreover, he insists that jazz was invented—literally—by Bras-Coupé. Beginning his autobiography not with the circumstances of his own birth but at a time and place before his birth where jazz was "being born," Bechet begins his personal history of the music in a conventional way by suggesting that the roots of jazz could be found in "the music they played at Congo Square." Telling this story through Bras-Coupé—renamed Omar in the book—Bechet stakes his claim that jazz was invented not by someone who took something away from Congo Square but by the "leader" who "beat out" the "rhythms" that "everyone followed" there. Following Cable and Asbury, Bechet repeats the old idea about Bras-Coupé's leadership in the performance, but he also takes things a step farther by making Bras-Coupé not only into the music's leader but also its point of origin. "It was Omar," he writes, who "started the song and all the good musicianers have been singing that song ever since." Before jazz, there was Congo Square. Before Congo Square, there was Bras-Coupé. Jazz is unleashed from an impulse that was already "there" in Bras-Coupé before he arrived at Congo Square.[42]

As if this were not enough, Bechet also claims that Bras-Coupé was his own grandfather. Bechet's kinship with Bras-Coupé is not merely the cultural connection that all jazz players have with the fugitive slave who invented their music. Bechet is related to Bras-Coupé by blood. John Chilton, Bechet's biographer, suggests that this family lineage was invented for the purposes of the book. According to Chilton, Bechet adapted the legend of Bras-Coupé to create the story of a grandfather who never existed. Other scholars continue to take Bechet at his word, understanding Omar as Bechet's flesh-and-blood ancestor. Whether we see Bechet's relation to Omar as blood ancestry or as

Sidney Bechet, one of the first great improvisers in jazz, claimed that Bras-Coupé was his grandfather. William P. Gottlieb, *Sidney Bechet at Jimmy Ryan's (Club), New York, NY, ca. June 1947,* William P. Gottlieb Collection, Library of Congress, Washington, D.C. Published with permission from Getty Images.

a creative experiment in elective kinship, it is important to recognize that Omar's characterization draws upon the Bras-Coupé legend to pose some profound questions about jazz tradition. We need to take these questions seriously. What does it mean to find, as the absence at the origin of jazz history, a slave maimed by the police? What would it mean to write a history of jazz that includes Bras-Coupé? These are things we have to ask, Bechet suggests, along the way to answering the question posed in the book's original title: "Where Did It Come From?"[43]

Bechet returns Bras-Coupé to Congo Square, and he also restores other details from the oral tradition: the maroon communities, the setting of the cypress swamp, the indulgent master who allows Bras-Coupé to go hunting on his own, the loss of the arm, the declaration of outlawry, the "big reward" offered for the fugitive, the "sheriff" sending "posses" in "all directions," the "wanted posters," the "dogs working the bayou all day long trying to pick up a trail." By restoring these incidents and settings to the legend, Bechet is able to offer an alternative account of the origin of jazz that grounds the music not in a spectacle witnessed at Congo Square but in the everyday experience of the slave community. In *Treat It Gentle*, jazz happens at Congo Square, but it also happens on street corners, in the cabarets, on the riverfront, and way back in the swamp. Jazz emerges from the slave experience without interces-sion, conditioned by a common experience of oppression that intensifies in the manhunt for Omar as masters become increasingly anxious and patrols fan out into the swamp. "The slaves felt a trouble on them," Bechet explains:

> Nights, they was talking low to themselves, trying superstitions to keep away more evil, keeping under cover, trying to stay out of the white man's way. And days, they had their trouble on them. The overseers were being more cruel; the meals had less food to them; the work, they made it harder and there was more and more whip behind it. There was a whole lot more slaves getting beatings these days. The only thing they had that couldn't be taken from them was their music. Their song, it was coming right up from the fields, settling itself in their feet and working right up, right up into their stomachs, their spirit, into their fear, into their longing. It was bewil-dered, this part of them. It was like it had no end, nowhere even to wait for an end, nowhere to hope for a change in things. But it had a beginning . . . it was a feeling in them, a memory that came from a long way back. It was like they were trying to work the music back to its beginning and then start it over again, start it over and build it to a place where it could stop some-how, to a place where the music could put an end to itself and become an-other music, a new beginning that could begin them over again. There were chants and drums and voices . . . and there was love and work and worry and waiting; there was being tired, and the sun, and the overseers following behind them so they didn't dare stop and look back. It was all in the music.

This passage finds a new origin for jazz in the manhunt for Bras-Coupé. Here the music rises up from the fields as a retort to the aggression experienced by slaves by virtue of their involuntary association with the outlaw. In this meditation, Bechet pushes jazz to a place where it can no longer be plotted on straight lines with beginnings, middles, and ends. For Bechet, the music expresses an experience of history that refuses the consolation of progress, a feeling that pools instead in feet and stomachs, that suspends time's animation by decomposing its development into longing, waiting, and worry. If history's endpoint is unavailable, its beginning is not so much known as felt, like the unseen authority of the "overseers following" so closely that these slaves do not even "dare stop and look back." By locating the music's genesis in the violence suffered by these slaves, Bechet revives the question that the first generation of jazz historians thought they had answered. For Bechet, the only way to find the origin of jazz is to start the story over again, rewinding to the historical setting of slavery.[44]

Concluding with Bechet's magisterial synthesis, this edition gathers the most crucial materials relevant to Bras-Coupé, from early newspaper articles, to the vernacular tradition, to the legend's adaptation in literature and history. Some of these adaptations reveal Cable's disproportionate influence, including *Koanga,* an opera composed by Frederick Delius between 1896 and 1897, which, following Gottschalk, brings not only creole melodies but also syncopation, blue notes, and African-derived instrumentation, including banjos and hand drums, into European art music. *Koanga* was one of the vehicles through which the legend of Bras-Coupé reached audiences outside the United States, as it was performed in Paris and London and revived in several places, including Trinidad, where it was performed for the first time with an all-black cast.[45]

Another adaptation of the legend, a short story by J. Andrew Gaulden, first appeared in *Negro Digest* (1942–1951), a Chicago-based, black-owned monthly magazine with a peak circulation in the hundreds of thousands. Modeled on *Reader's Digest, Negro Digest* included book summaries and articles reprinted from other sources as well as original works by authors including W.E.B. Du Bois, Langston Hughes, Zora Neale Hurston, and George Padmore. Gaulden's "Tiger of the Bayous" was an original story published by the magazine. Over the course of his career, Gaulden published many stories and was a featured columnist for African American newspapers such as the *Shreveport Sun, Houston Informer,* and *Los Angeles Sentinel.* He also published a magazine, *Negro Louisiana,* in the 1950s, and served as principal of public schools in northern Louisiana before joining Grambling University. "Tiger of the Bayous" is richly detailed. It features standard elements from the legend, including the indulgent master, the loss of the arm, the maroon settlements, the rumors of magic powers, the police patrols, the offered reward, the betrayal by Francisco Garcia, and the display of the corpse on the Place d'Armes. It describes Bras-Coupé at Congo Square leaping higher and shouting louder than anyone else, and quotes his booming voice: "Badoum! Badoum!" Gaulden also dramatizes scenes that do not appear in other versions of the legend, including Squire's final confrontation with DeBuys and the battles among outlaws on the riverfront and in the swamp.[46]

This edition also includes a version of the legend recomposed—somewhat cryptically—in Robert Penn Warren's historical romance *Band of Angels* (1955), a novel that was made into a would-be technicolor blockbuster in 1957 directed by Raoul Walsh and starring Sidney Poitier as Bras-Coupé (renamed Rau-Ru) and Clark Gable as William DeBuys (renamed Hamish Bond). Warren's novel follows Bras-Coupé (or "Rau-Ru") from his birth in a West African village under attack by slave raiders, where he is saved as an infant by Hamish Bond and then brought to New Orleans, a variation on the narrative of African origins suggested by Cable. As "k'la" (favored slave) to his indulgent master, Rau-Ru learns to shoot and to despise his bondage, roaming freely in New Orleans and in the cypress swamps beyond the Bond plantation at Point du Loup, before he escapes to lead the maroons, fighting against the police patrols sent to hunt him down. Warren includes winking acknowledgments to earlier versions of the legend. In *The Grandissimes*, for example, Bras-Coupé flees after he strikes his master, but in *Band of Angels* Rau-Ru escapes after striking the novel's villain, Charles de Marigny Prieur-Denis, whose name inverts and alludes to Mayor Denis Prieur, who outlawed Bras-Coupé in 1836. Following Cable, Warren leaves Rau-Ru with two arms intact, but he alludes to the missing limb in a scene where Rau-Ru "cuts off" a slave's "mangled and gangrenous arm . . . just above the elbow" using a "knife and saw" to sever the arm and a "white-hot iron" to cauterize the wound.[47]

Warren also extends Rau-Ru's career beyond the 1830s to imagine his participation in the Civil War and Reconstruction. When the Union Army comes to Louisiana, Rau-Ru leads his guerrilla band of maroons out of the swamps and joins their ranks. Rising quickly to lieutenant, he takes a new name, Oliver Cromwell Jones, by implication linking the American and En-

This still image is from Raoul Walsh's film adaptation of Robert Penn Warren's novel *Band of Angels*, with Sidney Poitier as Rau-Ru (Bras-Coupé) and Clark Gable as Hamish Bond (William DeBuys). Raoul Walsh, dir., "[Rau-Ru and Hamish Bond]," *Band of Angels* (Hollywood, Calif.: Warner Brothers, 1957). Published with permission from AF Archive/Alamy Photography.

glish Civil Wars. When New Orleans is occupied, Rau-Ru becomes an official in the government working for reform, before he is forced to flee back to the swamps, where he is gunned down.[48]

Bras-Coupé makes a number of other cameo appearances in literary history. There are early adaptations, for example, in long poems, mostly inspired by Cable, such as Mark Frederick Bigney's *Poetical History of Louisiana* (1885), Espy Williams's "Bras Coupé" (1892), and Henry Gilbert's *The Dance in Place Congo* (1922), and there are references in best-selling novels like Frank Yerby's *The Foxes of Harrow* (1946), historical epics like Marcus Christian's *I Am New Orleans* (1968), lyric poems like Tom Dent's "Secret Messages" (1976), plays like Aishah Rahman's *Anybody Seen Marie Laveau?* (1989), and short genre fiction like Kalamu ya Salaam's "Bras Coupe" (2004).[49]

The memory of Bras-Coupé is alive today in the vernacular culture of New Orleans, including in the tradition of the Mardi Gras Indians. This suit, paying homage to the legendary outlaw, was created and worn by Demond Melancon, Big Chief of the Young Seminole Hunters, in 2016. Published courtesy of Demond Melancon.

Together, all of these works remind us that Bras-Coupé is still with us in ways that we may not recognize. From the beginning, he was an enemy of the state—an example invoked to make the case that cities had to have police departments with heavy weapons and the right to deadly force. After his death he joined the company of legendary maroons—Nanny, Makandal, Three-Fingered Jack, Saint Malo—celebrated as heroes in oral tradition and claimed as freedom fighters by antislavery activists. He also helped to shape our historical knowledge of Congo Square and therefore our understanding of jazz—maybe most powerfully in cases where he is invisible but nonetheless important to cultural memory. As his legend was transformed in novels and plays and narrative poems, Bras-Coupé became a superhero, a star-crossed lover, a noble savage, a type of all slavery, a voodoo priest, a captive king, a dancer, a drummer, an adopted son, an army officer, a politician, and a grandfather. Not least he became a culture hero in New Orleans, anticipating a lineage that extends into the twentieth century through other outlaws, such as Robert Charles and Mark Essex. His memory is still kept alive by local artists, like Langston Allston and Henry Lipkis, whose public murals demonstrate the parallel between Bras-Coupé's struggles and current tensions over policing in New Orleans. His memory is also honored by Mardi Gras Indians, as shown, for example, in the beautiful Bras-Coupé suit that was created and worn by Demond Melancon, Big Chief of the Young Seminole Hunters, in 2016. Across its variations, the legend remains indispensable as a tradition stretching from slavery to the present.[50]

NOTES

1. This introduction extends the argument from Bryan Wagner, "The Strange Career of Bras-Coupé," in *Disturbing the Peace: Black Culture and the Police Power after Slavery* (Cambridge, Mass.: Harvard Univ. Press, 2009), 58–115, 258–273. Most critical analysis of Bras-Coupé has focused on George Washington Cable's adaptation of the legend in his novel *The Grandissimes*, with the following exceptions: Frederick W. Turner III, "Badmen, Black and White" (Ph.D. diss., University of Pennsylvania, 1965), 158–165; Robert O. Stephens, "Cable's Bras-Coupé and Merimeé's Tamango: The Case of the Missing Arm," *Mississippi Quarterly* 35 (1982): 387–405; John W. Roberts, *From Trickster to Badman: The Black Folk Hero from Slavery to Freedom* (Philadelphia: Univ. of Pennsylvania Press, 1989), 134–136; and Barbara Ladd, "'An Atmosphere of Hints and Allusions': Bras-Coupé and the Context of Black Insurrection in *The Grandissimes*," *Southern Quarterly* 29 (1991): 63–76.

2. On Nanny, see Karla Gottlieb, *The Mother of Us All: A History of Queen Nanny* (New York: Africa World Press, 2000). On Three-Fingered Jack, see the following works: Frances Botkin, *Thieving Three-Fingered Jack: Transatlantic Tales of a Jamaican Outlaw* (New Brunswick, N.J.: Rutgers Univ. Press, 2017); William Earle, *Obi: or, The History of Three-Fingered Jack*, ed. Srinivas Aravamudan (Peterborough, Ontario: Broadview Press, 2005); and Michael Warner, Natasha Hurley, Luis Iglesias, Sonia Di Loreto, Jeffrey Scraba, and Sandra Young, "A Soliloquy 'Lately Spoken at the African Theatre': Race and the Public Sphere in New York City, 1821," *American Literature* 73 (2001): 1–46. On Makandal and Boukman, see the following works: Jared Hickman, *Black Prometheus: Race and Radicalism in the Age of Atlantic Slavery* (New York: Oxford Univ. Press, 2016), 33–73; Laurent Dubois, *Avengers of the New World* (Cambridge, Mass.: Harvard Univ. Press, 2005), 51–57, 94–114; Colin [Joan] Dayan, *Haiti, History, and the Gods* (Berkeley: Univ. of California Press, 1995), 29–33, 46–47, 68–70; and C. L. R. James, *The Black Jacobins: Toussaint*

L'Ouverture and the San Domingo Revolution (1938; revised ed., New York: Vintage Books, 1963), 20–21, 86–87, 96.

3. Grace Elizabeth King, *Creole Families of New Orleans* (New York: Macmillan, 1921), 383, 386–387. There are records concerning a mulatto Squire owned by a Monsieur Gurly, and some scholars, including Marcus Christian, have wondered whether this Squire may have been the slave who became Bras-Coupé. Others, such as Lafcadio Hearn, have said that Squire's master was the auctioneer Joseph Le Carpentier, and that he was sold to John Freret before he escaped to the swamps. Vernon Loggins identifies Bras Coupé's master as a doctor who purchases him for $2,000 in the St. Louis Hotel slave market. Contemporary records from the mayor's office, the city guard, and the council of the city's Third Municipality, however, confirm that it was William DeBuys who owned Squire at the point that he became Bras-Coupé. Given the absence of conveyance documentation and the fact that the Squire owned by DeBuys is never described as a "mulatto," it seems unlikely that Gurly's slave is the same person as the Squire owned by DeBuys. On Gurly's mulatto Squire, see the following documents: New Orleans City Guard, Reports of the Captain of the Guard 1826–1836, 12–13 Janvier 1835, City Archives, Louisiana Division, New Orleans Public Library, New Orleans, Louisiana; and Marcus Christian, "Bras-Coupé," Marcus Christian Papers, Historical Research Materials, box 11, Archives and Manuscripts Division, Earl K. Long Library, University of New Orleans, New Orleans, Louisiana. For the contrasting claims by Hearn and Loggins, see the following works: Lafcadio Hearn, "The Original Bras-Coupe," *New Orleans Item* (27 October 1880), 2; and Vernon Loggins, *Where the World Ends: The Life of Louis Moreau Gottschalk* (Baton Rouge: Louisiana State Univ. Press, 1958), 27. William DeBuys's ownership of Squire is recorded in the arrest record that represents the injury that leads to the loss of the arm. New Orleans City Guard, Reports of the Captain of the Guard 1826–1836, 20–21 Janvier 1836, City Archives, Louisiana Division, New Orleans Public Library, New Orleans, Louisiana. Several important pieces of primary evidence on Squire, including new information about General William DeBuys, were found by Kevin Watson. See "Fugitive Slave (Squire)," Williams Research Center, Historic New Orleans Collection, New Orleans, Louisiana.

4. On the life of William DeBuys, see the following sources: Herman Boehm de Bachellé Seebold, *Old Louisiana Plantation Homes and Family Trees* (New Orleans: Pelican, 1941), 2:161; Weston Arthur Goodspeed, *The Province and the States: A History of the Province of Louisiana under France and Spain* (Madison, Wisc.: Western Historical Association, 1904), 110, 114–116, 243; and Arnold R. Hirsch and Joseph Logsdon, eds., *Creole New Orleans: Race and Americanization* (Baton Rouge: Louisiana State Univ. Press, 1992), 151, 154. On the original DeBuys residence on St. Louis Street, see the following: *The New-Orleans Guide; or, General Directory for 1837, Embracing the Three Municipalities, and Containing the Names, Professions and Residences of All the Heads of Families and Persons in Business, Together with Other Useful Information* (New Orleans: Gaux and Meynier, 1837), 15; and *Gibson's Guide and Directory of the State of Louisiana and the Cities of New Orleans and Lafayette* (New Orleans: J. Gibson, 1838), 54. On the DeBuys residence on Elmire Street and the sawmill located on the riverfront levee between Piety and Desire Streets, see the following sources: *New-Orleans Directory for 1842: Comprising the Names, Residences and Occupations of the Merchants, Business Men, Professional Gentlemen and Citizens* (New Orleans: Pitts and Clarke, 1842), 106; *New Orleans Annual and Commercial Register of 1846: Containing the Names, Residences and Professions of All the Heads of Families and Persons in Business* (New

Orleans: E. A. Michel, 1845), 198; and H. A. Cohen and Bennet Dowler, *Cohen's New Orleans and Lafayette Directory* (New Orleans: Printed at the Office of the Picayune, 1855), 66. On the location of the DeBuys cotton press, see Stephen E. Percy and Edward Auguste Michel, *The New Orleans Directory; Containing the Names, Professions and Residences of All the Heads of Families, and Persons in Business, of the City and Suburbs* (New Orleans: Stephen E. Percy and Company, 1832), 54. It is worth observing that while Lafcadio Hearn misidentifies Bras-Coupé's master, he does discuss the fact that his master owned a cotton press, a potential holdover from the vernacular tradition featuring William DeBuys. See Hearn, "The Original Bras-Coupe," 2. On DeBuys's reputation as an avid hunter and fisherman, see the following sources: Seebold, *Plantation Homes and Family Trees*, 2:161; "Death of Gen. DeBuys," *New Orleans Picayune* (25 May 1856), 2; and "General William De Buys," *Baltimore Sun* (31 May 1856), 2. For a description of the DeBuys estate in Grand Isle, see "Delightful Property Situated on Grand Isle," *New Orleans Picayune* (22 May 1857), 4. On DeBuys's indulgence of Squire, his favorite slave, see the following sources: Henry C. Castellanos, *New Orleans as It Was: Episodes of Louisiana Life* (New Orleans: L. Graham, 1895), 210–211; "Jackson Square Was the Old City's Heart," *New Orleans Picayune* (20 September 1897), 3; John Smith Kendall, *History of New Orleans* (Chicago: Lewis Publishing, 1922), 131–132; Hodding Carter, *Lower Mississippi* (New York: Farrar and Rinehart, 1942), 178–179; Herbert Asbury, *The French Quarter: An Informal History of the New Orleans Underworld* (New York: Knopf, 1936), 237–253; Lyle Saxon, Edward Dreyer, and Robert Tallant, eds., *Gumbo Ya-Ya: A Collection of Louisiana Folk Tales* (Boston: Houghton Mifflin, 1945), 253–254; J. Andrew Gaulden, "Tiger of the Bayous," *Negro Digest* 5 (1946): 25; Benjamin Albert Botkin, ed., *A Treasury of Southern Folklore: Stories, Ballads, Traditions, and Folkways of the People of the South* (New York: Crown Publishers, 1949), 328–330; James Lewicki, *The Life Treasury of American Folklore* (New York: Time Life, 1961), 180–181; M. A. Harris, Morris Levitt, Toni Morrison, Roger Furman, and Ernest Smith, *The Black Book* (New York: Random House, 1974), 142; and Jay Robert Nash, "The Legend of a One-Armed Murderer," in *The Almanac of World Crime* (New York: Bonanza, 1986), 310–311.

5. Hodding Carter describes Squire's early escapades as a *petit marron* as his taking "French leave" from his master. See Carter, *Lower Mississippi*, 178–179. On the genealogy of the concept of marronage, including its division into *petit* and *grand* forms, see Jean-Pierre Tardieu, "Cimarrón-Maroon-Marron: An Epistemological Note," *Outre-Mers: Revue d'Histoire* 94 (2006): 237–247. For the account from the slave who returned to her master from one of the maroon settlements outside the city, see "New Orleans," *New York Evening Post* (4 December 1827), 2. For historical overviews of marronage in Louisiana, particularly in the cypress swamp outside New Orleans, see the following works: Gwendolyn Midlo Hall, *Africans in Colonial Louisiana: The Development of Afro-Creole Culture in the Eighteenth Century* (Baton Rouge: Louisiana State Univ. Press, 1992), 97–155, 203–236, 284, 322–323; Lawrence N. Powell, *The Accidental City: Improvising New Orleans* (Cambridge, Mass.: Harvard Univ. Press, 2012), 23–31, 93–105, 238–240; and Sylviane A. Diouf, *Slavery's Exiles: The Story of the American Maroons* (New York: New York Univ. Press, 2014), 157–186. On the topography of the backswamp, see Richard Campanella, *Geographies of New Orleans: Urban Fabrics before the Storm* (New Orleans: Univ. of New Orleans Press, 2006), 33–66. These semi-aquatic areas were enclosed between 1890 and 1920. After the invention of the Wood screw pump, the whole of the backswamp was drained, divided into blocks, built out, and integrated into the city. See Pierce F. Lewis, *New Orleans: The Making of an Urban Landscape*, 2nd

ed. (Charlottesville: Univ. of Virginia Press, 2003), 37–100. On the global history of marronage, see the following classic works: Herbert Aptheker, "Maroons within the Present Limits of the United States," *Journal of Negro History* 24 (1939): 167–184; Richard Price, ed., *Maroon Societies: Rebel Slave Communities in the Americas* (Garden City, N.Y.: Anchor Press, 1973); Gonzalo Aguirre Bel-trán and Deward E. Walker, *Regions of Refuge* (Washington, D.C.: Society for Applied Anthropol-ogy, 1979); Pierre Clastres, *Society against the State: Essays in Political Anthropology* (New York: Zone Books, 1987); John Hope Franklin and Loren Schweninger, *Runaway Slaves: Rebels on the Plantation* (New York: Oxford Univ. Press, 1999); and Sally Price and Richard Price, *Maroon Arts: Cultural Vitality in the African Diaspora* (Boston: Beacon Press, 1999). On marronage in political philosophy, see Neil Roberts, *Freedom as Marronage* (Chicago: Univ. of Chicago Press, 2015).

6. "Necessity of Enforcing the Ordinances," *New Orleans Bee* (9 October 1839), 2. On an earlier police directive from Mayor Denis Prieur, scheduling a patrol to sweep the "upper incorporated faubourgs of the city," see "City Council," *New Orleans Argus* (18 March 1828), 2. On the ongoing battles between police and maroons in the 1830s, including the dismantling of a network of ma-roons on the Cane Bayou and a series of raids on maroon camps around Bayou Metairie, see Nath-alie Dessens, *Creole City: A Chronicle of Early American New Orleans* (Gainesville: Univ. of Florida Press, 2015), 154–156. See also Liliane Crété, *La Vie Quotidienne en Louisiane, 1815-1830* (Paris: Hachette Litterature, 1978), 84–86.

7. On borderland and hinterland maroons, see Diouf, *Slavery's Exiles*, 6–11. On the participa-tion of maroons in the local economy, see the following works: Hall, *Africans in Colonial Louisi-ana*, 97–155, 203–236, 284, 322–323; and Powell, *Accidental City*, 23–31, 93–105. For comparison, on trade and the task economy in the Dismal Swamp, see Ted Maris-Wolf, "Hidden in Plain Sight: Maroon Life and Labor in Virginia's Dismal Swamp," *Slavery and Abolition* 34 (2013): 446–464.

8. Evidence suggests Squire made the final decision to take up a more permanent residence in the cypress swamp at some point in the fall of 1835. When Squire was arrested in August 1835 for "jouer dans la rue" (playing in the street) in the Faubourg Marigny, he is listed as a slave be-longing to "W. Debuys," and DeBuys appears to have paid the fine for the infraction. In this record, Squire is not listed "comme marron." New Orleans City Guard, Reports of the Captain of the Guard 1826–1836, 16–17 Août 1835, City Archives, Louisiana Division, New Orleans Public Library, New Orleans, Louisiana. For the arrest record reporting his injury at the hands of the police, leading to the amputation of his arm, see New Orleans City Guard, Reports of the Captain of the Guard 1826–1836, 21–22 Janvier 1836, City Archives, Louisiana Division, New Orleans Public Library, New Orleans, Louisiana. The following is a transcription of this record in the original French: "Squire, nègre de Mr. Dubuyse [*sic*], conduit au Poste par la Patrouille bourgeoise du Bayou St. Jean, qui consistaite de Messrs: Coquet, B. Flaitasse, P. Massia, Auguste Brungier & Philippe Lambert, et qui l'ont arrêté dans une cabanne auprès du bois; mais comme le nègre ne voulait pas se rendre et comme lui ou son camarade avaient tiré un coup de fusil sur la Patrouille, elle a fait feu également et a blessé le dit nègre dangereusement. Un fusil deposé au Poste et le nègre mis à la geôle de police à 2 heures." Henry Castellanos also mentions "Monsieur Fleitas" as the person who shoots Squire in the arm. Castellanos, *New Orleans as It Was*, 211. Versions of the legend that represent the loss of the arm in terms broadly compatible with this arrest record include the following: Hearn, "Original Bras-Coupé," 2; Kendall, *History of New Orleans*, 131–132; Asbury, *French Quarter*, 245; Christian, "Bras Coupé"; Saxon et al., *Gumbo Ya-Ya*, 253–254; Carter, *Lower Mississippi*, 178–179; Botkin,

ed., *Treasury of Southern Folklore*, 328–330; Harris et al., *Black Book*, 142; and Nash, "Legend of a One-Armed Murderer," 310–311. Gaulden includes details about the loss of the arm and also adds another scene after the escape from the hospital in which Bras-Coupé returns to bid farewell to William DeBuys. "He had walked into his master's study late one night with the white man's shiny rifle in his one hand," Gaulden writes. "'I'm leaving,'" Bras-Coupé announces, "'And you can tell 'em they ain't going to get me no more.'" Gaulden, "Tiger of the Bayous," 25.

9. "[The Cypress Swamp]," *New Orleans Bee* (6 June 1836), 2. After Bras-Coupé was outlawed, a dispute erupted between Mayor Prieur and the Third Municipality council over who exactly had the legal authority to issue the proclamation. This dispute was an extension of the controversy between the mayor and the three municipal councils over the management of the city guard. On the outlawry proclamation, see the following municipal council minutes, mayoral proclamations, and newspaper editorials and articles: Ordinances and Resolutions, Third Municipality, vol. 1, Seance du 29 Juin 1836, City Archives, Louisiana Division, New Orleans Public Library, New Orleans, Louisiana; Ordinances and Resolutions, Third Municipality, vol. 1, Résolution du 2 Juillet 1836, City Archives, Louisiana Division, New Orleans Public Library, New Orleans, Louisiana; Office of the Mayor, Messages to the City Councils, subseries I, vol. 1, 6 July 1836, City Archives, Louisiana Division, New Orleans Public Library, New Orleans, Louisiana; "[Squire and James Outlawed]," *New Orleans Bee* (30 June 1836), 2; "Council of the Third Municipality," *New Orleans Bee* (1 July 1836), 2; and "Runaway Negroes in the Cypress Swamp," *Liberator* (2 July 1836), 107. On the murders on Bayou Cochon and the cypress swamp as a "ville de malheurs" (city of misfortune) populated by criminals, refugees, and marauding fugitive slaves, see also Sainte-Gême Papers, folder 271, Williams Research Center, Historic New Orleans Collection, New Orleans, Louisiana. The outlawing of Bras-Coupé is also discussed in the following newspaper articles: "[The Negro Squier]," *New Orleans Bee* (7 April 1837), 2; "Squire—the Outlaw!" *New Orleans Picayune* (19 July 1837), 2; "Death of Squier," *New Orleans Bee* (20 July 1837), 2. On Squire venturing into the old city and "taking over," see Gaulden, "Tiger of the Bayous," 26. See also Carter, *Lower Mississippi*, 178–179.

10. On the Panic of 1837, with attention to its impact on New Orleans, see Jessica M. Lepler, *The Many Panics of 1837: People, Politics, and the Creation of a Transatlantic Financial Crisis* (Cambridge: Cambridge Univ. Press, 2013). On the 1836 partition, see Joseph G. Tregle Jr., "Creoles and Americans," in *Creole New Orleans: Race and Americanization*, ed. Arnold R. Hirsch and Joseph Logsdon (Baton Rouge: Louisiana State Univ. Press, 1992), 131–185. For comparative analysis, see Mary Ryan, *Civic Wars: Democracy and Public Life in the American City during the Nineteenth Century* (Berkeley: Univ. of California Press, 1998), 21–134. On the many reform proposals for the city guard, see Dennis C. Rousey, *Policing the Southern City: New Orleans, 1805-1889* (Baton Rouge: Louisiana State Univ. Press, 1996), 11–39, 59–64.

11. Rousey, *Policing the Southern City*, 11–39; *A Digest of Ordinances, Resolutions, By-Laws, and Regulations of the Corporation of New Orleans and a Collection of the Laws of the Legislature Relative to the Said City* (New Orleans: Gaston Brusle, 1836), 105–115; Albert E. Fossier, *New Orleans: The Glamour Period, 1800-1840* (Gretna, La.: Pelican, 1998), 161–174. In an editorial demonstrating the high-flown rhetoric of the police reform campaign, the *Louisiana Advertiser* declares: "Founded on the customs, and continued by the prejudices of ancient despotic governments . . . our police establishment still remains a blot on the face of a free country, an ancient barbarism in a great commercial and republican city . . . a glaring remnant of despotism in a land of liberty. Are we

not sufficiently enlightened? Have we not sufficient energy and decision of character in our present city government to cast off this offending remnant of barbarism—annihilate this remaining leaven of ancient despotic custom and inherited prejudice—to dispense with the sword and pistol, the musket and bayonet, in our civil administration of republican laws?" "Our City," *Louisiana Advertiser* (14 February 1834), 2. The *Advertiser* also spoke archly to Mayor Denis Prieur, the principal opponent of police reform. "Our worthy mayor," the paper held, "is a wise and observing man," and "he will not stand in the way of the removal of such a foul stain upon the laws." "Our City," *Louisiana Advertiser* (18 February 1834), 2. These controversial editorials were reprinted in local newspapers across the political spectrum. See, for example, "Our City," *New Orleans Bee* (15 February 1834), 2. The ongoing controversy sparked by the *Advertiser*'s police reform editorials, including an violent attack on its offices by an angry mob, is detailed in the following reports: "New Orleans," *Baltimore Gazette* (19 September 1835), 2; "[A Second Disturbance]," *Daily Pennsylvanian* (22 September 1835), 2; "New Orleans," *Eastern Shore Whig and People's Advocate* (26 September 1835), 2; "Further Excitement in N. Orleans," *Portland Daily Evening Advertiser* (24 September 1835), 2; and "[The Late Excitement at New Orleans]," *Baltimore American* (29 September 1835), 2. Other newspapers were quick to defend the police's right to deadly force. Disputing the claim that "l'équipement des gardes de ville soit anti-republican" (the equipment of the city guard is anti-republican) or "desagreable à tout homme libre" (unpleasant to all free men), the *Bee* lampooned the farce of demilitarization, wondering if the reformers expected police to offer criminals an "honnête invitation" (honest invitation): "Pardon Monsieur le bandit, j'en suis bien faché mais je viens pour vous arrêter" (Pardon Mister Bandit, I'm very sorry, but I come to arrest you). "Police de La Ville," *New Orleans Bee* (21 July 1835), 2. For Prieur's statements on the proposed police reform in January 1836, see the following: Office of the Mayor, Messages to the City Councils, subseries I, vol. 1, 21 January 1836, 6 February 1836, 5 March 1836, City Archives, Louisiana Division, New Orleans Public Library, New Orleans, Louisiana. Demilitarization became a point of pride, at least for some city residents, in subsequent years. The *Picayune,* for instance, criticized the Natchez police for wielding pistols "which they keep cracking all night," noting that the New Orleans police "carry nothing more than batons" and are not "one whit less efficient than those who are armed with swords, cutlasses, pistols and blunderbusses." "[The City Guard at Natchez]," *New Orleans Picayune* (16 June 1838), 2.

12. Office of the Mayor, Messages to the City Councils, subseries I, vol. 1, 21 January 1836, City Archives, Louisiana Division, New Orleans Public Library, New Orleans, Louisiana. Prieur's initial objections to this proposed reorganization of the guard also appear in *New Orleans Bee* (25 January 1836), 2. See also Prieur's repeated assertions that demilitarization would render the police "inadequate." Office of the Mayor, Messages to the City Councils, subseries I, vol. 1, 17 May 1836, City Archives, Louisiana Division, New Orleans Public Library, New Orleans, Louisiana. For the text of the reform ordinance, see *A Digest of Ordinances*, 105. Prieur echoed other supporters of the city guard by citing Charleston as a counterexample, as shown in the comments published by the *Mercantile Advertiser* in response to the original editorial in the *Louisiana Advertiser*: "Are we the only city having an armed police such as our city guard? No—look at Charleston, we there find an armed police of tenfold extent to our own, yet there we hear no murmurs—there we do not see the people on every little occasion arrayed against the police, and yet it is armed in every respect as ours." "[The City Guard]," *New Orleans Mercantile Advertiser* (17 February 1834), 2. On Prieur's

earlier attempts to bolster the city guard, see Dessens, *Creole City*, 56–58. On the construction of the racially segregated state penitentiary across from Congo Square, which opened in 1837 while Bras-Coupé was still at large, see the following works: Rashauna Johnson, *Slavery's Metropolis: Unfree Labor in New Orleans during the Age of Revolutions* (Cambridge: Cambridge Univ. Press, 2016), 125–161; Jeff Forret, "Before Angola: Enslaved Prisoners in the Louisiana State Penitentiary," *Louisiana History* 54 (2013): 133–171; and Roulhac Toledano and Mary Louise Christovich, *New Orleans Architecture*, vol. 6, *Faubourg Tremé and the Bayou Road : North Rampart Street to North Broad Street, Canal Street to St. Bernard Avenue* (Gretna, La.: Pelican, 1980), 63.

13. "[Squire and James Outlawed]," *New Orleans Bee* (30 June 1836), 2; "Council of the Third Municipality," *New Orleans Bee* (1 July 1836), 2; "[The Negro Squier]," 2; "Squire—the Outlaw!" 2; and "Death of Squier," 2. For background on the city guard's history as a slave patrol, see Rousey, *Policing the Southern City*, 11–39. Police development accelerated after the 1811 slave revolt on the German Coast, as documented in the following works: Albert Thrasher, *On to New Orleans: Louisiana's Heroic 1811 Slave Revolt* (New Orleans: Cypress Press, 1996); Robert L. Paquette, "'A Horde of Brigands?' The Great Louisiana Slave Revolt of 1811 Reconsidered," *Historical Reflections/Reflexions Historiques* 35 (2009): 72–96; and Daniel Rasmussen, *American Uprising: The Untold Story of America's Largest Slave Revolt* (New York: Harper Collins, 2011).

14. Kendall, *History of New Orleans*, 131–132. Rumors about the reward circulated not only during 1836–1837, but also in later decades. Estimates range from $1,000, as reported by Lafcadio Hearn; to $3,000, as reported by the *Cleveland Daily Herald* and the *Philadelphia Public Ledger*; to "6000 piasters," as imagined by Louis-Armand Garreau. Others, like Henry Castellanos, simply speculated about a massive sum. The *Bee* reported that the "impression" that "very high rewards" had been offered by the mayor was a "mistake" and that the bounty was in fact a mere $250. Hearn, "Original Bras-Coupe," 2; "Squire, Notorious Negro Outlaw," *Cleveland Daily Herald* (1 August 1837), 1; "Squire, the Outlaw," *Philadelphia Public Ledger* (31 July 1837), 2; Louis-Armand Garreau, "Bras Coupé," *Les Cinq Centimes Illustrés* 2 (29 March 1856), 124; Castellanos, *New Orleans as It Was*, 214; and "Death of Squier," 2. On the rumored reward, see also the following: "Squire—the Outlaw," 2; "Bras Coupe," *Ouachita Telegraph* (19 November 1880), 1; [Henry C. Castellanos], "The Black Terror of the Bayous: A Runaway Slave Whose Death Made a Holiday in New Orleans," *Cleveland Plain Dealer* (2 July 1893), 10; Asbury, *French Quarter*, 246–247; Carter, *Lower Mississippi*, 178; Gaulden, "Tiger of the Bayous," 26; and Sidney Bechet, *Treat It Gentle: An Autobiography* (New York: Hill and Wang, 1960), 43.

15. "[The Negro Squier]," 2; "Communications," *Liberator* (28 April 1837), 4; and "Death of Squier," 2.

16. On the $250 paid to Francisco Garcia, see the following sources: Third Municipality Treasurer's Office, Journal 1836–1851, vol. 1, 19 July 1837, City Archives, Louisiana Division, New Orleans Public Library, New Orleans, Louisiana; and Third Municipality Treasurer's Office, Ledger 1836–1852, vol. 1, 20 July 1837, City Archives, Louisiana Division, New Orleans Public Library, New Orleans, Louisiana. These documents were discovered by Kevin Watson. J. Andrew Gaulden describes Garcia not as a member of Bras-Coupé's gang, but as one of the black-market brokers who linked the maroons to the economy of the city. According to Gaulden, Garcia maintained a "hut on the banks of Bayou St. John" where Bras-Coupé would come to exchange "news and products of the city for those of the bayous." Gaulden, "Tiger of the Bayous," 27.

17. Castellanos, *New Orleans as It Was*, 209–215. Castellanos's account of the Bras-Coupé legend was also published in a different version as "The Black Terror of the Bayous: A Runaway Slave Whose Death Made a Holiday in New Orleans" in the *New Orleans Times Democrat*. The original has not survived, but this article, part of a long-running series on local history, was reprinted elsewhere. See, for example, [Castellanos], "The Black Terror of the Bayous," 10. Following this gruesome display at the Place d'Armes, Bras Coupé became "indissolubly associated with the Cabildo" in public memory. See *The Picayune's Guide to New Orleans* (New Orleans: Picayune, 1900), 25. The exhibition of the corpse is also described in the following sources: "Squire—the Outlaw," 2; "Death of Squire," 2; Hearn, "Original Bras-Coupe," 2; Louis Moreau Gottschalk, *Notes of a Pianist*, ed. Clara Gottschalk (Philadelphia: J. B. Lippincott, 1881), 105; William Head Coleman, *The Historical Sketch-Book and Guide to New Orleans and Environs* (New York: W. H. Coleman, 1885), 21; "Bras Coupe," *Ouachita Telegraph* (19 November 1880), 1; "Jackson Square Was the Old City's Heart," 3; Kendall, *History of New Orleans*, 131; Asbury, *French Quarter*, 247; Aptheker, "Maroons within the Present Limits," 179–180; Carter, *Lower Mississippi*, 178; Saxon et al., *Gumbo Ya-Ya*, 254; and Gaulden, "Tiger of the Bayous," 27.

18. "Death of Squier," 2. See also "Mort du Nègre Squire," *New Orleans Bee* (20 July 1837), 3; and "Squire—the Outlaw!" 2. Reprints and elaborations of the *Picayune* obituary include the following. "Death of a Brigand," *Boston Courier* (31 July 1837); "Squire, the Outlaw," *Clarke County Post* (25 August 1837), 2; "[Negro Squire]," *Jacksonville Republican* (31 August 1837), 2; "[Squire, Notorious Negro Outlaw]"; "Squire, the Notorious Outlaw," *Vermont Phoenix* (18 August 1837), 1; "Squire, the Outlaw," *Huntsville Democrat* (15 August 1837), 2; "Squire, the Outlaw," *Jacksonville Republican* (24 August 1837), 2; "Squire, the Outlaw," *Liberator* (11 August 1837), 132; "Squire, the Outlaw," *Long-Island Star* (31 July 1837), 2; "Squire, the Outlaw," *Mississippi South-Western Farmer* (18 August 1837), 2; "Squire, the Outlaw," *Natchez Weekly Courier* (28 July 1837), 1; "Squire, the Outlaw," *New York Spectator* (31 July 1837); "Squire, the Outlaw," *Ohio Democrat* (22 September 1837); "Squire, the Outlaw," *Philadelphia Public Ledger* (27 July 1837), 1; "Squire, the Outlaw," *Wilmington Democrat and Herald* (22 September 1837), 1; and "[The Negro Outlaw, Recently Killed in the Swamp Back of New Orleans]," *Wisconsin Territorial Gazette* (17 August 1837).

19. "[Negroes in the Cypress Swamp]," *Liberator* (2 July 1836), 107; "Communications," 4; "Squire, the Outlaw," *Liberator* (11 August 1837), 132; "Anti-Slavery," *Liberator* (31 May 1839), 1; "Lecture IV," *Friend of Man* 3 (10 April 1839), 1; American Anti-Slavery Society, *American Anti-Slavery Almanac for 1839* (New York: S. W. Benedict, 1839), 43; and Aaron, *The Light and Truth of Slavery: Aaron's History* (Worcester, Mass.: Published by Author, 1845), 37. The *Human Rights* editorial and reply from the *Picayune* are in "Abolition Papers," *New Orleans Picayune* (28 September 1837), 2.

20. Garreau's short story exists in the following editions: Louis-Armand Garreau, "Bras Coupé," *Les Cinq Centimes Illustrés* 2 (29 March 1856), 122–126; Louis-Armand Garreau, "Bras Coupé," *Bras Coupé et Autres Récits Louisianais*, ed. Fabrice Leroy (Shreveport, La.: Centenary College of Louisiana, 2012), 61–78; and Louis-Armand Garreau, "Bras Coupé," trans. Sarah Jessica Johnson, *Transition* 117 (2015): 23–39. Johnson's is the first translation into English. It is included in this edition. On Garreau's career, see the following works: Edward Larocque Tinker, *Les Écrits de Langue Française en Louisiane au XIXe Siècle: Essais Biographiques et Bibliographiques* (Paris: D'Évreux, 1923), 214–217; Ruby Van Allen Caulfeild, *The French Literature of Louisiana* (New

York: Institute of French Studies, Columbia Univ. Press, 1929), 161; and Catharine Savage Brosman, *Louisiana Creole Literature: A Historical Study* (Jackson: Univ. Press of Mississippi, 2013), 63–64. For an important work anticipating Garreau in this literary milieu, believed to be the first short story published by an African American, see Victor Séjour, "Le Mulâtre," *Revue des Colonies* 3 (1837), 376–392.

21. Garreau, "Bras Coupé," 122–126; Louis-Armand Garreau, "Un Nègre Marron," *Les Cinq Centimes Illustrés* 2 (2 Février 1856): 57–58.

22. Coleman, *Historical Sketch-Book*, 21; Asbury, *French Quarter*, 246; Castellanos, *New Orleans as It Was*, 211. See also Gaulden, "Tiger of the Bayous," 25. The article from the *West Baton Rouge Planter* is lost, but it is reprinted as "Bras Coupe," *Ouachita Telegraph* (19 November 1880), 1. On the legend's prevalence "among both the white and colored races" in Louisiana, see Saxon et al., *Gumbo Ya-Ya*, 253. Generalizations about the oral tradition are also based on the following sources: George Washington Cable, "[How I Came to Write the Episode of Bras-Coupé]," George W. Cable Collection, Manuscripts Department, Howard Tilton Memorial Library, Tulane University, New Orleans, Louisiana; Hearn, "Original Bras Coupe," 2; Gottschalk, *Notes of a Pianist*, 105; Coleman, *Historical Sketch-Book*, 21–22; "Bras Coupe," *Ouachita Telegraph* (19 November 1880), 1; James S. Zacharie, *New Orleans Guide* (New Orleans: New Orleans News Company, 1885), 98; "Louisiana Outings: Rambles About Home," *New Orleans Picayune* (16 December 1888), 10; [Castellanos], "The Black Terror of the Bayous," 10; George Washington Cable, "New Orleans," *St. Nicholas* 21 (1893), 49; Castellanos, *New Orleans as It Was*, 209–215; "Jackson Square Was the Old City's Heart," 3; *Picayune's Guide*, 25; *Winter in New Orleans: Carnival, Racing, French Opera, the Old French Quarter* (Houston: Passenger Department, Southern Pacific Railroad, 1904), 40; Felix A. Koch, *A Little Journey through the Great Southwest* (Chicago: A. Flanagan Company, 1907), 13; *Creole Tourist's Guide and Sketch Book to the City of New Orleans* (New Orleans: Creole Publishing Company, 1910), 43; Kendall, *History of New Orleans*, 131–132; Corinne Hay, *Light and Shade 'Round Gulf and Bayou* (Boston: Roxburgh Publishing, 1921), 94–95; Charles Tenney Jackson, *Captain Sazarac* (Indianapolis, Ind.: Bobbs-Merrill, 1922), 60; Asbury, *French Quarter*, 244–247; Aptheker, "Maroons within the Present Limits," 179–180; Carter, *Lower Mississippi*, 178–179; Christian, "Bras Coupé"; Saxon et al., *Gumbo Ya-Ya*, 253–254; Botkin, ed., *Treasury of Southern Folklore*, 328–330; Gaulden, "Tiger of the Bayous," 23–27; Lewicki, *The Life Treasury of American Folklore*, 180–181; Harris et al., *Black Book*, 142; Mel Leavitt, *Great Characters of New Orleans* (San Francisco: Lexikos, 1984), 86–87; and Nash, "Legend of a One-Armed Murderer," 310–311.

23. On the premonition about the loss of the arm, see Asbury, *French Quarter*, 245. Asbury also mentions his being bulletproof and fireproof, and "detachments of soldiers" vanishing into a "cloud of mist." Asbury, *French Quarter*, 246. Gaulden explains that the outlaw was fireproof, bulletproof, and also able to teleport or disappear into a cloud of mist. Gaulden, "Tiger of the Bayous," 26. Gottschalk reports rumors about his ability to teleport or turn invisible and to "fascinate" with his gaze, and he includes the detail about bullets flattening against the fugitive's chest. Gottschalk, *Notes of a Pianist*, 105. Castellanos also reports the outlaw's supernatural "gift of ubiquity." Castellanos, *New Orleans as It Was*, 211. See also Coleman, *Historical Sketch-Book*, 21. On the bullets flattening against Bras Coupé and the power of his gaze to kill a pursuer, see also Loggins, *Where the World Ends*, 27–28. On bullets passing through the fugitive's body but doing no harm, see Saxon et al., *Gumbo Ya-Ya*, 253. On the "fearsome tales of Bras Coupe, the terror of the swamps

who preyed on human flesh and was proof to musket balls," see Jackson, *Captain Sazarac*, 60. On Bras-Coupé's "charmed" life and his pact with the devil, see "Bras Coupe," *Ouachita Telegraph* (19 November 1880) 1. Reflecting on Bras Coupé's treatment as a superhero, Charles Chesnutt imagines a model for black self-representation in literature. "If there are no super-Negroes," Chesnutt recommends, "make some, as Mr. Cable did in his Bras Coupé." Charles W. Chesnutt, "The Negro in Art: How Shall He Be Portrayed?" *Crisis* 31 (1926): 28–29.

24. George Washington Cable, "Creole Slave Songs," *Century Magazine* 23 (1886): 812, 814, 823; George Washington Cable, "The Dance in Place Congo," *Century Magazine* 31 (1886): 517–532. Dimitry, Petersen, Hearn, and Krehbiel all contributed materials to Cable's essays. Hearn claimed it was Dimitry who told Cable the story of Bras-Coupé (Hearn, "Original Bras-Coupe," 2). Cable claimed he heard about Bras-Coupé from an "old darkey," but he credited Dimitry with collecting the dirge about Saint Malo (Cable, "[How I Came to Write]"). On Cable and Hearn's collaboration, see the overview in Van Wyck Brooks, *The Times of Melville and Whitman* (Boston: Dutton, 1947), 385–388. For examples of folklore collected by this group, see also the following works: Lafcadio Hearn, *Children of the Levee* (Lexington: Univ. of Kentucky Press, 1957); Clara Gottschalk Peterson, *Creole Songs from New Orleans in the Negro Dialect* (New Orleans: L. Gruenwald Company, 1902); and Henry Edward Krehbiel, *Afro-American Folksongs: A Study in Racial and National Music* (New York: G. Schirmer, 1914). On Saint Malo and the maroons in Bas du Fleuve, see the following works: Hall, *Africans in Colonial Louisiana*, 201–236; Gilbert C. Din, *Spaniards, Planters, and Slaves: The Spanish Regulation of Slavery in Louisiana* (College Station: Texas A&M Univ. Press, 1999), 89–115; and Diouf, *Slavery's Exiles*, 157–185.

25. George W. Cable, "After-Thoughts of a Story-Teller," *North American Review* 158 (1894): 18; Cable, "[How I Came to Write]"; Frederick Delius and Charles F. Keary, *Koanga, Opera in Three Acts*, rev. Thomas Beecham and Edward Agate (1897; rev. London: Boosey and Hawkes, 1935); Asbury, *French Quarter*, 244–247. On Cable's work with the legend, from his efforts to sell the story "Bibi" (now lost) during 1872–1873 to the legend's gradual incorporation into *The Grandissimes* during 1876–1880, see the following works: Arlin Turner, *George W. Cable: A Biography* (Durham, N.C.: Duke Univ. Press, 1956), 54–55, 94–100; Louis D. Rubin Jr., *George W. Cable: The Life and Times of a Southern Heretic* (New York: Pegasus, 1969), 77–85; and Barbara Ladd, *Nationalism and the Color Line in George W. Cable, Mark Twain, and William Faulkner* (Baton Rouge: Louisiana State Univ. Press, 1997), 51–53, 71–76. On the local reception of *The Grandissimes* and Cable's retreat from New Orleans, see Rien Fertel, *Imagining the Creole City: The Rise of Literary Culture in Nineteenth-Century New Orleans* (Baton Rouge: Louisiana State Univ. Press, 2014), 71–95. Later in life, Cable published another version of the story, adjusting its diction and syntax for younger readers. See George Washington Cable, "The Story of Bras-Coupé," in *The Cable Story Book: Selections for School Reading*, ed. Mary Elizabeth Burt and Lucy Leffingwell Cable Biklé (New York: Charles Scribner's Sons, 1906), 26–65.

26. George Washington Cable, *The Grandissimes: A Story of Creole Life* (New York: Charles Scribner's Sons, 1880), 219, 2–3, 236, 239–240. On the DeBuys family legend about the presence of their ancestors at founding of New Orleans, see King, *Creole Families*, 383.

27. Critics, starting with Arlin Turner and Louis Rubin, have observed that this setting after the Louisiana Purchase facilitates an analogy between the past represented in the novel and the present world where the novel was being read. The Louisiana Purchase is equivalent to Recon-

struction; the Anglo-Americans flooding into the city, including the novel's protagonist, Joseph Frowenfeld, are equivalent to the carpetbaggers and other Yankee transplants; and the incumbent creoles, prideful and provincial to an almost ludicrous extreme, are equivalent to the city's unrepentant would-be patricians dedicated to the incipient Lost Cause. Turner, *George W. Cable*, 93. Rubin, *George W. Cable*, 77–85. Cable's subsequent essays on civil rights similarly represent the pursuit of racial justice as a struggle to supersede primitive governance. George Washington Cable, "The Convict Lease System in the Southern States," *Century Magazine* 27 (1884): 582–599; George Washington Cable, "The Freedman's Case in Equity," *Century Magazine* 29 (1885): 409–418; George Washington Cable, "The Silent South," *Century Magazine* 30 (1885): 674–691.

28. Cable, *Grandissimes*, 219, 414.

29. Ibid., 248–249. Cable's encounter with the Code Noir is described in Cable, "[How I Came to Write]." See also Lawrence N. Powell, ed., *The New Orleans of George Washington Cable: The 1887 Census Office Report* (Baton Rouge: Louisiana State Univ. Press, 2008), 73. For the original version of this slave code, which transitioned over time with the turnover in government, see *Le Code Noir ou Edit du Roy* (Paris: Claude Girard, 1735).

30. Cable, *Grandissimes*, 219, 221; Cable, "[How I Came to Write]"; Stephens, "Cable's Bras-Coupé," 387–397.

31. Cable, *Grandissimes*, 220, 221. Cable identifies Bras-Coupé as Arada in "[How I Came to Write]." He labels Bras-Coupé as Jaloff (or more commonly Wolof) in *Grandissimes*, 221. Aphra Behn, *The History of Oroonoko: or, The Royal Slave*, 9th ed. (Doncaster, UK: C. Plummer, 1770); John Ferriar, *The Prince of Angola* (Manchester, UK: J. Harrop 1788); [Peter Newby], *The Wrongs of Almoona, or The African's Revenge* (Liverpool: H. Hodgson, 1788); *The Royal African: or, Memoirs of the Young Prince of Annamaboe* (London: W. Reeve, G. Woodfall, and J. Barnes, 1749); Henry Mackenzie, *Julia de Roubigné* (Dublin: J. Byrn and Son, 1777); Anna Maria Mackenzie, *Slavery, or the Times* (London: G. G. J. Robinson, 1792); William Cullen Bryant, "The African Chief," in *Poems* (New York: Harper and Brothers, 1836), 111–113; Henry Wadsworth Longfellow, "The Slave's Dream," in *Poems on Slavery* (Cambridge, Mass.: John Owen, 1842), 11–14; Herman Melville, "Benito Cereno," *Putnam's Monthly* 6 (1855): 353–367, 459–473, 633–644. On the topos of enslaved royalty, see Wylie Sypher, *Guinea's Captive Kings: British Anti-Slavery Literature of the XVIIIth Century* (Chapel Hill: Univ. of North Carolina Press, 1942). One intriguing possibility is that the identification of Bras-Coupé as a captive king may have developed prior to Cable in the oral tradition on the basis of his leadership of the maroons. As Jeroen Dewulf notes, there is a tradition both in Louisiana and elsewhere in the African diaspora of referring to chosen leaders of mutual-aid and burial societies as "kings," a tradition descending from the succession rituals of Kongo brotherhoods. When travelers like J. G. Flügel witnessed slave celebrations in New Orleans and claimed to have spotted "negroes" who "were formerly Kings or Chiefs in Congo," Dewulf suggests that it is likely they were looking at decorated leaders of local groups and not enslaved royals. Jeroen Dewulf, *From the Kingdom of Kongo to Congo Square: Kongo Dances and the Origins of the Mardi Gras Indians* (Lafayette: Center for Louisiana Studies, University of Louisiana at Lafayette, 2017), 11–12, 63; Johan Gottfried Flügel, "Pages from a Journal of a Voyage down the Mississippi to New Orleans in 1817," ed. Felix Flügel, *Louisiana Historical Quarterly* 7 (1924): 432. Concerning the identification of local leaders as African kings, see also Samuel Kinser, *Carnival, American Style: Mardi Gras at New Orleans and Mobile* (Chicago: Univ. of Chicago Press, 1990), 43.

32. On New Orleans and the domestic slave trade, see Walter Johnson, *Soul by Soul: Life Inside the Antebellum Slave Market* (Cambridge, Mass.: Harvard Univ. Press, 1999). Ship manifests and conveyance records, including the William Boswell indexes, are available in the following repositories: Slave Manifests of Vessels at New Orleans, Louisiana, 1807–1860, Records of the US Customs Service, National Archives and Records Administration, Washington, D.C.; and Notarial Archives of the Office of the Clerk of Civil District Court for Orleans Parish, New Orleans, Louisiana. Garreau says Bras-Coupé is from Virginia. See Louis-Armand Garreau, "Bras Coupé," *Les Cinq Centimes Illustrés* 2 (29 March 1856), 122.

33. Cable, *Grandissimes*, 236–237. For examples of attention to the police campaign and the display on the Place d'Armes in the oral tradition, see the following sources: "Squire—the Outlaw," 2; "Death of Squier," 2; Hearn, "Original Bras-Coupe," 2; Gottschalk, *Notes of a Pianist*, 105; Coleman, *Historical Sketch-Book*, 21; "Bras Coupe," *Ouachita Telegraph* (19 November 1880), 1; Kendall, *History of New Orleans*, 131; Asbury, *French Quarter*, 247; Carter, *Lower Mississippi*, 178; and Saxon et al., *Gumbo Ya-Ya*, 254.

34. Cable, *Grandissimes*, 246–248. The dances at Congo Square only peaked after 1817, when an ordinance was passed banning such assemblies except in places and times designated by the mayor. It was decided that slaves could "gather in a crowd" only in Congo Square and only on Sunday afternoon, under the supervision of a police officer who would designate with a gunshot when the dancing was to begin and end. Slaves "assembled" elsewhere would be "arrested by the police" and punished with "ten to twenty-five lashes." Ordinance Concerning the Slaves of the City, Suburbs and Places Adjacent to New Orleans, Conseil de Ville, Resolutions and Ordinances, 15 October 1817, City Archives, Louisiana Division, New Orleans Public Library, New Orleans, Louisiana. On Congo Square and its importance to cultural retention in the African diaspora, see the following works: Freddi Williams Evans, *Congo Square: African Roots in New Orleans* (Lafayette: Center for Louisiana Studies, Univ. of Louisiana at Lafayette Press, 2011); Matt Sakakeeny, "New Orleans Music as a Circulatory System," *Black Music Research Journal* 31 (2011): 291–325; Ned Sublette, *The World that Made New Orleans: From Spanish Silver to Congo Square* (Chicago: Chicago Review Press, 2008); Samuel A. Floyd Jr., *The Power of Black Music: Interpreting Its History from Africa to the United States* (New York: Oxford Univ. Press, 1995); Jerah Johnson, "New Orleans's Congo Square: An Urban Setting for Early Afro-American Culture Formation," *Louisiana History* 32 (1991): 117–157; David C. Estes, "Traditional Dances and Processions of Blacks in New Orleans as Witnessed by Antebellum Travelers," *Louisiana Folklore Miscellany* 6 (1990): 1–14; Gary A. Donaldson, "A Window on Slave Culture: Dances at Congo Square in New Orleans, 1800–1862," *Journal of Negro History* 69 (1984): 63–72; and Toledano and Christovich, *New Orleans Architecture*, 6:6, 63–66, 95.

35. Garreau, "Bras Coupé," 122–126; Gottschalk, *Notes of a Pianist*, 104–105; Cable, "The Dance in Place Congo," 517–532.

36. Ladd, "'An Atmosphere of Hints and Allusions,'" 63–76. On Makandal, see Dubois, *Avengers of the New World*, 51–57. Médéric Louis Élie Moreau de Saint-Méry, *Description Topographique, Physique, Civile, Politique et Historique de la Partie Française de L'isle Saint-Domingue*, eds. Blanche Maurel and Étienne Taillemite (1797–1798; reprint, Paris: Société d'histoire des colonies françaises, 1958). Cable also draws description from Médéric Louis Élie Moreau de Saint-Méry, *De La Danse* (Parme: Giambattista Bodoni, 1803). On Cable's use of these sources, see the following

THE LIFE AND LEGEND OF BRAS-COUPÉ

works: Turner, *George W. Cable*, 227–242; and Gilbert Chase, *America's Music: From the Pilgrims to the Present* (New York: McGraw-Hill, 1955), 305–314. In addition to ethnographic sources and travel writings representing dances at Congo Square and elsewhere, Cable draws at length from the following historical sketch: "The Congo Dance—A Glimpse of the Old Square of a Sunday Afternoon Sixty Years Ago," *New Orleans Picayune* (12 October 1879), 2.

37. Hearn, "Original Bras Coupe," 2. For city guides and local-color literature treating Cable's innovations as historical truths, see the following works: Zacharie, *New Orleans Guide*, 98; *Winter in New Orleans*, 40; Koch, *A Little Journey through the Great Southwest*, 13; and *Creole Tourist's Guide*, 43.

38. Asbury, *French Quarter*, 244–245; Botkin, ed., *Treasury of Southern Folklore*, 328–330; Marshall Stearns, *The Story of Jazz* (New York: Oxford Univ. Press, 1956), 51; Harris et al., *Black Book*, 142; and Lynne Fauley Emery, *Black Dance in the United States from 1619 to 1970* (Palo Alto, Calif.: National Press Books, 1972), 154–156. Even in the cases when scholars are careful to separate Cable's fiction and nonfiction, they remain willing to draw on his novels as sources of ethnographic information. Melville Herskovits, for example, confirms the importance of Cable's "articles" on African American culture, but he also refers to *The Grandissimes* as one of the "richest stores of data pertaining to Negro custom" with "special significance for research." Melville J. Herskovits, *The Myth of the Negro Past* (New York: Harper and Brothers, 1941), 246. In *The Story of Jazz*, Marshall Stearns cites Herskovits to support his own mixing together of Cable's essays and *The Grandissimes* as sources on the ritual practices at Congo Square. See Stearns, *Story of Jazz*, 40.

39. Loggins, *Where the World Ends*, 27, 14, 64, 71; Louis Moreau Gottschalk, *Bamboula: Danse des Nègres: Fantaisie pour Piano, Op. 2* (Paris: Au Bureau Central de Musique, 1849).

40. S. Frederick Starr, *Bamboula!: The Life and Times of Louis Moreau Gottschalk* (New York: Oxford Univ. Press, 1995), 32–45, 62–77; Gottschalk, *Notes of a Pianist*, 104–105. Even before *Where the World Ends* was published, others were already questioning Loggins's propagation of this myth. See, for example, Chase, *America's Music*, 305–314. The story about Gottschalk's inspiration at Congo Square also appears in Federal Writers' Project, *New Orleans City Guide* (Boston: Houghton Mifflin, 1938), 135. These claims are anticipated by others who figure Gottschalk, in a broad sense, as a genius who distills and thus preserves the city's vernacular tradition. Henry Krehbiel, for example, identifies Gottschalk as an "[alchemist] of musical science" who extracts "perfume" from the "strangest black flowers." Krehbiel, *Afro-American Folksongs*, 39. For other accounts of Gottschalk's salvage mission, see Henry Didimus, "L. M. Gottschalk," *Graham's Magazine* 42 (1853): 61–69; Asbury, *French Quarter*, 243; Cable, "Dance in Place Congo," 523–525. It is worth realizing that none of the Bamboula songs given in Cable's "Dance in Place Congo" actually come from Congo Square. Gottschalk's version, as Starr has shown, is an adaptation without an immediate connection to Congo Square, and the version that Cable takes from *Slave Songs of the United States* (1967) comes from Good Hope Plantation in St. Charles Parish, Louisiana. For the source for this song, see William Francis Allen, Charles Pickard Ware, and Lucy McKim Garrison, *Slave Songs of the United States* (Chapel Hill, N.C.: Courier Corporation, 1867), 113. It is also worth noting that scholars like Asbury and Loggins have retrospectively shaped our appreciation of "Dance in Place Congo" to the point where its account of the bamboula and its most famous illustration by E. W. Kemble have been explicitly connected to Bras-Coupé. Kemble's iconic illustration "The Bamboula" is in Cable, "Dance in Place Congo," 525. This illustration is identified as an image of Bras-Coupé,

for example, in Jay Robert Nash, *The Great Pictorial History of World Crime* (Lanham, Md.: Scarecrow Press, 2004), 1337. On Kemble's engraving and its prominence in the study of black music, see Eileen Southern and Josephine Wright, *Images: Iconography of Music in African American Culture, 1770s–1920s* (New York: Garland Publishing, 2000), 33–39.

41. *Jazzmen*, for example, makes much of the fact that Bolden "was already in his teens before the Congo Dances were discontinued." "In New Orleans," *Jazzmen* suggests, "you could still hear the bamboula on Congo Square when Buddy Bolden cut his first chorus on cornet." In *Shining Trumpets*, Rudi Blesh frames the same observation as an open question: "Much has been made of the fact that Buddy Bolden was a boy when the Congo Square activity reached its last stages of decline in the 1880s. . . . What, then must have been the effect of this African survival at its height, on the children and youths who, in future years, formed the first street bands? May not some of them have danced and sung, drummed or blown wooden trumpets in the historic square?" Frederic Ramsey Jr. and Charles E. Smith, eds., *Jazzmen* (New York: Harcourt Brace, 1939), 5, 9; Rudi Blesh, *Shining Trumpets: A History of Jazz* (New York: Knopf, 1946), 157–158. See also Robert Goffin, *Jazz: From the Congo to the Metropolitan*, trans. Walter Schaap and Leonard Feather (Garden City, N.Y.: Doubleday, 1944), 13–14. Even in cases where Bolden is not featured as the dramatic lead, it remains important to these histories that the dances at Congo Square lasted into the 1880s, when they would have been observed by the younger generation of musicians who would soon develop jazz. Different time lines are suggested by different scholars. Lynne Emery suggests that the dances continued into the 1880s. Marshall Stearns says the dances concluded in 1885. Barry Ulanov and Russell Roth propose that they were closed down by 1890. Whatever the exact time line, the early consensus was that the dances there lasted long enough to have "midwifed into existence what we know as jazz." Emery, *Black Dance*, 156; Stearns, *Story of Jazz*, 50–51, 55; Barry Ulanov, *A History of Jazz in America* (New York: Viking Press, 1952), 46; Russell Roth, "On the Instrumental Origins of Jazz," *American Quarterly* 4 (1952): 313. For the metaphor of the midwife, see Roth, "Instrumental Origins," 306. In all of these cases, the implication is self-evident: Bolden, and other early jazz musicians, had to have had some direct experience at Congo Square, and this experience must have influenced their early playing style. Proximity in time and space becomes the warrant for assuming cause and effect. On this assumption, see Boyd Bruce Raeburn, *New Orleans Style and the Writing of American Jazz History* (Ann Arbor: Univ. of Michigan Press, 2009), 38–80. A final irony about the argument for direct transmission is that it depends on a misreading of Cable's essay, "The Dance in Place Congo." The dances at Congo Square ended in the 1840s around the time when Cable was born. Most of these historians, however, have assumed that Cable was writing about dances he saw with his own eyes at the time he was writing the essay. Their assumption that musicians like Buddy Bolden could have seen the dances depends on their persisting into the 1880s. The argument for immediate transmission made by these historians would not be possible were it not for their misunderstanding of Cable's essay. On this problem, see Henry Kmen, "The Roots of Jazz in Place Congo: A Re-Appraisal," *Inter-American Musical Research Yearbook* 8 (1972): 5–16. Marshall and Jean Stearns portray Cable as an "observant contemporary" and "acute eyewitness" at Congo Square. Marshall Stearns, *Jazz Dance: The Story of American Vernacular Dance* (New York: Macmillan, 1968), 19; Stearns, *Story of Jazz*, 39. The consensus now is that the dances were outlawed at some point in the 1840s, although they may have been revived briefly in the next decade. See Evans, *Congo Square*, 28–33. On Bolden's birth and the chronology of his early life, see Donald

Marquis, *In Search of Buddy Bolden: First Man of Jazz* (Baton Rouge: Louisiana State Univ. Press, 2005). Attributed and unattributed variations on the line "Badoum! Badoum!" are in the following sources: Asbury, *French Quarter*, 244; Loggins, *Where the World Ends*, 27; Ramsey and Smith, *Jazzmen*, 8; Goffin, *Jazz*, 14; Stearns, *Story of Jazz*, 51.

    42. Bechet, *Treat It Gentle*, 8, 6, 202.

    43. Ibid., 6–44. "When *Treat it Gentle* was eventually published," Chilton explains, "the saga of Omar . . . raised eyebrows amongst many of those who knew Sidney well." In his biography of Bechet, Chilton carefully reconstructs the family tree to reveal an affluent lineage of artisans and cabinet makers but no Bras-Coupé. John Chilton, *Sidney Bechet: The Wizard of Jazz* (New York: Oxford Univ. Press, 1987), 291–292, 18. The likeness between Omar and Bras-Coupé is also noted in Lawrence W. Levine, *Black Culture and Black Consciousness* (New York: Oxford Univ. Press, 1977), 388. A number of critics have assumed that Omar is Bechet's grandfather without noting the similarity between Omar and Bras-Coupé. Martin Williams, *Jazz Masters of New Orleans* (New York: Macmillan, 1967), 140; Rudi Blesh, *Combo U.S.A.: Eight Lives in Jazz* (Philadelphia: Chilton Book Company, 1971), 35–36; Whitney Balliett, *Jelly Roll, Jabbo, and Fats* (New York: Oxford Univ. Press, 1983), 39–40; Raymond Horricks, *Profiles in Jazz: From Sidney Bechet to John Coltrane* (New Brunswick, N.J.: Transaction Publishers, 1991), 13; Grace Lichtenstein and Laura Dankner, *Musical Gumbo: The Music of New Orleans* (New York: Norton, 1993), 41; Floyd, *Power of Black Music*, 37, 810; Ted Gioia, *The History of Jazz* (New York: Oxford Univ. Press, 1997), 36; George E. Lewis, "Singing Omar's Song: A (Re)construction of Great Black Music," *Lenox Avenue* 4 (1998): 71, 87; Robert M. Crunden, *Body and Soul: The Making of American Modernism* (New York: Basic Books, 2000), 153–154; Farah Jasmine Griffin, "Children of Omar: Resistance and Resilience in the Expressive Cultures of Black New Orleans," *Journal of Urban History* 35 (2009): 656–667; Richard Brent Turner, *Jazz Religion, the Second Line, and Black New Orleans* (Bloomington: Indiana Univ. Press, 2009), 50. On the composition of *Treat It Gentle*, see the following: Chilton, *Sidney Bechet*, 290–292; "[John Ciardi to Jason Berry, 16 February 1976]," Jason Berry Papers, series 1, box 1, folder 4, Amistad Research Center, Tulane University, New Orleans, Louisiana; John Ciardi, "Writing Treat It Gentle," in *John Ciardi: Measure of the Man*, ed. Vince Clemente (Fayetteville: Univ. of Arkansas Press, 1987), 82–83; Edward M. Cifelli, *John Ciardi: A Biography* (Fayetteville: Univ. of Arkansas Press, 1997), 153–155. On *Treat It Gentle* and African American literature, see Jason Berry, "Jazz Literature: Through a Rhythm Joyously," *Village Voice* (8 May 1978), 61–82. Bechet's autobiography is influenced by the style of important precursors including the following works: Mezz Mezzrow, *Really the Blues* (New York: Random House, 1946); Louis Armstrong, *Satchmo: My Life in New Orleans* (New York: Prentice Hall, 1954); Alan Lomax, *Mister Jelly Roll: The Fortunes of Jelly Roll Morton, New Orleans Creole and "Inventor of Jazz"* (New York: Duell, Sloan, and Pearce, 1950).

    44. Bechet, *Treat It Gentle*, 27, 25, 27, 20, 28, 30. Current research supports Bechet's suggestion that music and dance were happening all over the city. Congo Square was distinct in scale and in its accessibility to outside observation, but in other respects the square was only the most conspicuous manifestation of a vibrant social life that was happening everywhere all the time. "Planters," Lawrence Powell writes, "wailed that cimarrones were infesting the city and its faubourgs, carousing in grog shops and cabarets, dancing and singing after sunset. This suggests that

the transmission and exchange of musical and dance-step ideas were not confined to the Congo Plain." See Powell, *Accidental City,* 272. On the evolution of these various open venues in the late eighteenth century, see the following works: Sublette, *The World that Made New Orleans,* 118–123; Kimberley S. Hanger, *Bounded Lives, Bounded Places: Free Black Society in Colonial New Orleans,* 1769–1803 (Durham, N.C.: Duke Univ. Press, 1997), 136–149; Johnson, "New Orleans's Congo Square," 127–128; and Henry A. Kmen, *Music in New Orleans: The Formative Years 1791-1841* (Baton Rouge: Louisiana State Univ. Press, 1966), 42–45. Freddi Evans draws from municipal codes, police records, and newspaper reporting on unlawful assemblies to indicate the persistence and range of these gatherings across the antebellum decades. See Evans, *Congo Square,* 135–157. On neighborhood social life, see Johnson, *Slavery's Metropolis,* 85–124. For first-person accounts by travelers and other observers describing cabarets, taverns, ballrooms, and outdoor venues admitting slaves, see the following works: Francis Baily, *Journal of a Tour in Unsettled Parts of North America* (Carbondale: Southern Illinois Univ. Press, 1969), 173; James Pitot, *Observations on the Colony of Louisiana, from 1796 to 1802* (Baton Rouge: Louisiana State Univ. Press, 1979), 29; Berquin Duvallon, *Travels in Louisiana and the Floridas in the Year 1802, Giving a Correct Picture of Those Countries,* trans. John Davis (New York: I. Riley, 1806), 26–27, 53–54; and *New Orleans as It Is: Manners and Customs, Morals, Fashionable Life, Profanation of the Sabbath, Prostitution, Licentiousness, Slave Markets and Slavery* (Utica, N.Y.: DeWitt C. Grove, 1849), 33, 34, 46–48. On the levee as a gathering place and outdoor performance venue, see the following works: Reuben Gold Thwaites, ed., *Early Western Travels, 1748-1846,* 32 vols. (Cleveland: A. H. Clark Co., 1904–1907), 4:363; John Fanning Watson, "Notitia of Incidents at New Orleans in 1804 and 1805," *American Pioneer* 2 (1843): 227, 232–236, 237; "Important," *New Orleans Picayune* (28 August 1837), 2; Fortescue Cumming, *Sketches of a Tour to the Western Country* (Pittsburgh, Pa.: Cramer, Speer, and Eichbaum, 1810), 333, 336; and "Negro Audacity," *New Orleans Daily Picayune* (19 November 1840), 2. On the outdoor dances and parties held at the legendary "Camp" clearing in the swamp by Lake Pontchartrain, see the following sources: Georges Joyaux, "Forest's Voyage aux États-Unis de l'Amérique en 1831," *Louisiana Historical Quarterly* 39 (1956): 468–469; and "Dancing Under Difficulty," *New Orleans Weekly Picayune* (15 July 1844), 2. On gatherings on Dumaine Street, see Hearn, "The Scenes of Cable's Romances," 45.

45. Delius and Keary, *Koanga, Opera in Three Acts.* Delius was English but lived in Florida from 1884 to 1886, a sojourn when he became interested in African American music, an influence shown in *Koanga.* The libretto by novelist Charles Francis Keary adapts Cable's version of the legend, including major themes (such as the fugitive's royal lineage) and subsidiary characters and scenes that are unique to the novel. Broken into three acts, the opera features long passages of music to reinforce its tropical atmosphere and an original epilogue in which the legend is told on a plantation to a group of girls by their Uncle Joe. Performed privately in Paris and in London in 1899, the opera had its public premiere in Elberfeld (in North Rhine-Westphalia), for which the libretto was translated into German. In these early performances, Bras-Coupé appears in blackface. Koanga was revived in 1972 for London's Camden Festival, for its first staging in the United States at the Opera Society of Washington in 1970–1971, and then in Port-of-Spain, Trinidad, in 1995. On the history of *Koanga* and its reworking of *The Grandissimes,* see William Randel, "'Koanga' and Its Libretto," *Music and Letters* 52 (1971): 141–156.

46. On *Negro Digest,* see Adam Green, *Selling the Race: Culture, Community, and Black Chicago* (Chicago: Univ. of Chicago Press, 2007), 136–140, 238–239, 257. Information on J. Andrew Gaulden's life and career was provided by Mae and Mark Gaulden.

47. Warren pushes in new directions even as he settles the legend into more-or-less conventional genre patterns (historical romance on the scale of *Gone with the Wind*) and character types (Amantha's tragic mulatta, ambivalent about her racial identity and therefore haunted by Rau-Ru's moral commitment). When Warren's novel was subsequently adapted by Warner Brothers studio screenwriters, the legend was further tempered in an effort to play to assumed audience expectations, as the novel's tragic conclusion was given a new happy ending in which Sidney Poitier helps Clark Gable to reconcile with Yvonne DeCarlo and evade the Union Army, waving to them as they float into the sunset. Robert Penn Warren, *Band of Angels* (1955; reprint, Baton Rouge: Louisiana State Univ. Press, 1983), 102, 106–108, 118–120, 141–145, 154–157, 199–200. Raoul Walsh, dir., *Band of Angels* (Hollywood, Calif.: Warner Brothers, 1957). On Poitier's recollection of this role, see Aram Goudsouzian, *Sidney Poitier: Man, Actor, Icon* (Chapel Hill: Univ. of North Carolina Press, 2004), 138.

48. Warren, *Band of Angels,* 260–262, 269–272, 280–281, 299–333, 354–365. On the political conflicts that form the backdrop for these later episodes, see James G. Hollandsworth Jr., *An Absolute Massacre: The New Orleans Race Riot of July 30, 1866* (Baton Rouge: Louisiana State Univ. Press, 2004).

49. Mark Frederick Bigney, *Poetical History of Louisiana, to Which Is Attached Columbia, a Centennial Poem, Respectfully Dedicated to Exposition Visitors* (New Orleans: E. A. Brandao, 1885), 7; Espy Williams, "Bras-Coupé," in *The Dream of Art and Other Poems* (New York: G. P. Putnam's Sons, 1892), 23; Henry F. Gilbert, *The Dance in Place Congo; Symphonic Poem, after George W. Cable* (New York: H. W. Gray Company, 1922); Frank Yerby, *The Foxes of Harrow* (New York: Dial Press, 1946), 209; Marcus Bruce Christian, *I Am New Orleans: A Poem Published in Commemoration of the 250th Anniversary Celebration of the Founding of the Crescent City, 1718–1968* (New Orleans: Published by the Author, 1968), 5; Tom Dent, "Secret Messages," in *Magnolia Street* (New Orleans: Published by the Author, 1976), 61; Aishah Rahman, *Anybody Seen Marie Laveau?* (1989; reprint, Alexandria, Va.: Alexander Street Press, 2002); Kalamu ya Salaam, "Bras Coupe," in *The Collected Stories of Kalamu ya Salaam* (2004; reprint, Alexandria, Va.: Alexander Street Press, 2005), 19–52.

50. On Robert Charles, who was outlawed by Mayor Paul Capdevielle in 1900, see the following works: Ida B. Wells-Barnett, *Mob Rule in New Orleans: Robert Charles and His Fight to Death, the Story of His Life, Burning Human Beings Alive, Other Lynching Statistics* (Chicago: Published by the Author, 1900); William Ivy Hair, *Carnival of Fury: Robert Charles and the New Orleans Race Riot of 1900* (Baton Rouge: Louisiana State Univ. Press, 1976); and K. Stephen Prince, "Remembering Robert Charles: Violence and Memory in Jim Crow New Orleans," *Journal of Southern History* 83 (2017): 297–328. For Bechet's account of Robert Charles, see *Treat It Gentle,* 53–55. On Mark Essex, see Leonard N. Moore, *Black Rage in New Orleans: Police Brutality and African American Activism from World War II to Hurricane Katrina* (Baton Rouge: Louisiana State Univ. Press, 2010), 96–114.

Death Notices (1837)

After Bras-Coupé was killed and his body displayed on the Place d'Armes opposite the Cabildo, two death notices were published in New Orleans newspapers. These notices provide an overview of the fugitive's career, and they were instrumental in helping to launch his legend. They also formed the basis for articles on Bras-Coupé that subsequently appeared in newspapers throughout the United States, including in abolitionist publications, such as the Liberator *and* Human Rights, *which offered critical responses to the coverage of Bras-Coupé in the New Orleans press. Both articles refer to Bras-Coupé by his original slave name, Squire. The* New Orleans Picayune *printed "Squire—the Outlaw!" on July 19, 1837. The* Picayune *was established only seven months before it published its notice on Squire; the paper was named after its initial cost, which was one picayune, a Spanish coin roughly equivalent to a nickel. An English language newspaper, it merged with several other publications over the course of its history and remains in circulation to this day as the* Times-Picayune. *The* New Orleans Bee *(or* L'Abeille de la Nouvelle-Orléans*) printed "Death of Squier" on July 20, 1837. The* Bee *was a bilingual newspaper printed in French and English. Founded in 1827, with offices between Bourbon and Royal Streets, it was the most influential newspaper in New Orleans during the 1830s, with a conservative political orientation that was closely aligned with the city's established creole elite.*

Squire—the Outlaw!
New Orleans Picayune (July 19, 1837)

This notorious black scoundrel was yesterday killed by a Spaniard in the swamp near the Bayou road. It will be remembered by all our citizens that Squire was the negro who has so long prowled about the marshes in the rear of the city, a terror to the community, and for whose head a reward of two thousand dollars was offered some years ago.

The life of this negro has been one of crime and total depravity. The annals of the city furnish records of his cruelty, crime and murder. He had killed several white men in this place before he fled to the swamp, and has up to the time of his death, eluded, with a dexterity worthy of a more educated villain, all the searching efforts of justice to capture him. He has lived for the last three years an outlaw in the marshes in the rear of the city. Many years since he had his right arm shot off; he is said, notwithstanding this deprivation, to have been an excellent marksman, with but the use of his left arm. Inured by hardships and exposure to climate, he has subsisted in the woods and carried on, until this time, his deeds of robbery and murder with the most perfect impunity—the marshes surrounding the city being almost impenetrable to our citizens.

This demi-devil has for a long time ruled as the "Brigand of the Swamp." A supposition has always found believers that there was an encampment of outlaw negroes near the city, and that Squire was their leader. He was a fiend in human shape and has done much mischief in the way of decoying slaves to his camp, and in committing depredations upon the premises of those who live on the outskirts of the city. His destruction is hailed, by old and young, as a benefit to society.

A Spaniard was yesterday morning in the swamp, and proved the successful foe of this enemy to society. Squire raised his gun to shoot him, but failed, the gun having snapped. Immediately the Spaniard rushed upon him with a big stick—he gave him a blow which brought him to the ground, when his brains were literally beat out by the infuriated man. Proud of his victory, the conqueror came into the city and reported what he had done. On hearing that Squire was dead the authorities determined to have his body hauled to the city and forthwith appointed a guard of men to repair to the swamp and bring it.

About two o'clock yesterday his body exhibited on the public square of the First Municipality. For the sake of example, two or three thousand slaves were encouraged to go and see it. Squire was so well known to the negroes of the city, it was thought it would have a salutary effect to let them gaze upon the outlaw and murderer as he lay bleeding and weltering in his gore. So enormous have been the crimes of this negro that the large multitude of slaves assembled to see the last of him, shuddered at the bare recital of his bloody and murderous deeds.

It is to be hoped that the death of this leader of the outlaw negroes supposed to be in the swamp will lead to the scouring of the swamp round about the city. This nest of desperadoes should be broken up. While they can support a gang and have a camp, we may expect our slaves to run away and harrowing depredations to be committed upon society.

"Death of Squier"
New Orleans Bee (July 20, 1837)

The negro Squier so celebrated for his brigandism and who had obtained the appellation of *bras coupé* from the circumstance of his having lost one of his arms in resisting the patrol who attempted to arrest him, has at length paid the forfeiture of his accumulated crimes and enormities. It will be recollected, that this same fellow was reported to have been left dead by some men of the guard, whom he had attacked some months ago. When he lost his arm, which was by a shot from one of the Messrs. Fleitas, he was secured and sent to the hospital for the recovery of his wounds, where after some time he was attacked by a dysentery which reduced him to such a state of feebleness that the guardian relinquished an active surveillance over him, which he availed himself of, to make his escape and avoid the punishment he so justly merited. No sooner had he made good his retreat than he gave himself up more than ever to the natural ferocity of his disposition, and it is reported that having made captive of a white woman, after detaining her in his camp for several days, he suspended her to a tree by one of her arms; and retreating a few steps shot her dead on the spot.

On Monday last, a man named, Francisco Garcia, who was fishing at the entrance of *Petit Rivière* left his boat for a few moments for the purpose of hauling to shore the car that contained the fish he had caught. He held in his hand a kind of crow bar to which he intended to make fast, and was proceeding, when he heard the detonation of a cap from a gun, and saw at a little distance from him a negro who was endeavoring to fit another cap in the place of the one that had exploded without effect. He hesitated not a moment, but coming up to him, struck him three blows, with the bar he held in his hand, the latter of which was so affectual as to strike him dead. The body was brought up on Tuesday about one o'clock in the evening, and was exposed to inspection on the public square, where it remained for some time. The marks of the wounds given by one of the city guard who had left this brigand for dead, were very visible, and completely corroborated the story told by him, against which some discredit had been thrown.

Many persons are under the impression that the three municipalities had offered very high rewards for the arrest of Squier. This is a mistake. The third Municipality alone offered $250, for which amount Garcia received a warrant from the Mayor yesterday.

"Bras Coupé"

LOUIS-ARMAND GARREAU (1856)

Garreau was a writer and educator born in Cognac, France, and educated in Paris. He divided his adult life between France and Louisiana, opening a school for boys at the intersection of Rampart and Dumaine, across from Congo Square. Printed in a feuilleton based in Paris, Les Cinq Centimes Illustrés, *Garreau's short story is the first attempt to represent Bras-Coupé in fiction, coming close on the heels of a companion story, "Un Nègre Marron," that Garreau published in the preceding issue. In many respects, Garreau's "Bras Coupé" is close to the oral tradition, but Garreau does make the choice to embed the legend in a love story, an innovation that anticipates plots subsequently introduced by George Washington Cable and Sidney Bechet. Garreau's story was republished for the first time in an edition produced by Fabrice Leroy in the Éditions Tintamarre series based at Centenary College at Shreveport, Louisiana. The following is an English translation by Sarah Jessica Johnson.*

In 1836, on the edge of the Bayou Saint-Jean, the canal that connects New Orleans with Lake Pontchartrain, there was a small wooden structure in which an old Irishman and his wife had established a tavern and a grocery.

This Irishman, named Hinclay, did a good deal of business with the negroes of the neighboring plantations, to whom he sold—at great profit (and in secret)—tafia, whiskey, brandy, as well as (in the light of day) ham, oil, fruit, seeds, and so on.

One Sunday, the Hinclay store was crowded with its usual black clientele. All the daylong, the *picaillon* and *escalin* coins of the slaves poured onto the grocer's counter. But the day's profit had not left the grocer in a more accommodating mood; for, that night, having surprised a negress at the very moment she was snatching two or three bananas from a bunch hanging from the door, the old Irishman took her by the arm and shoved her into the store. There he overwhelmed her with insults, pummeled her with blows, and tried to make her pay the sum of all the month's petty thefts of which he claimed to be victim.

This negress belonged to Monsieur D—, of whom we have spoken in another account. She was called Elsie. A young woman in her twenties, she was in the late stages of pregnancy. The unhappy woman cried and begged the grocer to let her go, promising to send him all the money he wanted the next day.

Hinclay finally allowed her to leave, giving her twenty-four hours to pay him twenty dollars (his estimate of losses for that month), while threatening to go and complain to Monsieur D— if the sum was not accounted for in the allotted time.

Elsie left; but less than an hour later, her "husband," another slave of Monsieur D—, entered the tavern. He was a man of thirty, six English feet tall, bull-necked with an enormous head, a back slightly bowed, and gifted with terrific strength. He was regarded as the best slave on the plantation. Moreover, he came from the state of Virginia, and it is from there that one typically acquires the slaves most highly valued in Louisiana. Active, industrious, suited to all forms of work, with a gentle nature, they rarely give themselves over to the vices through which other slaves often seek deplorable distractions. They are, on the other hand, of an incorrigible stubbornness.

Elsie's husband was named Jim, and had until then been considered to be the most gentle and least offensive slave on the ten neighboring plantations.

—Mouché (Mista) Hinclay, he said to the grocer with complete contriteness, Elsie rob you, is it true?

—Yes, my boy, and it has probably happened ten times before, for now I strongly suspect her to be the culprit of many a theft that I have suffered over many days.

—Oh! Dose other times, it wadn't her, for sure, me tell you!

—It is her who I found; it is her who will pay.

—You ask her twenty dolla'?

—Twenty dollars, as you say.

—Believe me, Mouché Hinclay, we don' have money like dat.

—Too bad for her!

—You see, my good masta', she pregnant, and so she want all dat she see.

—The princess is not so difficult to please.

—But 'course, she no thief.

—Anyways, have you come here to pay me? said the grocer, growing impatient.

—Listen masta', me bring you ten dolla'; dats all me have right now!

—I want twenty dollars, or I will denounce her to Monsieur D—.

—Oh! No, don't do dat, kind masta', the boss likely to kill Elsie.

—She had better pay me then.

—Me have two prize chickens; Me give you dem, if you want!

—No, it must be my twenty dollars, Hinclay repeated harshly.

—But we don't have it, masta'; you know me, right? You know me a good slave, me no liar, no drunkard for sho,' no slacker! So! Me give you de ten other dolla' next month.

—I want them on the spot.

—You is mean, Mouché Hinclay, you no good at all for de po' slave.

—So leave me alone then; I am no good for the poor slave when they steal from me, *that's* true!

—One word more, Mouché Hinclay. If de boss hit Elsie for you, true! . . . you be sorry later, me tell you dat!

—Are you threatening me, you scoundrel?

—You no want ten dolla'?

—No!

—With two chickens who grow like turkeys?

—No!

—You gonna get Elsie beaten?

—Certainly.

—Well! Do it, Mouché Hinclay, if you can. Me no ingrate, go on!

Jim seemed calm as he left, but his limbs were trembling and his eyes were bloodshot.

The next day, the twenty dollars had not appeared on the Irishman's counter. Jim had been truthful. All of his savings amounted to no more than ten dollars.

Following through on his threat, Mister Hinclay went to complain to Monsieur D— of the numerous thefts to which he had fallen victim, and he attributed these thefts to Elsie, whom he had surprised the day before robbing him of a whole bunch of bananas.

The plantation owner called for the accused. She lowered her head without daring to defend herself.

—Well! said the planter. Wait here, Mister Hinclay, and you will see for yourself how well I know how to punish my thieving slaves.

Elsie, as we have said, was pregnant. This circumstance required certain precautions that one would not normally use. Two other slaves dug a hole in the ground so that the stomach of the unhappy negress would not support all the weight of her body while she was stretched out on the dirt. To make impossible any writhing of her body from the pain (which could have been dangerous in her state), her four limbs were attached to four stakes driven into the earth, and, so stretched like a cross, her stomach filling the hole made for that purpose, Elsie was stripped of her clothes down to the waist, and given fifteen lashes of the whip.

It would be difficult to imagine the screams and pleas of the unfortunate slave.

When the torture had ended, the negress, all bloodied, was untied and made to stand up. She was in a ghastly state: foam bubbled from the two corners of her mouth, a cold sweat bathed her face. Her chest rose with effort as she let out indescribable groans. Two negroes held her up.

The Irishman Hinclay, ashamed of what he had done, slipped to the back of the camp and disappeared.

As soon as Elsie could speak, she cried out, struggling:

—Let me go! I'll die me! I'll go throw my head in the canal! Let me go!

It is common for all slaves, in moments of great vexation, to threaten their masters with suicide. The former understand well that it is in the interest of the latter to put a stop to this plan, which the negroes themselves have the least desire in the world to execute.

But for a long time now, Monsieur D— had warned his slaves that the first of them to utter this threat would be forced to go through with it in spite of themselves. In hearing the words wrested from the miserable Elsie by her torture, the planter approached her, frowning.

—What did you say? he demanded, full of anger.

—I'll die me! the slave exclaimed again.

—Repeat that! cried her master.

—Yes! repeated Elsie while vainly trying to escape the grasp of those holding her. Yes, I go kill me and my baby!

Monsieur D— grew livid, went inside the plantation house for an instant and came out almost immediately with a pistol in each hand.

—Let go of her! he said to the slaves holding Elsie. They obeyed. The negress took off running as fast as she could towards the canal.

Many of her friends were prepared to follow her; Monsieur D— stopped them with a word:

—Stay there! No one move!

All the negroes looked at each other with dread.

The planter marched quickly, close on her heels.

The canal was a fairly long distance from the plantation house; by the time Elsie arrived there, she had calmed down a bit, and, what's more, the instinct of self-preservation had awakened in her; she stopped.

Out of the corner of her eyes, she perceived her master advancing towards her—his pistols still in his hands. A glacial shiver ran down the young woman's spine; she suddenly remembered all the cruelties for which they reproached the planter; she covered her eyes as if to escape a terrifying nightmare.

—Ah, well! said Monsieur D—, who arrived at that moment.

The slave did not respond, but she glanced at the greenish water of the canal with terror, and turned away in horror.

—Hurry up! said her master in a ferocious voice. You threatened to throw yourself in the water, and I'm waiting.

—Mercy! Elsie murmured then, letting herself fall to her knees on the levee, holding out to the planter her pleading hands.

—I am fed up with these foolish threats. I want it known that they do not intimidate me. Go on!

The planter approached, and the butt of his pistol grazed the negress's forehead. The glacial touch of the steel made Elsie jump; she stood suddenly and found herself face to face with her master. The physiognomy of the latter was so somber and so fierce that the poor woman drew back a step. Monsieur D—, his arm still extended, advanced one step to match hers. The slave stepped back again, but she was on the edge of the levee; her foot missed, and she slipped into the canal, letting out a terrible cry.

She disappeared for an instant into this miry water, but her efforts soon brought her back to the surface, and, with all the energy of despair, she tried clinging to the grass of the bank; but the foot of her master pushed down on her head and sent her back into the middle of the canal. Twice Elsie's utmost efforts brought her back to the shore, and twice her executioner shoved her back into the depths.

Finally, the miserable slave did not reappear. The bubbling of the blackish water indicated the spot where the unfortunate woman still struggled in her death throes at the bottom of the bayou. Then, the canal stilled, regaining its sickly green appearance, and it was done!

The planter put his pistols back into their holsters, and calmly returned home where his dinner awaited him. He seemed uneasy. He did not believe his conscience to be stained by any crime, but he found himself one slave the poorer! That was it!

The same night, the grocer Hinclay heard a knock on his door. He had already been in bed; he cautiously peeked out the window to see who had come to disturb him at that hour.

A large negro stood facing the house.

—Mouché Hinclay, said the negro in a gloomy voice, Elsie. . . . she dead! Watch out! It me, de *nèg* Jim, who tell you dis. *Adieu!*

And the slave disappeared into the darkness.

The next day, Monsieur D— searched in vain for his negro; Jim had left the slave quarters.

A week later, in the middle of the night, the Irishman's house went up in flames. Negroes and even farmers from five or six neighboring plantations came to aid the grocer, but no one could find Hinclay or his wife near the burning house. Still, they tried with all their might to put out the fire, the flames of which they finally extinguished before the house was completely ruined. And then they entered the Irishman's grocery, whereupon they found two bodies stretched out near the counter: it was the Hinclays. Their faces were livid, eyes coming out of their sockets, and their necks were ringed with a black mark, showing clearly enough that they had been strangled.

Otherwise, nothing had been disturbed in the grocer's store, and one could see that theft had not been the motive for the crime.

Jim's name spread quickly through the astonished crowd.

Monsieur D— was equally convinced that Elsie's husband was responsible for the death of the Irish couple. He knew the boundless energy of his slave, and the planter, in spite of his own indisputable nerve, began to fear for his own life. If Jim had so cruelly taken his revenge upon Hinclay, whatever could await the killer of poor Elsie?

Monsieur D— returned home posthaste, and, disturbed all the way by even the least noise, threw fearful anguished glances in every direction.

He entered his room and, counter to his habit, closed all the doors and windows, but not before inspecting every corner. Just as he was getting into bed, Monsieur D— suddenly blanched. Trembling, he stopped as if petrified: His frenzied eyes were fixed upon the bedpost above his head.

The handkerchief that Elsie wore in her hair on the day of her death was nailed with a dagger to that bedpost. There was nothing to misunderstand: it was a death threat addressed to the planter.

The very next day, all the nearby residents formed a hunting party to find the runaway, *le nègre marron*. Over fifty hunters, armed to the teeth, followed by many slave-catching dogs, spread out through the cypress forest across a twenty-mile radius. Yet it was impossible to track Jim down. Authorities in New Orleans and the surrounding parishes were warned of a runaway negro capable of murder and arson. His description was given, and a $250 reward was promised to whomever could capture the criminal or reveal his whereabouts.

These efforts were futile. For three months there was no news of Jim.

Even so, Monsieur D— was not lulled into a false sense of security. He knew that a rebel negro was capable of anything. Fear of even the most horrid torture would not stop him from seeking the vengeance he desired. And so the planter was on guard night and day.

One evening, as he returned from his usual inspection of the slave quarters, he was stopped by a little mulatto boy, who said:

—Massa! Me saw Jim!

—Jim? said Monsieur D—, reaching for his holsters.

—Yes! Me see him real quick! Him slide thru da canes just like a snake. Me hid 'hind da tree yonda, an' him no see me.

—Good! said Monsieur D—, bringing the little mulatto boy with him so that he would not speak to anyone else.

The planter called the overseer and gave him his instructions. The overseer returned to the quarters, and with no pretense of alarm resumed his usual task of surveying the property. Then, when the quarters were calm, he slipped away to the yard of the plantation house where the planter waited with two or three of his most trusted slaves.

Three hours passed without a sound to interrupt the silence of the night, but soon enough they heard, near the wooden fence surrounding the yard, a scraping noise so faint that it might have been mistaken for the whistling of the breeze through the trees, or the fluttering of a night bird's wings. At that instant, there appeared above the fence a large black head. Each of the lookouts held his breath, frozen in his hiding place.

The black head stayed perfectly still for a while. Its eyes glowed in the darkness. Finally, little by little, the head rose up, and a body to whom the darkness lent gigantic proportions soon towered over the fence. This body started to lower itself down into the interior of the yard, suspended there by the arms.

That moment: a flash of light, an explosion, and the black shadow that clung to the fence falls, letting out a scream; but the shadow has barely hit the ground before jumping back up. Jim, for it is indeed him, has no time to gather himself. He is tied up before he can make his next move.

The gunshot had been fired by the overseer, who had not been able to hold off any longer. The left arm of the slave had received the shot's full force, and this mutilated arm hung inert at his side.

Apart from the cry he made while falling, not another sound was heard from the negro.

—Ah! I've got you, brigand! cried Monsieur D—, relieved of a fear that had so long consumed him. You will hang, you villain! Quick, he said to the overseer, a cart and some horses! I want this bandit off my plantation and not a moment too soon!

And so, Jim, chained, bloody, was laid in the back of a cart and, escorted by Monsieur D— and two trusted negroes, quickly driven to New Orleans, where they arrived at the break of day.

The magistrate in charge of the arraignment of criminals had Jim taken to the Saint-Louis Hospital after consulting a doctor. The negro had been found unconscious in the cart. The doctor declared his state to be very serious and judged that an immediate amputation was necessary.

—Try to save him, said the magistrate to the doctor. He is a known outlaw and we need to make a terrible example of him, as a warning.

That night, Elsie's husband lay in the bed of an isolated hospital room. They had cut off his left arm. His feet were in chains, the ends of which were fixed to the wall. Besides this, two orderlies kept watch at the door of his room, and every hour a policeman was relieved of his watch at the hospital's entrance.

All these precautions seemed perfectly unnecessary, since the patient could barely open his eyes. He had not been heard to complain, not even during the amputation. The doctor declared him beset by a violent fever, and the two orderlies keeping watch over him believed he would succumb to it before morning.

What happened next that night? What are the details of the negro's super-human struggle? No one knows. But the next day, the whole town was talking about it. It was said that Jim, in the middle of the night, broke his irons, which he then used as a weapon to knock out the two orderlies; that he broke down the two doors; and that, completely naked, having leveled not only the policeman but also the watchmen who hurried to the cries, he had managed to escape. Everywhere he went, he left bloody footprints. These could be traced as far as the Carondelet Canal.

The story seemed unbelievable at first, but the facts had to be acknowledged.

When Monsieur D— learned of his negro's escape, he cried:

—Oh! If I stay here, I am a dead man!

An hour later, the planter had quit his plantation without telling a soul the location of his retreat. This was the most prudent decision.

Nevertheless, there immediately began a most active search for Elsie's husband, who was from then on referred to only as *le Bras-Coupé*, the Severed Arm. The entire police force was put on alert.

A large number of hunters joined to make a complete sweep of the cypress forest surrounding the city. Two months later, there was still no trace of the fugitive. The conclusion was drawn that, without the treatment that his

63

wound required, he had perished in the swamp and been devoured by the crocodiles.

This belief was not long-lived. Soon not a day passed without talk of Bras-Coupé. The audacious negro had come, by night, as far as the outskirts of town; he had broken into and ransacked shops—above all, those where he could get hold of whiskey, gunpowder, and ammunition.

The Creoles, those most ardent hunters, no longer ventured into the forest unless they were in large parties. The imprudent ones who risked going out alone returned stripped of their shotguns, ammunition, often their clothes, and sometimes they did not return at all: these last had undoubtedly resisted in some way, and had paid for their reckless courage with their lives.

When a man was missing upon the return of a hunting party, no one sought the culprit; each and every person whispered the name of the terrible Bras-Coupé.

Soon, they counted over forty people fallen victim to the blows of the *nègre marron*. It was first feared that he would encourage other slaves to join him and form a redoubtable band of runaways, but he did none of this. He took an aversion to the human species and wanted no other being with him, neither man nor woman, white nor black. He treated everyone he came across as an enemy, and his name became, by the end of a few months, the terror of the land.

The New Orleans magistrates were moved to take action. They promised $6000 (over 30,000 franc) as a reward to whomever delivered Bras-Coupé, dead or alive. Every state newspaper published this enticing reward and broadsides were placed in the most frequented public places. All impatiently awaited the results of the offer.

A few days later, a Spaniard came upriver in a boat loaded with hunted game. Upon landing at the ferry dock across from Sainte-Anne Street, he moored his skiff at one of the piles where other small vessels loaded with fruit bobbed up and down with the tide.

—Well, hey, look here! It's Jacoppo Burmudez! said the captain of a nearby skiff. Have you given up the fruit trade then, Jacoppo?

—*Oui!* said Jacoppo. With the end of summer coming, I decided to take poor Juan Lopez's place.

—Let's hope you fare better than he did. . . . Do we know yet who killed him?

—How could we know? They found him on the deck of his ship with a bullet in his brain, just drifting away. The steamboat L'Union came across him at the Detour des Anglais. I knew the channels where he went to hunt his game, so went to find those who had hunted for him. I arranged everything with them, and this is my second voyage.

—Go on then! Good luck!

—*Merci!*

Jacoppo's boat was unloaded of its many pieces of venison, and he settled his accounts with the eight or ten merchants he traded with. He then headed to the Café du Petit-Goave, where he ordered a *champouras:* a strange mix of ten different liqueurs, some *biter,* some *pepermen*—that is, the most bitter of bitters, the roughest. Only in Louisiana could such a drink be conceived and consumed, for it is only there that one finds gullets capable of braving the fire ignited by such a combination. And they say it refreshes them.

So once Jacoppo had "cooled off" with a glass of *champouras,* he went inside a nearby grocery and bought a powder keg, many boxes of capsules, bags of buckshot, and one bag of bullets, all of which he put onto his ship and stored away in a hiding place tucked under the stern. Then, being the true Spaniard that he was, Jacoppo stretched out atop a woolen blanket and took his two-hour nap. Upon waking, as he had only come down river the previous morning, and feeling his pockets sufficiently lined, he set out to explore the city.

At the moment he was crossing the Place des Armes his eyes involuntarily fell upon a large pasted sign on which read in enormous letters:

$6000 Reward!

Jacoppo started to move on, for he was not so dazzled by the amount of that magnificent reward. He figured that it concerned some well-filled pocketbook lost by a local nabob, and since he had found no such pocketbook, he started to go on, as we say, about his way—that is until his eyes saw, a few lines below, the name Bras-Coupé. The Spaniard stopped, rubbed his eyes and walked closer to the sign. He was not mistaken. The poster was signed by the mayor and the governor.

Jacoppo reread the official notice from top to bottom ten times over. His olive skin deepened a shade; his brow furrowed, creating two deep lines; his mouth tensed.

So, instead of continuing his stroll through the city, he anxiously headed back to his ship. He opened the little hiding place where he had locked up his provisions, took out an old munitions rifle and examined it for a good while. After this examination, he took his purse and emptied it onto a handkerchief stretched out on his knees. He counted his treasure, which amounted to thirty-something dollars, and put it back into his pocket.

—There's enough! he murmured, getting up.

He threw the rifle over his shoulder, headed quickly towards Chartres Street, and stopped at the first gunsmith he found. When he left, he had no more than a dozen dollars in his pocket. But he had exchanged his old rifle for a good hunting rifle.

The next day at dawn, Jacoppo's boat was no longer docked at the Ferry; she was gliding rapidly downriver, aided by a good northeasterly breeze that filled her square sail. Around noon, the Spaniard folded up his sail and entered one of the many bayous that traverse the cypress forest on their way to toss their reddish-water into the Mississippi. One can only move through the bayous with the use of oars. It was early November, but the heat was still excessive; sweat dripped from Jacoppo's face.

He had no more than an hour of daylight left when he finally stopped.

The forest was thick around him. The vines vigorously climbed up the reddish trunks of the cypresses; the Spanish moss, *barbe espagnole,* hung so dark and so dense from the tip of each branch that even the most experienced eye could see no more than ten feet ahead through this potent and savage vegetation.

From the deck of his boat, Jacoppo took a brass cornet and sounded three long notes.

—Me here! came a quick short voice from behind the Spaniard.

The latter spun around, startled. Close to him, on the edge of the bayou, leaning against the trunk of a tree, stood a negro of enormous stature. It was Jim. His single arm was wrapped around the barrel of a gun, the butt resting on his foot. His intense, defiant eyes were fixed on Jacoppo, who felt uneasy under such a searching gaze.

—What dat you bring me? demanded the negro.

—Some powder, capsules, buckshot, bullets, and some whiskey, responded the Spaniard.

—Good! Put it all there!

Jacoppo brought out all the provisions that he had declared and put them on the bayou's edge, not daring to look at Bras-Coupé, whose eyes were fixed on him.

—Now go! said the negro to the Spaniard when the latter had finished. You come 'morrow heah, an' you see much game!

Without a word, Jacoppo took back up his oars and descended the bayou down to where it met the river. There, he attached his boat to a tree and stretched out on the deck to sleep, but his mind was too preoccupied and sleep did not come.

In the middle of the night, he untied his boat and slowly ascended the bayou to the place where he had met Jim. There he stopped, climbed silently down onto the bank, and slipped from tree to tree, throwing curious glances in every direction.

All of a sudden, a blow to his shoulder sent him to his knees, and Jacoppo knew he was done for.

—Listen! said Jim, in a voice that made him shiver. Juan Lopez too curious! Juan Lopez make much money wid me; but Juan Lopez did like wolf: him prowl all de night, an' him see Jim cabin! . . . Juan Lopez him die! . . . You see what me tellin' you?

—I'm not looking to find where you sleep, my brave Jim, you can believe me.

—You liar! Get out! Stay in boat there 'til mornin,' an' try ta sleep!

The Spaniard, happy to see another day, retired to his boat without a word. Stretched out on his blanket, not daring to move an inch, he eventually fell asleep.

When he awoke it was broad daylight. He rose up and saw on the bank of the bayou a heap of wild ducks, teals, squirrels, rabbits, and three roe deer that the negro had put there during his sleep. He first occupied himself with transporting all the game onto his boat; but as he went from the skiff to the shore and from the shore to the skiff, he stole some looks at the forest around him. He noticed traces of Bras-Coupé's footprints near the game; it must have taken multiple trips to move everything that the Spaniard had just loaded onto his boat.

Jacoppo took a moment for self-reflection. When that was over he sat for a moment on the bank, his eyes still fixed on Jim's footprints; he clearly suffered from some kind of hesitation. Finally he got up, opened the hiding space in his boat, took out his rifle, and jumped back onto the bank, saying:

—For $6000, I'd even risk my own life!

He made sure that a long knife, his trusty friend, was indeed in its case, tucked away in his shirt, and then slipped away, creeping alongside the negro's footprints. At each step, he stopped to listen and check his surroundings. For half an hour, he crawled on his hands and knees. Finally he heard loud snoring. There was no mistaking it; it had to be the sleeping negro.

The noise came from a circle where the looser vines and thinner trees made a clearing draped in green moss. A magnolia tree rose majestically from the middle of the clearing. Its green canopy broke up the grey and black background of the large hanging moss of the nearby cypress trees.

At the foot of this magnolia tree slept the negro Jim. His rifle lay across his stomach, and even in his sleep his hand remained on the butt of his terrible arm.

Jacoppo crept up, his heart beat rapidly, his lips convulsed, his face was livid. When he came very close to Elsie's husband, he straightened himself up, took his rifle in a trembling hand, pressed the barrel of the gun into the negro's forehead, and pulled the trigger. The hammer fell with a dry noise. In dragging the rifle behind him, Jacoppo had dropped the capsule.

At this noise, Jim leapt up, as if propelled by an invisible force.

Jacoppo, at first taken aback, regained his calm in the face of danger. Accustomed to his munitions rifle, he'd forgotten that his new arm had two shots. Seeing the negro rise up terrible and menacing, Jacoppo recovered his senses; the barrel of his rifle was still on the forehead of Bras-Coupé. He pulled the trigger. This time the shot fired. Jim let out a hoarse cry; opened his eyes wide, and his arm escaped his grasp; he fell on his face, vomiting up a pool of blood.

The Spaniard took a moment to compose himself. Even he was stunned by what he had done. He contemplated this terrible man who had made so many tremble, and whom Jacoppo Bermudez had just made into a corpse.

The next day, carrying a bloody head in his handkerchief, Jacoppo went to claim the promised $6000 from the governor of Louisiana. It was a fortune, for the price of which he had so easily agreed to become a murderer, six thousand dollars for which he had sold his arm to men and his soul to hell.

They refused—we do not know under what pretext—to pay him the promised amount. He had to be satisfied with $600! They profited from his action, but now that Bras-Coupé was no longer a threat, they found that fear had priced the value of the negro a bit too high.

We judge not the act, we recount it.

As soon as word spread of Bras-Coupé's death, Monsieur D— returned to his plantation, but he was no more humane than before towards his unhappy slaves.

From *The Grandissimes*

GEORGE WASHINGTON CABLE (1880)

George Washington Cable is one of the most renowned American novelists and essayists of the late nineteenth century. Cable's fictional representation of Bras-Coupé in his novel The Grandissimes *had a strong influence on subsequent versions of the legend. Cable was born in New Orleans in 1844 to parents who had recently moved to the city. He is best known for his fictional representation of New Orleans society, especially the city's creole elite, which is considered an important contribution to literary regionalism (or "local color"). Cable also published important studies on vernacular culture and controversial essays criticizing segregation and the convict lease system. Cable claimed that he learned about Bras-Coupé in the 1870s from an African American porter in the counting room where he worked as a bookkeeper. Cable decided to "make a story" about Bras-Coupé, which was rejected by several magazines on the grounds that it was too disturbing. Cable incorporated the story into his first novel,* The Grandissimes, *which was published serially in 1879–1880. His novel introduces several key changes to the legend. It pushes the story back in time from the 1830s to the 1790s, and it states that Bras-Coupé never loses an arm, that he is an African prince, that he lives alone in the swamp, and that he is the most famous performer at Congo Square.*

Bras-Coupé, they said, had been, in Africa and under another name, a prince among his people. In a certain war of conquest, to which he had been driven by *ennui,* he was captured, stripped of his royalty, marched down upon the beach of the Atlantic, and, attired as a true son of Adam, with two goodly arms intact, became a commodity. Passing out of first hands in barter for a looking-glass, he was shipped in good order and condition on board the good schooner *Egalité,* whereof Blank was master, to be delivered without delay at the port of Nouvelle Orleans (the dangers of fire and navigation excepted), unto Blank Blank. In witness whereof, He that made men's skins of different colors, but all blood of one, hath entered the same upon His book, and sealed it to the day of judgment.

Of the voyage little is recorded—here below; the less the better. Part of the living merchandise failed to keep; the weather was rough, the cargo large, the vessel small. However, the captain discovered there was room over the side, and there—all flesh is grass—from time to time during the voyage he jettisoned the unmerchantable.

Yet, when the reopened hatches let in the sweet smell of the land, Bras-Coupé had come to the upper—the favored—the buttered side of the world; the anchor slid with a rumble of relief down through the muddy fathoms of the Mississippi, and the prince could hear through the schooner's side the savage current of the river, leaping and licking about the bows, and whimpering low welcomes home. A splendid picture to the eyes of the royal captive, as his head came up out of the hatchway, was the little Franco-Spanish-American city that lay on the low, brimming bank. There were little forts that showed their whitewashed teeth; there was a green parade-ground, and yellow barracks, and cabildo, and hospital, and cavalry stables, and custom-house, and a most inviting jail, convenient to the cathedral—all of dazzling white and yellow, with a black stripe marking the track of the conflagration of 1794, and here and there among the low roofs a lofty one with round-topped dormer windows and a breezy belvidere looking out upon the plantations of coffee and indigo beyond the town.

When Bras-Coupé staggered ashore, he stood but a moment among a drove of "likely boys," before Agricola Fusilier, managing the business adventures of the Grandissime estate, as well as the residents thereon, and struck with admiration for the physical beauties of the chieftain (a man may even fancy a negro—as a negro), bought the lot, and, loth to resell him with the rest to some unappreciative 'Cadian, induced Don José Martinez' overseer to become his purchaser.

Down in the rich parish of St. Bernard (whose boundary line now touches that of the distended city) lay the plantation, known before Bras-Coupé passed away as La Renaissance. Here it was that he entered at once upon a chapter of agreeable surprises. He was humanely met, presented with a clean garment, lifted into a cart drawn by oxen, taken to a whitewashed cabin of logs, finer than his palace at home, and made to comprehend that it was a free gift. He was also given some clean food, whereupon he fell sick. At home it would have been the part of piety for the magnate next the throne to launch him heavenward at once; but now, healing doses were administered, and to his amazement he recovered. It reminded him that he was no longer king.

His name, he replied to an inquiry touching that subject, was —— ——, something in the Jaloff tongue, which he by and by condescended to render into Congo: Mioko-Koanga, in French Bras-Coupé, the Arm Cut Off. Truly it would have been easy to admit, had this been his meaning, that his tribe, in losing him, had lost its strong right arm close off at the shoulder; not so easy for his high-paying purchaser to allow, if this other was his intent; that the arm which might no longer shake the spear or swing the wooden sword, was no better than a useless stump never to be lifted for aught else. But whether easy to allow or not, that was his meaning. He made himself a type of all Slavery, turning into flesh and blood the truth that all Slavery is maiming.

He beheld more luxury in a week than all his subjects had seen in a century. Here Congo girls were dressed in cottons and flannels worth, where he came from, an elephant's tusk apiece. Everybody wore clothes—children and lads alone excepted. Not a lion had invaded the settlement since his immigration. The serpents were as nothing; an occasional one coming up through the floor— that was all. True, there was more emaciation than unassisted conjecture could explain—a profusion of enlarged joints and diminished muscles, which, thank God, was even then confined to a narrow section and disappeared with Spanish rule. He had no experimental knowledge of it; nay, regular meals, on the contrary, gave him anxious concern, yet had the effect—spite of his apprehension that he was being fattened for a purpose—of restoring the herculean puissance which formerly in Africa had made him the terror of the battle.

When one day he had come to be quite himself, he was invited out into the sunshine, and escorted by the driver (a sort of foreman to the overseer), went forth dimly wondering. They reached a field where some men and women were hoeing. He had seen men and women—subjects of his—labor—a little—in Africa. The driver handed him a hoe; he examined it with silent interest—until by signs he was requested to join the pastime.

"What?"

He spoke, not with his lips, but with the recoil of his splendid frame and the ferocious expansion of his eyes. This invitation was a cataract of lightning leaping down an ink-black sky. In one instant of all-pervading clearness he read his sentence—WORK.

Bras-Coupé was six feet five. With a sweep as quick as instinct the back of the hoe smote the driver full in the head. Next, the prince lifted the nearest Congo crosswise, brought thirty-two teeth together in his wildly kicking leg and cast him away as a bad morsel; then, throwing another into the branches of a willow, and a woman over his head into a draining-ditch, he made one bound for freedom, and fell to his knees, rocking from side to side under the effect of a pistol-ball from the overseer. It had struck him in the forehead, and running around the skull in search of a penetrable spot, tradition—which sometimes jests—says came out despairingly, exactly where it had entered.

It so happened that, except the overseer, the whole company were black. Why should the trivial scandal be blabbed? A plaster or two made every-thing even in a short time, except in the driver's case—for the driver died. The woman whom Bras-Coupé had thrown over his head lived to sell calas to Joseph Frowenfeld.

Don José, young and austere, knew nothing about agriculture and cared as much about human nature. The overseer often thought this, but never said it; he would not trust even himself with the dangerous criticism. When he ventured to reveal the foregoing incidents to the señor he laid all the blame possible upon the man whom death had removed beyond the reach of cor-rection, and brought his account to a climax by hazarding the assertion that Bras-Coupé was an animal that could not be whipped.

"Caramba!" exclaimed the master, with gentle emphasis, "how so?"

"Perhaps señor had better ride down to the quarters," replied the overseer.

It was a great sacrifice of dignity, but the master made it.

"Bring him out."

They brought him out—chains on his feet, chains on his wrists, an iron yoke on his neck. The Spanish-Creole master had often seen the bull, with his long, keen horns and blazing eye, standing in the arena; but this was as though he had come face to face with a rhinoceros.

"This man is not a Congo," he said.

"He is a Jaloff," replied the encouraged overseer. "See his fine, straight nose; moreover, he is a *candio*—a prince. If I whip him he will die."

The dauntless captive and fearless master stood looking into each other's eyes until each recognized in the other his peer in physical courage, and each was struck with an admiration for the other which no after difference was sufficient entirely to destroy. Had Bras-Coupé's eye quailed but once—just for one little instant—he would have got the lash; but, as it was—

"Get an interpreter," said Don José; then, more privately, "and come to an understanding. I shall require it of you."

Where might one find an interpreter—one not merely able to render a Jaloff's meaning into Creole French, or Spanish, but with such a turn for diplomatic correspondence as would bring about an "understanding" with this African buffalo? The overseer was left standing and thinking, and Clemence, who had not forgotten who threw her into the draining-ditch, cunningly passed by.

"Ah, Clemence— "

"*Mo pas capabe! Mo pas capabe!* (I cannot, I cannot!) *Ya, ya, ya! 'oir Miché Agricol' Fusilier! ouala yune bon monture, oui!*"—which was to signify that Agricola could interpret the very Papa Lébat.

"Agricola Fusilier! The last man on earth to make peace."

But there seemed to be no choice, and to Agricola the overseer went. It was but a little ride to the Grandissime place.

"I, Agricola Fusilier, stand as an interpreter to a negro? Sir!"

"But I thought you might know of some person," said the weakening applicant, rubbing his ear with his hand.

"Ah!" replied Agricola, addressing the surrounding scenery, "if I did not—who would? You may take Palmyre."

The overseer softly smote his hands together at the happy thought.

"Yes," said Agricola, "take Palmyre; she has picked up as many negro dialects as I know European languages."

And she went to the don's plantation as interpretess, followed by Agricola's prayer to Fate that she might in some way be overtaken by disaster. The two hated each other with all the strength they had. He knew not only her pride, but her passion for the absent Honoré. He hated her, also, for her intelligence, for the high favor in which she stood with her mistress, and for her invincible spirit, which was more offensively patent to him than to others, since he was himself the chief object of her silent detestation.

It was Palmyre's habit to do nothing without painstaking. "When Mademoiselle comes to be Señora," thought she—she knew that her mistress and the don were affianced—" it will be well to have a Señor's esteem. I shall endeavor to succeed." It was from this motive, then, that with the aid of her mistress she attired herself in a resplendence of scarlet and beads and feathers that could not fail the double purpose of connecting her with the children of Ethiopia and commanding the captive's instant admiration.

Alas for those who succeed too well! No sooner did the African turn his tiger glance upon her than the fire of his eyes died out; and when she spoke to him in the dear accents of his native tongue, the matter of strife vanished from his mind. He loved.

He sat down tamely in his irons and listened to Palmyre's argument as a wrecked mariner would listen to ghostly church-bells. He would give a short assent, feast his eyes, again assent, and feast his ears; but when at length she made bold to approach the actual issue, and finally uttered the loathed word, *Work*, he rose up, six feet five, a statue of indignation in black marble.

And then Palmyre, too, rose up, glorying in him, and went to explain to master and overseer. Bras-Coupé understood, she said, that he was a slave—it was the fortune of war, and he was a warrior; but, according to a generally recognized principle in African international law, he could not reasonably be expected to work.

"As señor will remember I told him," remarked the overseer; "how can a man expect to plow with a zebra?"

Here he recalled a fact in his earlier experience. An African of this stripe had been found to answer admirably as a "driver" to make others work. A second and third parley, extending through two or three days, were held with the prince, looking to his appointment to the vacant office of driver; yet what was the master's amazement to learn at length that his Highness declined the proffered honor.

* * *

"Stop!" spoke the overseer again, detecting a look of alarm in Palmyre's face as she turned away, "he doesn't do any such thing. If Señor will let me take the man to Agricola—"

"No!" cried Palmyre, with an agonized look, "I will tell. He will take the place and fill it if you will give me to him for his own—but oh, messieurs, for the love of God—I do not want to be his wife!"

The overseer looked at the Señor, ready to approve whatever he should decide. Bras-Coupé's intrepid audacity took the Spaniard's heart by irresistible assault.

"I leave it entirely with Señor Fusilier," he said.

"But he is not my master; he has no right—"

"Silence!"

And she was silent; and so, sometimes, is fire in the wall.

Agricola's consent was given with malicious promptness, and as Bras-Coupé's fetters fell off it was decreed that, should he fill his office efficiently, there should be a wedding on the rear veranda of the Grandissime mansion simultaneously with the one already appointed to take place in the grand hall of the same house six months from that present day. In the meanwhile Palmyre should remain with Mademoiselle, who had promptly but quietly made up her mind that Palmyre should not be wed unless she wished to be. Bras-Coupé made no objection, was royally worthless for a time, but learned fast, mastered the "gumbo" dialect in a few weeks, and in six months was the most valuable man ever bought for gourde dollars. Nevertheless, there were but three persons within as many square miles who were not most vividly afraid of him.

The first was Palmyre. His bearing in her presence was ever one of solemn, exalted respect, which, whether from pure magnanimity in himself, or by reason of her magnetic eye, was something worth being there to see. "It was royal!" said the overseer.

The second was not that official. When Bras-Coupé said—as, at stated intervals, he did say—"*Mo courri c'ez Agricole Fusilier 'pou oir' n'amourouse* (I go to Agricola Fusilier to see my betrothed,)" the overseer would sooner have intercepted a score of painted Chickasaws than that one lover. He would look after him and shake a prophetic head. "Trouble coming; better not deceive that fellow"; yet that was the very thing Palmyre dared do. Her admiration for Bras-Coupé was almost boundless. She rejoiced in his stature; she revelled in

the contemplation of his untamable spirit; he seemed to her the gigantic em-
bodiment of her own dark, fierce will, the expanded realization of her lifetime
longing for terrible strength. But the single deficiency in all this impassioned
regard was—what so many fairer loves have found impossible to explain to so
many gentler lovers—an entire absence of preference; her heart she could not
give him—she did not have it. Yet after her first prayer to the Spaniard and his
overseer for deliverance, to the secret surprise and chagrin of her young mistress, she simulated content. It was artifice; she knew Agricola's power, and to
seem to consent was her one chance with him. He might thus be beguiled into
withdrawing his own consent. That failing, she had Mademoiselle's promise
to come to the rescue, which she could use at the last moment; and that failing, there was a dirk in her bosom, for which a certain hard breast was not too
hard. Another element of safety, of which she knew nothing, was a letter from
the Cannes Brulée. The word had reached there that love had conquered—
that, despite all hard words, and rancor, and positive injury, the Grandissime
hand—the fairest of Grandissime hands—was about to be laid into that of
one who without much stretch might be called a De Grapion; that there was,
moreover, positive effort being made to induce a restitution of old gaming-
table spoils. Honoré and Mademoiselle, his sister, one on each side of the
Atlantic, were striving for this end. Don José sent this intelligence to his kinsman as glad tidings (a lover never imagines there are two sides to that which
makes him happy), and, to add a touch of humor, told how Palmyre, also, was
given to the chieftain. The letter that came back to the young Spaniard did
not blame him so much: *he* was ignorant of all the facts; but a very formal
one to Agricola begged to notify him that if Palmyre's union with Bras-Coupé
should be completed, as sure as there was a God in heaven, the writer would
have the life of the man who knowingly had thus endeavored to dishonor
one who *shared the blood of the De Grapions.* Thereupon Agricola, contrary
to his general character, began to drop hints to Don José that the engagement of Bras-Coupé and Palmyre need not be considered irreversible; but
the don was not desirous of disappointing his terrible pet. Palmyre, unluckily,
played her game a little too deeply. She thought the moment had come for
herself to insist on the match, and thus provoke Agricola to forbid it. To her
incalculable dismay she saw him a second time reconsider and become silent.

The second person who did not fear Bras-Coupé was Mademoiselle. On
one of the giant's earliest visits to see Palmyre he obeyed the summons which

she brought him, to appear before the lady. A more artificial man might have objected on the score of dress, his attire being a single gaudy garment tightly enveloping the waist and thighs. As his eyes fell upon the beautiful white lady he prostrated himself upon the ground, his arms outstretched before him. He would not move till she was gone. Then he arose like a hermit who has seen a vision. *"Bras-Coupé 'n pas oulé oir zombis* (Bras-Coupé dares not look upon a spirit)." From that hour he worshipped. He saw her often; every time, after one glance at her countenance, he would prostrate his gigantic length with his face in the dust.

The third person who did not fear him was—Agricola? Nay, it was the Spaniard—a man whose capability to fear anything in nature or beyond had never been discovered.

Long before the end of his probation Bras-Coupé would have slipped the entanglements of bondage, though as yet he felt them only as one feels a spider's web across the face, had not the master, according to a little affectation of the times, promoted him to be his game-keeper. Many a day did these two living magazines of wrath spend together in the dismal swamps and on the meagre intersecting ridges, making war upon deer and bear and wildcat; or on the Mississippi after wild goose and pelican; when even a word misplaced would have made either the slayer of the other. Yet the months ran smoothly round and the wedding night drew nigh.* A goodly company had assembled. All things were ready. The bride was dressed, the bridegroom had come. On the great back piazza, which had been inclosed with sail-cloth and lighted with lanterns, was Palmyre, full of a new and deep design and playing her deceit to the last, robed in costly garments to whose beauty was added the charm of their having been worn once, and once only, by her beloved Mademoiselle.

But where was Bras-Coupé?

The question was asked of Palmyre by Agricola with a gaze that meant in English, "No tricks, girl!"

Among the servants who huddled at the windows and door to see the inner magnificence a frightened whisper was already going round.

---

* An over-zealous Franciscan once complained bitterly to the bishop of Havana, that people were being married in Louisiana in their own houses after dark and thinking nothing of it. It is not certain that he had reference to the Grandissime mansion; at any rate he was tittered down by the whole community.

"We have made a sad discovery, Miché Fusilier," said the overseer. "Bras-Coupé is here; we have him in a room just yonder. But—the truth is, sir, Bras-Coupé is a voudou."

"Well, and suppose he is; what of it? Only hush; do not let his master know it. It is nothing; all the blacks are voudous, more or less."

"But he declines to dress himself—has painted himself all rings and stripes, antelope fashion."

"Tell him Agricola Fusilier says, 'dress immediately!'"

"Oh, Miché, we have said that five times already, and his answer—you will pardon me—his answer is—spitting on the ground—that you are a contempt-ible *dotchian* (white trash)."

There is nothing to do but privily to call the very bride—the lady herself. She comes forth in all her glory, small, but oh, so beautiful! Slam! Bras-Coupé is upon his face, his finger-tips touching the tips of her snowy slippers. She gently bids him go and dress, and at once he goes.

Ah! now the question may be answered without whispering. There is Bras-Coupé, towering above all heads, in ridiculous red and blue regimentals, but with a look of savage dignity upon him that keeps every one from laugh-ing. The murmur of admiration that passed along the thronged gallery leaped up into a shout in the bosom of Palmyre. Oh, Bras-Coupé—heroic soul! She would not falter. She would let the silly priest say his say—then her cunning should help her *not to be* his wife, yet to show his mighty arm how and when to strike.

"He is looking for Palmyre," said some, and at that moment he saw her.

"Ho-o-o-o-o!"

Agricola's best roar was a penny trumpet to Bras-Coupé's note of joy. The whole masculine half of the indoor company flocked out to see what the mat-ter was. Bras-Coupé was taking her hand in one of his and laying his other upon her head; and as some one made an unnecessary gesture for silence, he sang, beating slow and solemn time with his naked foot and with the hand that dropped hers to smite his breast:

> "'En haut la montagne, zami,
> Mo pé coupé canne, zami,
> Pou' fé l'a'zen' zami,
> Pou' mo baille Palmyre.

Ah! Palmyre, Palmyre mo c'ere,
Mo l'aimé 'ou'—mo l'aimé ou.'"

"*Montagne?*" asked one slave of another, "*qui ci çà, montagne? gnia pas quiç' ose comme çà dans la Louisiana?* (What's a mountain? We haven't such things in Louisiana.)"
"*Mein ye gagnein plein montagnes dans l'Afrique,* listen!"

"'Ah! Palmyre, Palmyre, mo' piti zozo,'
Mo l'aimé 'ou'—mo l'aimé, l'aimé ou.'"

"Bravissimo!—" but just then a counter-attraction drew the white company back into the house. An old French priest with sandalled feet and a dirty face had arrived. There was a moment of hand-shaking with the good father, then a moment of palpitation and holding of the breath, and then— you would have known it by the turning away of two or three feminine heads in tears—the lily hand became the don's, to have and to hold, by authority of the Church and the Spanish king. And all was merry, save that outside there was coming up as villainous a night as ever cast black looks in through snug windows.

It was just as the newly wed Spaniard, with Agricola and all the guests, were concluding the by-play of marrying the darker couple, that the hurricane struck the dwelling. The holy and jovial father had made faint pretence of kissing this second bride; the ladies, colonels, dons, etc.,—though the joke struck them as a trifle coarse—were beginning to laugh and clap hands again and the gowned jester to bow to right and left, when Bras-Coupé, tardily realizing the consummation of his hopes, stepped forward to embrace his wife.

"Bras-Coupé!"

The voice was that of Palmyre's mistress. She had not been able to comprehend her maid's behavior, but now Palmyre had darted upon her an appealing look.

The warrior stopped as if a javelin had flashed over his head and stuck in the wall.

"Bras-Coupé must wait till I give him his wife."

He sank, with hidden face, slowly to the floor.

"Bras-Coupé hears the voice of zombis; the voice is sweet, but the words are very strong; from the same sugar-cane comes *sirop* and *tafia;* Bras-Coupé says to zombis, 'Bras-Coupé will wait; but if the *dotchians* deceive Bras-Coupé——" he rose to his feet with his eyes closed and his great black fist lifted over his head—"Bras-Coupé will call Voudou-Magnan!"

The crowd retreated and the storm fell like a burst of infernal applause. A whiff like fifty witches flouted up the canvas curtain of the gallery and a fierce black cloud, drawing the moon under its cloak, belched forth a stream of fire that seemed to flood the ground; a peal of thunder followed as if the sky had fallen in, the house quivered, the great oaks groaned, and every lesser thing bowed down before the awful blast. Every lip held its breath for a minute— or an hour, no one knew—there was a sudden lull of the wind, and the floods came down. Have you heard it thunder and rain in those Louisiana low-lands? Every clap seems to crack the world. It has rained a moment; you peer through the black pane—your house is an island, all the land is sea.

However, the supper was spread in the hall and in due time the guests were filled. Then a supper was spread in the big hall in the basement, below stairs, the sons and daughters of Ham came down like the fowls of the air upon a rice-field, and Bras-Coupé, throwing his heels about with the joy-ous carelessness of a smutted Mercury, for the first time in his life tasted the blood of the grape. A second, a fifth, a tenth time he tasted it, drinking more deeply each time, and would have taken it ten times more had not his bride cunningly concealed it. It was like stealing a tiger's kittens.

The moment quickly came when he wanted his eleventh bumper. As he presented his request a silent shiver of consternation ran through the dark company; and when, in what the prince meant as a remonstrative tone, he repeated the petition—splitting the table with his fist by way of punctuation— there ensued a hustling up staircases and a cramming into dim corners that left him alone at the banquet.

Leaving the table, he strode upstairs and into the chirruping and dancing of the grand salon. There was a halt in the cotillion and a hush of amaze-ment like the shutting off of steam. Bras-Coupé strode straight to his master, laid his paw upon his fellow-bridegroom's shoulder and in a thunder-tone demanded:

"More!"

The master swore a Spanish oath, lifted his hand and—fell, beneath the terrific fist of his slave, with a bang that jingled the candelabra. Dolorous stroke!—for the dealer of it. Given, apparently to him—poor, tipsy savage—in self-defence, punishable, in a white offender, by a small fine or a few days' imprisonment, it assured Bras-Coupé the death of a felon; such was the old *Code Noir*. (We have a *Code Noir* now, but the new one is a mental reservation, not an enactment.)

The guests stood for an instant as if frozen, smitten stiff with the instant expectation of insurrection, conflagration and rapine (just as we do to-day whenever some poor swaggering Pompey rolls up his fist and gets a ball through his body), while, single-handed and naked-fisted in a room full of swords, the giant stood over his master, making strange signs and passes and rolling out in wrathful words of his mother tongue what it needed no interpreter to tell his swarming enemies was a voudou malediction.

"*Nous sommes grigis!*" screamed two or three ladies, "we are bewitched!"

"Look to your wives and daughters!" shouted a Brahmin-Mandarin.

"Shoot the black devils without mercy!" cried a Mandarin-Fusilier, unconsciously putting into a single outflash of words the whole Creole treatment of race troubles.

With a single bound Bras-Coupé reached the drawing-room door; his gaudy regimentals made a red and blue streak down the hall; there was a rush of frilled and powdered gentlemen to the rear veranda, an avalanche of lightning with Bras-Coupé in the midst making for the swamp, and then all without was blackness of darkness and all within was a wild commingled chatter of Creole, French, and Spanish tongues,—in the midst of which the reluctant Agricola returned his dress-sword to its scabbard.

While the wet lanterns swung on crazily in the trees along the way by which the bridegroom was to have borne his bride; while Madame Grandissime prepared an impromptu bridal-chamber; while the Spaniard bathed his eye and the blue gash on his cheek-bone; while Palmyre paced her room in a fever and wild tremor of conflicting emotions throughout the night and the guests splashed home after the storm as best they could, Bras-Coupé was practically declaring his independence on a slight rise of ground hardly sixty feet in circumference and lifted scarce above the water in the inmost depths of the swamp.

And what surroundings! Endless colonnades of cypresses; long, motionless drapings of gray moss; broad sheets of noisome waters, pitchy black, resting on bottomless ooze; cypress knees studding the surface; patches of floating green, gleaming brilliantly here and there; yonder where the sunbeams wedge themselves in, constellations of water-lilies, the many-hued iris, and a multitude of flowers that no man had named; here, too, serpents great and small, of wonderful colorings, and the dull and loathsome moccasin sliding warily off the dead tree; in dimmer recesses the cow alligator, with her nest hard by; turtles a century old; owls and bats, raccoons, opossums, rats, centipedes and creatures of like vileness; great vines of beautiful leaf and scarlet fruit in deadly clusters; maddening mosquitoes, parasitic insects, gorgeous dragon-flies and pretty water-lizards: the blue heron, the snowy crane, the red-bird, the moss-bird, the night-hawk and the chuckwill's widow; a solemn stillness and stifled air only now and then disturbed by the call or whir of the summer duck, the dismal ventriloquous note of the rain-crow, or the splash of a dead branch falling into the clear but lifeless bayou.

The pack of Cuban hounds that howl from Don José's kennels cannot snuff the trail of the stolen canoe that glides through the sombre blue vapors of the African's fastnesses. His arrows send no tell-tale reverberations to the distant clearing. Many a wretch in his native wilderness has Bras-Coupé himself, in palmier days, driven to just such an existence, to escape the chains and horrors of the barracoons; therefore not a whit broods he over man's inhumanity, but, taking the affair as a matter of course, casts about him for a future.

Bras-Coupé let the autumn pass, and wintered in his den.

Don José, in a majestic way, endeavored to be happy. He took his señora to his hall, and under her rule it took on for a while a look and feeling which turned it from a hunting-lodge into a home. Wherever the lady's steps turned— or it is as correct to say wherever the proud tread of Palmyre turned—the features of bachelor's hall disappeared; guns, dogs, oars, saddles, nets, went their way into proper banishment, and the broad halls and lofty chambers— the floors now muffled with mats of palmetto-leaf—no longer re-echoed the tread of a lonely master, but breathed a redolence of flowers and a rippling murmur of well-contented song.

But the song was not from the throat of Bras-Coupé's "*piti zozo*." Silent and severe by day, she moaned away whole nights heaping reproaches upon herself for the impulse—now to her, because it had failed, inexplicable in its folly—which had permitted her hand to lie in Bras-Coupé's and the priest to bind them together.

For in the audacity of her pride, or, as Agricola would have said, in the immensity of her impudence, she had held herself consecrate to a hopeless love. But now she was a black man's wife! and even he unable to sit at her feet and learn the lesson she had hoped to teach him. She had heard of San Domingo, and for months the fierce heart within her silent bosom had been leaping and shouting and seeing visions of fire and blood, and when she brooded over the nearness of Agricola and the remoteness of Honoré these visions got from her a sort of mad consent. The lesson she would have taught the giant was Insurrection. But it was too late. Letting her dagger sleep in her bosom, and with an undefined belief in imaginary resources, she had consented to join hands with her giant hero before the priest; and when the wedding had come and gone, like a white sail, she was seized with a lasting, fierce despair. A wild aggressiveness that had formerly characterized her glance in moments of anger—moments which had grown more and more infrequent under the softening influence of her Mademoiselle's nature—now came back intensified and blazed in her eye perpetually. Whatever her secret love may have been in kind, its sinking beyond hope below the horizon had left her fifty times the mutineer she had been before—the mutineer who has nothing to lose.

"She loves her *candio*," said the negroes.

"Simple creatures!" said the overseer, who prided himself on his discernment, "she loves nothing; she hates Agricola; it's a case of hate at first sight—the strongest kind."

Both were partly right; her feelings were wonderfully knit to the African; and she now dedicated herself to Agricola's ruin.

The señor, it has been said, endeavored to be happy; but now his heart conceived and brought forth its first-born fear, sired by superstition—the fear that he was bewitched. The negroes said that Bras-Coupé had cursed the land. Morning after morning the master looked out with apprehension toward his fields, until one night the worm came upon the indigo and between sunset and sunrise every green leaf had been eaten up, and there was nothing left for either insect or apprehension to feed upon.

And then he said—and the echo came back from the Cannes Brulées—that the very bottom culpability of this thing rested on the Grandissimes, and specifically on their fugleman Agricola, through his putting the hellish African upon him. Moreover, fever and death, to a degree unknown before, fell upon his slaves. Those to whom life was spared—but to whom strength did not return—wandered about the place like scarecrows, looking for shelter, and made the very air dismal with the reiteration, "*No' ouanga* (we are bewitched), *Bras-Coupé fe moi des grigis* (the voudou's spells are on me)." The ripple of song was hushed and the flowers fell upon the floor.

"I have heard an English maxim," wrote Colonel De Grapion to his kinsman, "which I would recommend you to put into practice—'Fight the devil with fire.'"

No, he would not recognize devils as belligerents.

But if Rome commissioned exorcists, could not he employ one?

No, he would not! If his hounds could not catch Bras-Coupé, why, let him go. The overseer tried the hounds once more and came home with the best one across his saddle-bow, an arrow run half through its side.

Once the blacks attempted by certain familiar rum-pourings and nocturnal charm-singing to lift the curse; but the moment the master heard the wild monotone of their infernal worship, he stopped it with a word.

Early in February came the spring, and with it some resurrection of hope and courage. It may have been—it certainly was, in part—because young Honoré Grandissime had returned. He was like the sun's warmth wherever he went; and the other Honoré was like his shadow. The fairer one quickly saw the meaning of these things, hastened to cheer the young don with hopes of a better future, and to effect, if he could, the restoration of Bras-Coupé to his master's favor. But this latter effort was an idle one. He had long sittings with his uncle Agricola to the same end, but they always ended fruitless and often angrily.

His dark half-brother had seen Palmyre and loved her. Honoré would gladly have solved one or two riddles by effecting their honorable union in marriage. The previous ceremony on the Grandissime back piazza need be no impediment; all slave-owners understood those things. Following Honoré's advice, the f.m.c., who had come into possession of his paternal portion, sent to Cannes Brulées a written offer, to buy Palmyre at any price that her master might name, stating his intention to free her and make her his wife. Colonel De Grapion could hardly hope to settle Palmyre's fate more satisfactorily, yet he could not forego an opportunity to indulge his pride by following up the threat he had hung over Agricola to kill whosoever should give Palmyre to a black man. He referred the subject and the would-be purchaser to him. It would open up to the old braggart a line of retreat, thought the planter of the Cannes Brulées.

But the idea of retreat had left Citizen Fusilier.

"She is already married," said he to M. Honoré Grandissime, f.m.c. "She is the lawful wife of Bras-Coupé; and what God has joined together let no man put asunder. You know it, sirrah. You did this for impudence, to make a show of your wealth. You intended it as an insinuation of equality. I overlook the impertinence for the sake of the man whose white blood you carry; but mark you, if ever you bring your Parisian airs and self-sufficient face on a level with mine again, I will slap it."

The quadroon, three nights after, was so indiscreet as to give him the opportunity, and he did it—at that quadroon ball to which Dr. Keene alluded in talking to Frowenfeld.

But Don José, we say, plucked up new spirit..

"Last year's disasters were but fortune's freaks," he said. "See, others' crops have failed all about us."

The overseer shook his head.

"*C'est ce maudit cocodri' la bas* (It is that accursed alligator, Bras-Coupé, down yonder in the swamp)."

And by and by the master was again smitten with the same belief. He and his neighbors put in their crops afresh. The spring waned, summer passed, the fevers returned, the year wore round, but no harvest smiled. "Alas!" cried the planters, "we are all poor men!" The worst among the worst were the fields of Bras-Coupé's master—parched and shrivelled. "He does not understand planting," said his neighbors; "neither does his overseer. Maybe, too, it is true as he says, that he is voudoued."

One day at high noon the master was taken sick with fever.

The third noon after—the sad wife sitting by the bedside—suddenly, right in the centre of the room, with the door open behind him, stood the magnificent, half-nude form of Bras-Coupé. He did not fall down as the mistress's eyes met his, though all his flesh quivered. The master was lying with his eyes closed. The fever had done a fearful three days' work.

"*Mioko-koanga oulé so' femme* (Bras-Coupé wants his wife)."

The master started wildly and stared upon his slave.

86

"*Bras-Coupé oulé so' femme!*" repeated the black.

"Seize him!" cried the sick man, trying to rise.

But, though several servants had ventured in with frightened faces, none dared molest the giant. The master turned his entreating eyes upon his wife, but she seemed stunned, and only covered her face with her hands and sat as if paralyzed by a foreknowledge of what was coming.

Bras-Coupé lifted his great, black palm and commenced:

"*Mo cé voudrai que la maison ci là et tout ça qui pas femme' ici s'raient encore maudits!* (May this house and all in it who are not women be accursed)."

The master fell back upon his pillow with a groan of helpless wrath.

The African pointed his finger through the open window.

"May its fields not know the plough nor nourish the cattle that overrun it."

The domestics, who had thus far stood their ground, suddenly rushed from the room like stampeded cattle, and at that moment appeared Palmyre.

"Speak to him," faintly cried the panting invalid.

She went firmly up to her husband and lifted her hand. With an easy motion, but quick as lightning, as a lion sets foot on a dog, he caught her by the arm.

"*Bras-Coupé oulé so' femme,*" he said, and just then Palmyre would have gone with him to the equator.

"You shall not have her!" gasped the master.

The African seemed to rise in height, and still holding his wife at arm's length, resumed his malediction:

"May weeds cover the ground until the air is full of their odor and the wild beasts of the forest come and lie down under their cover."

With a frantic effort the master lifted himself upon his elbow and extended his clenched fist in speechless defiance; but his brain reeled, his sight went out, and when again he saw, Palmyre and her mistress were bending over him, the overseer stood awkwardly by, and Bras-Coupé was gone.

The plantation became an invalid camp. The words of the voudou found fulfilment on every side. The plough went not out; the herds wandered through broken hedges from field to field and came up with staring bones and shrunken sides; a frenzied mob of weeds and thorns wrestled and throttled each other in a struggle for standing-room—rag-weed, smart-weed, sneeze-weed, bind-weed, iron-weed—until the burning skies of midsummer checked their growth and crowned their unshorn tops with rank and dingy flowers.

"Why in the name of—St. Francis," asked the priest of the overseer, "didn't the señora use her power over the black scoundrel when he stood and cursed, that day?"

"Why, to tell you the truth, father," said the overseer, in a discreet whisper, "I can only suppose she thought Bras-Coupé had half a right to do it."

"Ah, ah, I see; like her brother Honoré—looks at both sides of a question—a miserable practice; but why couldn't Palmyre use *her* eyes? They would have stopped him."

"Palmyre? Why Palmyre has become the best *monture* (Plutonian medium) in the parish. Agricola Fusilier himself is afraid of her. Sir, I think sometimes Bras-Coupé is dead and his spirit has gone into Palmyre. She would rather add to his curse than take from it."

"Ah!" said the jovial divine, with a fat smile, "castigation would help her case; the whip is a great sanctifier. I fancy it would even make a Christian of the inexpugnable Bras-Coupé."

But Bras-Coupé kept beyond the reach alike of the lash and of the Latin Bible.

By and by came a man with a rumor, whom the overseer brought to the master's sick-room, to tell that an enterprising Frenchman was attempting to produce a new staple in Louisiana, one that worms would not annihilate. It was that year of history when the despairing planters saw ruin hovering so close over them that they cried to heaven for succor. Providence raised up Etienne de Boré. "And if Etienne is successful," cried the news-bearer, "and gets the juice of the sugar-cane to crystallize, so shall all of us, after him, and shall yet save our lands and homes. Oh, Señor, it will make you strong again to see these fields all cane and the long rows of negroes and negresses cutting it, while they sing their song of those droll African numerals, counting the canes they cut," and the bearer of good tidings sang them for very joy:

An-o-qué, An-o-bia, Bia-tail-la, Que-re-que, Nal-le-oua,
Au-mon-de, Au-tap-o-té, Au-pé-to-té, Au qué-ré-qué, Bo.

"And Honoré Grandissime is going to introduce it on his lands," said Don José.

"That is true," said Agricola Fusilier, coming in. Honoré, the indefatigable peace-maker, had brought his uncle and his brother-in-law for the moment not only to speaking, but to friendly terms.

The señor smiled.

"I have some good tidings, too," he said; "my beloved lady has borne me a son."

"Another scion of the house of Grand—I mean Martinez!" exclaimed Agricola. "And now, Don José, let me say that *I* have an item of rare intelligence!"

The don lifted his feeble head and opened his inquiring eyes with a sudden, savage light in them.

"No," said Agricola, "he is not exactly taken yet, but they are on his track."

"Who?"

"The police. We may say he is virtually in our grasp."

It was on a Sabbath afternoon that a band of Choctaws having just played a game of racquette behind the city and a similar game being about to end between the white champions of two rival faubourgs, the beating of tom-toms, rattling of mules' jaw-bones and sounding of wooden horns drew the populace across the fields to a spot whose present name of Congo Square still preserves a reminder of its old barbaric pastimes. On a grassy plain under the ramparts, the performers of these hideous discords sat upon the ground facing each other, and in their midst the dancers danced. They gyrated in couples, a few at a time, throwing their bodies into the most startling attitudes and the wildest contortions, while the whole company of black lookers-on, incited by the tones of the weird music and the violent posturing of the dancers, swayed and writhed in passionate sympathy, beating their breasts, palms and thighs in time with the bones and drums, and at frequent intervals lifting, in that wild African unison no more to be described than forgotten, the unutterable songs of the Babouille and Counjaille dances, with their ejaculatory burdens of "*Aie! Aie! Voudou Magnan!*" and "*Aie Calinda! Dancé Calinda!*" The volume of sound rose and fell with the augmentation or diminution of the dancers' extravagances. Now a fresh man, young and supple, bounding into the ring, revived the flagging rattlers, drummers and trumpeters; now a wearied dancer, finding his strength going, gathered all his force at the cry of *"Dancé zisqu'a mort!"* rallied to a grand finale and with one magnificent antic fell, foaming at the mouth.

The amusement had reached its height. Many participants had been lugged out by the neck to avoid their being danced on, and the enthusiasm had risen to a frenzy, when there bounded into the ring the blackest of black men, an athlete of superb figure, in breeches of "Indienne"—the stuff used for slave women's best dresses—jingling with bells, his feet in moccasins, his tight, crisp hair decked out with feathers, a necklace of alligator's teeth rattling on his breast and a living serpent twined about his neck.

It chanced that but one couple was dancing. Whether they had been sent there by advice of Agricola is not certain. Snatching a tambourine from a bystander as he entered, the stranger thrust the male dancer aside, faced the woman and began a series of saturnalian antics, compared with which all that had gone before was tame and sluggish; and as he finally leaped, with tinkling heels, clean over his bewildered partner's head, the multitude howled with rapture.

Ill-starred Bras-Coupé. He was in that extra-hazardous and irresponsible condition of mind and body known in the undignified present as "drunk again."

By the strangest fortune, if not, as we have just hinted, by some design, the man whom he had once deposited in the willow bushes, and the woman Clemence, were the very two dancers, and no other, whom he had interrupted. The man first stupidly regarded, next admiringly gazed upon, and then distinctly recognized, his whilom driver. Five minutes later the Spanish police were putting their heads together to devise a quick and permanent capture; and in the midst of the sixth minute, as the wonderful fellow was rising in a yet more astounding leap than his last, a lasso fell about his neck and brought him, crashing like a burnt tree, face upward upon the turf.

"The runaway slave," said the old French code, continued in force by the Spaniards, "the runaway slave who shall continue to be so for one month from the day of his being denounced to the officers of justice, shall have his ears cut off and shall be branded with the flower de luce on the shoulder; and on a second offence of the same nature, persisted in during one month of his being denounced, he shall be hamstrung, and be marked with the flower de luce on the other shoulder. On the third offence he shall die." Bras-Coupé had run away only twice. "But," said Agricola, "these 'bossals' must be taught their place. Besides, there is Article 27 of the same code: 'The slave who, having struck his master, shall have produced a bruise, shall suffer capital punishment'—a very necessary law!" He concluded with a scowl upon Palmyre, who shot back a glance which he never forgot.

The Spaniard showed himself very merciful—for a Spaniard; he spared the captive's life. He might have been more merciful still; but Honoré Grandissime said some indignant things in the African's favor, and as much to teach the Grandissimes a lesson as to punish the runaway, he would have repented his clemency, as he repented the momentary truce with Agricola, but for the tearful pleading of the señora and the hot, dry eyes of her maid. Because of these he overlooked the offence against his person and estate, and delivered Bras-Coupé to the law to suffer only the penalties of the crime he had committed against society by attempting to be a free man.

We repeat it for the credit of Palmyre, that she pleaded for Bras-Coupé. But what it cost her to make that intercession, knowing that his death would leave her free, and that if he lived she must be his wife, let us not attempt to say.

In the midst of the ancient town, in a part which is now crumbling away, stood the Calaboza, with its humid vaults, grated cells, iron cages and its whips; and there, soon enough, they strapped Bras-Coupé face downward and laid on the lash. And yet not a sound came from the mutilated but unconquered African to annoy the ear of the sleeping city.

("And you suffered this thing to take place?" asked Joseph Frowenfeld of Honoré Grandissime.

"My-de'-seh!" exclaimed the Creole, "they lied to me—said they would not harm him!")

He was brought at sunrise to the plantation. The air was sweet with the smell of the weed-grown fields. The long-horned oxen that drew him and the naked boy that drove the team stopped before his cabin.

"You cannot put that creature in there," said the thoughtful overseer. "He would suffocate under a roof—he has been too long out-of-doors for that. Put him on my cottage porch." There, at last, Palmyre burst into tears and sank down, while before her, on a soft bed of dry grass, rested the helpless form of the captive giant, a cloth thrown over his galled back, his ears shorn from his head, and the tendons behind his knees severed. His eyes were dry, but there was in them that unspeakable despair that fills the eye of the charger when, fallen in battle, he gazes with sidewise-bended neck upon the ruin wrought upon him. His eye turned sometimes slowly to his wife. He need not demand her now—she was always by him.

There was much talk over him—much idle talk; no power or circumstance has ever been found that will keep a Creole from talking. He merely lay still under it with a fixed frown; but once some incautious tongue dropped the name of Agricola. The black man's eyes came so quickly round to Palmyre that she thought he would speak; but no; his words were all in his eyes. She answered their gleam with a fierce affirmative glance, whereupon he slowly bent his head and spat upon the floor.

There was yet one more trial of his wild nature. The mandate came from his master's sick-bed that he must lift the curse.

Bras-Coupé merely smiled. God keep thy enemy from such a smile!

The overseer, with a policy less Spanish than his master's, endeavored to use persuasion. But the fallen prince would not so much as turn one glance from his parted hamstrings. Palmyre was then besought to intercede. She made one poor attempt, but her husband was nearer doing her an unkindness than ever he had been before; he made a slow sign for silence—with his fist; and every mouth was stopped.

At midnight following, there came, on the breeze that blew from the mansion, a sound of running here and there, of wailing and sobbing—another Bridegroom was coming, and the Spaniard, with much such a lamp in hand as most of us shall be found with, neither burning brightly nor wholly gone out, went forth to meet Him.

"Bras-Coupé," said Palmyre, next evening, speaking low in his mangled ear, "the master is dead; he is just buried. As he was dying, Bras-Coupé, he asked that you would forgive him."

The maimed man looked steadfastly at his wife. He had not spoken since the lash struck him, and he spoke not now; but in those large, clear eyes, where his remaining strength seemed to have taken refuge as in a citadel, the old fierceness flared up for a moment, and then, like an expiring beacon, went out.

"Is your mistress well enough by this time to venture here?" whispered the overseer to Palmyre. "Let her come. Tell her not to fear, but to bring the babe—in her own arms, tell her—quickly!"

The lady came, her infant boy in her arms, knelt down beside the bed of sweet grass and set the child within the hollow of the African's arm. Bras-Coupé turned his gaze upon it; it smiled, its mother's smile, and put its hand upon the runaway's face, and the first tears of Bras-Coupé's life, the dying testimony of his humanity, gushed from his eyes and rolled down his cheek upon the infant's hand. He laid his own tenderly upon the babe's forehead, then removing it, waved it abroad, inaudibly moved his lips, dropped his arm, and closed his eyes. The curse was lifted.

"*Le pauv' dgiab'!*" said the overseer, wiping his eyes and looking fieldward. "Palmyre, you must get the priest."

The priest came, in the identical gown in which he had appeared the night of the two weddings. To the good father's many tender questions Bras-Coupé turned a failing eye that gave no answers; until, at length:

"Do you know where you are going?" asked the holy man.

"Yes," answered his eyes, brightening.

"Where?"

He did not reply; he was lost in contemplation, and seemed looking far away.

So the question was repeated.

"Do you know where you are going?"

And again the answer of the eyes. He knew.

"Where?"

The overseer at the edge of the porch, the widow with her babe, and Palmyre and the priest bending over the dying bed, turned an eager ear to catch the answer.

"To—" the voice failed a moment; the departing hero essayed again; again it failed; he tried once more, lifted his hand, and with an ecstatic, upward smile, whispered, "To—Africa"—and was gone.

"The Original Bras-Coupe"

LAFCADIO HEARN (1880)

Lafcadio Hearn was born in 1850 in Greece, and lived in France, England, Ireland, New York, and Cincinnati before moving to New Orleans. He published important ethnographic sketches, including a series of articles on songs and stories recorded from African American levee workers; folklore collections like Gombo Zhèbes: Little Dictionary of Creole Proverbs *(1885); and regional fiction, such as* Chita: A Memory of Last Island *(1889). Cable's friend and sometime collaborator, Hearn wrote "The Original Bras-Coupe" for the* New Orleans Item *in order to distinguish Bras-Coupé, the historical person, from the fictional character in Cable's novel. Hearn claims that Cable learned about Bras-Coupé from Alexander Dimitry, a creole who owned a bookstore in Exchange Alley. Hearn reminds his readers about key aspects—the missing arm, the battles in the swamp, Francisco Garcia's betrayal—that Cable excised from the legend, but he is also wrong on several points. He claims, for example, that Bras-Coupé died around 1857 (rather than 1837) and that he was slave to Joseph Le Carpentier and John Freret (rather than General William DeBuys).*

While reading Mr. Cable's eloquent novel *The Grandissimes,* many Southern readers have doubtless asked themselves: Was there ever a Bras-Coupe? and is it possible that such a tragedy occurred in Louisiana?

The story is founded on facts; but the author took the poet's license and used it to advantage. He made Bras-Coupe great, valiant, large-hearted;—a savage prince fighting for liberty against the whole force of a civilized community, with such weapons as nature had given him. The artistic effect is superb; and the figure of Bras-Coupe towers up above the dramatic persons of the novel like a statue of black basalt, with that weird grimness which Egyptian sculptors gave to their collosi. But the original of the story was a less epic hero and a more human one, perhaps, whom we must admire and perhaps pity less than the giant Jalot of the story.

Now it comes to pass some days ago that we, being in search of wisdom chanced to meet its personification in Alexander Dimitry, whose Aristophanic and silver-bearded face we did perceive in the shadowy labyrinths of a quaint bookstore in Exchange Alley. And we spoke among other things concerning the history of Bras-Coupe. What the hellenic sage told us we shall attempt to tell in our feeble way, not holding ourselves strictly responsible in the matter of dates and names, inasmuch as we are not gifted with such a memory or the memory of he that narrated it.

About 1857 was the period in which Bras-Coupe flourished. He was an intelligent negro, and had been the property of Joseph Le Carpentier, then a large auctioneer in New Orleans. While working for Le Carpentier he was known simply as "Squire," was industrious and obedient and well-treated. It was his business to open boxes and barrels and pack up goods sold; and he had learned this business so thoroughly that it was seldom found necessary to give him an order. Finally Le Carpentier became involved, and was obliged to sell Squire. Squire was sold to John Freret, who owned a cotton press at that time where Fulton Street now is. The work was laborious, and especially so for Squire, who had been accustomed to light tasks, and knew nothing of cotton press work. He did not succeed well in his new calling; and one day becoming involved in a quarrel with the overseer raised his hand against him. The overseer, with an iron bar, shattered the uplifted arm; and Squire had to be removed to the hospital, where it was found necessary to amputate the injured limb. It was then that he became, indeed, the Bras-Coupe.

Now it was death for a slave to raise his hand against a white man; and Bras-Coupe knew well what was awaiting him. As soon as he had recovered, he escaped from the hospital and took to the woods then lying between Bayou Cochon and Bayou Sauvage. There he succeeded in gaining the confidence and apparent good will of a Spaniard who furnished him with arms and clothing and helped him to eke out the life of a hunted animal amid the swamps.

After a long while, Bras-Coupe became a robber. Market-women and gardeners coming into town by the Gentilly road were halted and robbed, and several colored women were ravished. Repeated complaints were made to the city authorities; and the complaintants always said that the footpad was a one-armed negro. It became necessary to speak of him as Bras-Coupe, the Man whose arm was cut off.

So Bras-Coupe became a terror to lonely wayfarers, and as fear increases the magnitude of a real danger, extraordinary stories were told about him. Finally, after two years, the City Council offered a reward of one thousand dollars for Bras-Coupe, dead or alive.

Then it came to pass that the Spaniard, who had aided Bras-Coupe for those two long years, and had shared perhaps in the proceeds of the robbery, was moved by the announcement of the reward promised to betray the unfortunate outlaw. He watched his opportunity; and one day crushed Bras-Coupe's skull with a bar of iron, while the fugitive slept under the shadow of a tree.

The body was borne into the city, and was placed under the arcade of the quaint Spanish building on Jackson Square, where the court is now held, and where hundreds came to look at all that was left of horrible Bras-Coupe. And then it was found out that the great robber, and outlaw and marron was only poor old "Squire," the unhappy slave of Joseph Le Carpentier.

"Bras Coupe"

ANONYMOUS (1880)

Nothing is known about the anonymous author of this article. Originally published in a Louisiana newspaper, the West Baton Rouge Sugar Planter, *the only surviving copy comes from the* Ouachita Telegraph, *a newspaper from a nearby parish, where the article was reprinted. This article is valuable as it offers a firsthand account of the fantastic stories told about Bras-Coupé. It attests to the power of the oral tradition both in New Orleans and throughout Louisiana.*

A late number of the N. O. City Item contained an article upon this individual who, some forty years ago, was a terror to the boys of that city who were wont to harry the back country in search of blackberries or small birds with the common shot gun of the time. Everybody knew that Bras Coupe was a negro with one arm and that all sorts of crime were laid to his charge which, in the main, were true. He was a great villain and had often been shot at by more courageous hunters, but always escaped without a wound, until, at last, it was commonly believed that he bore a charmed life, being under the special care of the Evil One. Parents would scare refractory small children into the most abject submission by simply threatening them with old Bras Coupe, while those of a larger growth could be frightened from any mischief they had in contemplation by suggesting a probable encounter with that demon of the swamps. The writer, time and again in his youthful days, took to his heels, with his companions, when wandering in search of blackberries near Daniel Clark's house on the old basin or bathing in its not over clean waters, when some mischievous urchin would yelp out: "Here he comes!" He was the terror of New Orleans for a number of years; and notwithstanding the large rewards offered for his apprehension, no one seemed daring enough to risk securing the prize. The police force of the three municipalities in those days were not remarkable for vigilance, energy, or bravery, being selected from the lowest classes, and whose most arduous duty was to collect their pay in the shinplasters of the period and then dispose of them at an enormous discount. But at last the remains of Bras Coupe were brought in and exposed to view in the old Place d'Armes where hundreds of visitors viewed them from day to day until their condition compelled their removal. Current rumor at the time had it that the old Spaniard who killed him never reaped the reward of his valor, which was very likely the case. Once in a while old stories are raked up from the misty past in which youthful recollections are brought freshly back to memory and one almost feels young again as he hears them. Old Bras Coupe of forty or more years ago was an object of the greatest terror to the little boys of the first municipality and to none more than the writer.

From *Notes of a Pianist*

LOUIS MOREAU GOTTSCHALK (1881)

Louis Moreau Gottschalk was a popular classical composer and pianist best known for works that drew on musical themes from vernacular traditions in the Caribbean and southern United States, most significantly from his hometown, New Orleans. In his memoir, Notes of a Pianist, *Gottschalk recalls stories told by Sally, an "old negress," to the children and slaves assembled around the fireplace in the family's home. Many stories featured tricksters such as "Compé Lapin," known in English as Brer Rabbit. Among his favorite stories, Gottschalk says, were ones concerning a one-armed fugitive who served as "captain of the runaway negroes."*

I embarked at Havana on June 3 for St. Thomas. On the 6th we were in sight of the coast of Hayti. The night began to fall. All the passengers went below. I remained alone. Leaning against the rigging, I contemplated the desolate country which opened out before me: High mountains, whose angular peaks seemed as if they wished to pierce the clouds. Solitary palm-trees hanging sadly over the desert shore. A horizon whose lines were lost on stormy sky. Altogether, and more especially the name of St. Domingo, seemed to speak to my imagination by recalling to me the bloody episodes of the insurrection, so closely associated with my childhood memories. When very young, I was never tired of hearing my grandmother relate the terrible strife which our family, like all the rest of the colonists, had to sustain at this epoch; the narrative of the massacre at the Cape, and the combat fought in the 'mornes' by my great-grandfather against the negroes of the 'gouiaves.' My recollections, drawn towards them by a mysterious affinity, rose one by one in a striking and lucid manner from the long-forgotten past. I again found myself before the large fireplace of our dwelling on the street "des Ramparts" at New Orleans, where in the evening, squatting on the matting, the negroes, myself, and the children of the house formed a circle around my grandmother, and listened, by the trembling fire on the hearth, under the coals of which Sally, the old negress, baked her sweet potatoes, to the recital of this terrible negro insurrection. It was the same old Sally who, while listening all the time, spoke in a low voice to a portrait of Napoleon hung above the fireplace, and which she obstinately believed was bewitched because it seemed to look at her, in every corner of the room, wherever she might be. We cast fearful glances under the old bed with its baldachins, and drew closer together by creeping the one between the other, while my grandmother continued. I was without any doubt the favourite of Sally, to judge by the stories with which she filled my head. I was not tired of listening for the hundredth time to the marvellous adventures of Compé Bouqui (the clown of the negroes), and the knavery of Compé Lapin, whose type represents our punchinello of Europe. We listened to Sally so well that we knew the whole of her *stories* by heart—with an interest that continues till to-day, and still makes me find an inexpressible charm in all these naive legends of our old negroes. I should like to relate, in their picturesque language and their exquisite originality, some of those Creole ballads whose simple and touching melody goes right to the heart and makes you dream of unknown worlds. To return to the recitals of my grandmother. One of my favourite stories was that of John bras Coupé, captain of the runaway negroes of bayou Sarah, who filled the whole of Louisiana with the report of his sanguinary exploits. He resisted alone, this hero of our savannas, all the expeditions sent in pursuit of him. Strange rumours were in circulation on this subject. Sometimes it was a detachment of troops that had ventured to the haunt of this brigand, who disappeared without any one being able to discover any trace of him. Sometimes it was the hunter, whose ball was flattened against the breast of bras Coupé, whose skin was rendered invulnerable by certain herbs with which he rubbed it. The negroes asserted that his look fascinated, and that he fed on human flesh. He was finally captured, and condemned to be hung in the 'square' opposite the Spanish Cathedral. He had been attacked by a terrible scurvy, and the infecting odours exhaled by his corpse two hours after his execution made them bury him, contrary to the law that condemned him to remain suspended to the gallows for two days. Sometimes Sally interrupted the narrative of my grandmother to exorcise 'zombi,' of which, she said, she felt the impure breath on her face. We narrowed our circle, shivering with fright, around my grandmother, who, after crossing herself and scolding Sally, took up her story where she had left off.

"The Dance in Place Congo"

GEORGE WASHINGTON CABLE (1886)

This essay does not mention Bras-Coupé by name, but it remains inextricable from his legend. Cable's research into performance traditions at Congo Square was used both in this essay and in his novel, The Grandissimes, *in which Bras-Coupé is a spectacular dancer. Soon after they were published, the essay and the novel would become fused together in cultural commentary, as ethnographic sketches, tourist brochures, and local histories offered their own accounts of Congo Square based on both sources. Frequently, these accounts would mention that Bras-Coupé was the most famous performer at Congo Square, failing to distinguish Cable's fiction from the putative facts in this essay. Some histories compound this mistake by identifying the essay's most famous illustration, E. W. Kemble's "The Bamboula," as an image of Bras-Coupé.*

I. Congo Square

Whoever has been to New Orleans with eyes not totally abandoned to buying and selling will, of course, remember St. Louis Cathedral, looking south-
eastward—riverward—across quaint Jackson Square, the old Place d'Armes.
And if he has any feeling for flowers, he has not forgotten the little garden
behind the cathedral, so antique and unexpected, named for the beloved old
priest Père Antoine.

The old Rue Royale lies across the sleeping garden's foot. On the street's
farther side another street lets away at right angles, north-westward, straight,
and imperceptibly downward from the cathedral and garden toward the rear
of the city. It is lined mostly with humble ground-floor-and-garret houses of
stuccoed brick, their wooden doorsteps on the brick sidewalks. This is Orleans street, so named when the city was founded.

Its rugged round-stone pavement is at times nearly as sunny and silent as
the landward side of a coral reef. Thus for about half a mile; and then Rampart street, where the palisade wall of the town used to run in Spanish days,
crosses it, and a public square just beyond draws a grateful canopy of oak and
sycamore boughs. That is the place. One may shut his buff umbrella there,
wipe the beading sweat from the brow, and fan himself with his hat. Many's
the bull-fight has taken place on that spot Sunday afternoons of the old time.
That is Congo Square.

The trees are modern. So are the buildings about the four sides, for all
their aged looks. So are all the grounds' adornments. Trémé market, off, beyond, toward the swamp, is not so very old, and the scowling, ill-smelling
prison on the right, so Spanish-looking and dilapidated, is not a third the age
it seems; not fifty-five. In that climate every year of a building's age counts
for ten. Before any of these M. Cayetano's circus and menagerie were here.
Cayetane the negroes called him. He was the Barnum of that region and day.

"Miché Cayetane, qui sortie de l'Havane,
Avec so chouals et somacaques."

That is, "who came from Havana with his horses and baboons." Up at the
other end of Orleans street, hid only by the old padre's garden and the cathedral, glistens the ancient Place d'Armes. In the early days it stood for all that
was best; the place for political rallying, the retail quarter of all fine goods

and wares, and at sunset and by moonlight the promenade of good society and the haunt of true lovers; not only in the military, but also in the most un-warlike sense the place of arms, and of hearts and hands, and of words tender as well as words noble.

The Place Congo, at the opposite end of the street, was at the opposite end of everything. One was on the highest ground; the other on the lowest. The one was the rendezvous of the rich man, the master, the military officer—of all that went to make up the ruling class; the other of the butcher and baker, the raftsman, the sailor, the quadroon, the painted girl, and the negro slave. No meaner name could be given the spot. The negro was the most despised of human creatures and the Congo the plebeian among negroes. The white man's plaza had the army and navy on its right and left, the court-house, the council-hall and the church at its back, and the world before it. The black man's was outside the rear gate, the poisonous wilderness on three sides and the proud man's contumely on its front.

Before the city overgrew its flimsy palisade walls, and closing in about this old stamping ground gave it set bounds, it was known as Congo Plains. There was wide room for much field sport, and the Indian villagers of the town's outskirts and the lower class of white Creoles made it the ground of their wild ball game of *raquette*. Sunday afternoons were the time for it. Hence, beside these diversions there was, notably, another.

The hour was the slave's term of momentary liberty, and his simple, sav-age, musical and superstitious nature dedicated it to amatory song and dance tinctured with his rude notions of supernatural influences.

II. Grand Orchestra

The booming of African drums and blast of huge wooden horns called to the gathering. It was these notes of invitation, reaching beyond those of other outlandish instruments, that caught the Ethiopian ear, put alacrity into the dark foot, and brought their owners, male and female, trooping from all quarters. The drums were very long, hollowed, often from a single piece of wood, open at one end and having a sheep or goat skin stretched across the other. One was large, the other much smaller. The tight skin heads were not held up to be struck; the drums were laid along on the turf and the drum-mers bestrode them, and beat them on the head madly with fingers, fists, and feet,—with slow vehemence on the great drum, and fiercely and rapidly on the small one. Sometimes an extra performer sat on the ground behind the larger drum, at its open end, and "beat upon the wooden sides of it with two sticks." The smaller drum was often made from a joint or two of very large bamboo, in the West Indies where such could be got, and this is said to be the origin of its name; for it was called the *Bamboula*.

In stolen hours of night or the basking-hour of noon the black man contrived to fashion these rude instruments and others. The drummers, I say, bestrode the drums; the other musicians sat about them in an arc, cross-legged on the ground. One important instrument was a gourd partly filled with pebbles or grains of corn, flourished violently at the end of a stout staff with one hand and beaten upon the palm of the other. Other performers rang triangles, and others twanged from jew's-harps an astonishing amount of sound. Another instrument was the jawbone of some ox, horse, or mule, and a key rattled rhythmically along its weather-beaten teeth. At times the drums were reënforced by one or more empty barrels or casks beaten on the head with the shank-bones of cattle.

A queer thing that went with these when the affair was pretentious—full dress, as it were—at least it was so in the West Indies, whence Congo Plains drew all inspirations—was the Marimba brett, a union of reed and string principles. A single strand of wire ran lengthwise of a bit of wooden board, sometimes a shallow box of thin wood, some eight inches long by four or five in width, across which, under the wire, were several joints of reed about a quarter of an inch in diameter and of graduated lengths. The performer, sitting cross-legged, held the board in both hands and plucked the ends of the reeds with his thumb-nails. The result was called—music.

But the grand instrument at last, the first violin, as one might say, was the banjo. It had but four strings, not six: beware of the dictionary. It is not the "favorite musical instrument of the negroes of the Southern States of America." Uncle Remus says truly that that is the fiddle; but for the true African dance, a dance not so much of legs and feet as of the upper half of the body, a sensual, devilish thing tolerated only by Latin-American masters, there was wanted the dark inspiration of African drums and the banjo's thrump and strum.

And then there was that long-drawn human cry of tremendous volume, richness, and resound, to which no instrument within their reach could make the faintest approach:

"Eh! pou' la belle Layotte ma mourri 'nocent,
Oui 'nocent ma mourri!"

all the instruments silent while it rises and swells with mighty energy and
dies away distantly, "Yea-a-a-a-a-a!"—then the crash of savage drums, horns,
and rattles—

"For the fair Layotte I must crazy die!
Yes, crazy I must die!"

To all this there was sometimes added a Pan's-pipe of but three reeds,
made from single joints of the common brake cane, and called by English-
speaking negroes "the quills." One may even at this day hear the black lad,
sauntering home at sunset behind a few cows that he has found near the edge
of the canebrake whence he has also cut his three quills, blowing and hooting,
over and over. . . .

Such was the full band. All the values of contrast that discord can furnish
must have been present, with whatever there is of ecstasy in maddening rep-
etition, for of this the African can never have too much.

And yet there was entertaining variety. Where? In the dance! There was
constant, exhilarating novelty—endless invention—in the turning, bowing,
arm-swinging, posturing and leaping of the dancers. Moreover, the music of
Congo Plains was not tamed to mere monotone. Monotone became subordi-
nate to many striking qualities. The strain was wild. Its contact with French
taste gave it often great tenderness of sentiment. It grew in fervor, and rose
and sank, and rose again, with the play of emotion in the singers and dancers.

III. The Gathering

It was a weird one. The negro of colonial Louisiana was a most grotesque figure. He was nearly naked. Often his neck and arms, thighs, shanks, and splay
feet were shrunken, tough, sinewy like a monkey's. Sometimes it was scant
diet and cruel labor that had made them so. Even the requirement of law
was only that he should have not less than a barrel of corn—nothing else,—a
month, nor get more than thirty lashes to the twenty-four hours. The whole
world was cruder those times than now; we must not judge them by our own.

Often the slave's attire was only a cotton shirt, or a pair of pantaloons hanging in indecent tatters to his naked waist. The bondwoman was well clad who had on as much as a coarse chemise and petticoat. To add a *tignon*—a Madras handkerchief twisted into a turban—was high gentility, and the number of kerchiefs beyond that one was the measure of absolute wealth. Some were rich in *tignons;* especially those who served within the house, and pleased the mistress, or even the master—there were Hagars in those days. However, Congo Plains did not gather the house-servants so much as the "field-hands."

These came in troops. See them; wilder than gypsies; wilder than the Moors and Arabs whose strong blood and features one sees at a glance in so many of them; gangs—as they were called—gangs and gangs of them, from this and that and yonder direction; tall, well-knit Senegalese from Cape Verde, black as ebony, with intelligent, kindly eyes and long, straight, shapely noses; Mandingoes, from the Gambia River, lighter of color of cruder form, and a cunning that shows in the countenance; whose enslavement seems specially a shame, their nation the "merchants of Africa," dwelling in towns, industrious, thrifty, skilled in commerce and husbandry, and expert in the working of metals, even to silver and gold; and Foulahs, playfully miscalled "*Poulards*"—fat chickens,—of goodly stature, and with a perceptible rose tint in the cheeks; and Sosos, famous warriors, dexterous with the African targe; and in contrast to these, with small ears, thick eyebrows, bright eyes, flat, upturned noses, shining skin, wide mouths and white teeth, the negroes of Guinea, true and unmixed, from the Gold Coast, the Slave Coast, and the Cape of Palms—not from the Grain Coast; the English had that trade. See them come! Popoes, Cotocolies, Fidas, Socoes, Agwas, short, copper-colored Mines—what havoc the slavers did make!—and from interior Africa others equally proud and warlike: fierce Nagoes and Fonds; tawny Awassas; Iboes, so light-colored that one could not tell them from mulattoes but for their national tattooing; and the half-civilized and quick-witted but ferocious Arada, the original Voudou worshiper. And how many more! For here come, also, men and women from all that great Congo coast,—Angola, Malimbe, Ambrice, etc.,—small, good-natured, sprightly "boys," and gay, garrulous "gals," thick-lipped but not tattooed; chattering, chaffering, singing, and guffawing as they come: these are they for whom the dance and the place are named, the most numerous sort of negro in the colonies, the Congoes and Franc-

Congoes, and though serpent worshipers, yet the gentlest and kindliest na-
tures that came from Africa. Such was the company. Among these *bossals*—
that is, native Africans—there was, of course, an ever-growing number of
negroes who proudly called themselves Creole negroes, that is, born in America;* and at the present time there is only here and there an old native African
to be met with, vain of his singularity and trembling on his staff.

IV. The Bamboula

The gathering throng closed in around, leaving unoccupied the circle indicated by the crescent of musicians. The short, harsh turf was the dancing-
floor. The crowd stood. Fancy the picture. The pack of dark, tattered figures
touched off every here and there with the bright colors of a Madras *tignon.*
The squatting, cross-legged musicians. The lowroofed, embowered town off
in front, with here and there a spire lifting a finger of feeble remonstrance;
the flat, grassy plain stretching around and behind, dotted with black stumps;
in the distance the pale-green willow undergrowth, behind it the *cyprière*—
the cypress swamp—and in the pale, seven-times-heated sky the sun, only a
little declined to south and westward, pouring down its beams. With what
particular musical movements the occasion began does not now appear. May
be with very slow and measured ones; they had such that were strange and
typical. I have heard the negroes sing one—though it was not of the dance-
ground but of the cane-field—that showed the emphatic barbarism of five
bars to the line, and was confined to four notes of the open horn.

But I can only say that with some such slow and quiet strain the dance
may have been preluded. It suits the Ethiopian fancy for a beginning to be
dull and repetitious; the bottom of the ladder must be on the ground.

The singers almost at the first note are many. At the end of the first line
every voice is lifted up. The strain is given the second time with growing
spirit. Yonder glistening black Hercules, who plants one foot forward, lifts
his head and bare, shining chest, and rolls out the song from a mouth and
throat like a cavern, is a *candio,* a chief, or was before he was overthrown in

---

* This broader use of the term is very common. The Creole "dialect" is the broken English *of the
Creoles,* while the Creole *patois* is the corrupt French, not of the Creoles, but rather of the former
slave race in the country of the Creoles. So of Creole negroes and Creole dances and songs.

battle and dragged away, his village burning behind him, from the mountains of High Soudan. That is an African amulet that hangs about his neck—a *greegree*. He is of the Bambaras, as you may know by his solemn visage and the long tattoo streaks running down from the temples to the neck, broadest in the middle, like knife-gashes. See his play of restrained enthusiasm catch from one bystander to another. They swing and bow to right and left, in slow time to the piercing treble of the Congo women. Some are responsive; others are competitive. Hear that bare foot slap the ground! one sudden stroke only, as it were the foot of a stag. The musicians warm up at the sound. A smiting of breasts with open hands begins very softly and becomes vigorous. The women's voices rise to a tremulous intensity. Among the chorus of Franc-Congo singing-girls is one of extra good voice, who thrusts in, now and again, an improvisation. This girl here, so tall and straight, is a Yaloff. You see it in her almost Hindoo features, and hear it in the plaintive melody of her voice. Now the chorus is more piercing than ever. The women clap their hands in time, or standing with arms akimbo receive with faint courtesies and head-liftings the low bows of the men, who deliver them swinging this way and that.

See! Yonder brisk and sinewy fellow has taken one short, nervy step into the ring, chanting with rising energy. Now he takes another, and stands and sings and looks here and there, rising upon his broad toes and sinking and rising again, with what wonderful lightness! How tall and lithe he is. Notice his brawn shining through his rags. He too, is a *candio,* and by the three long rays of tattooing on each side of his face, a Kiamba. The music has got into his feet. He moves off to the farther edge of the circle, still singing, takes the prompt hand of an unsmiling Congo girl, leads her into the ring, and leaving the chant to the throng, stands her before him for the dance.

Will they dance to that measure? Wait! A sudden frenzy seizes the musicians. The measure quickens, the swaying, attitudinizing crowd starts into extra activity, the female voices grow sharp and staccato, and suddenly the dance is the furious Bamboula.

Now for the frantic leaps! Now for frenzy! Another pair are in the ring! The man wears a belt of little bells, or, as a substitute, little tin vials of shot, "bram-bram sonnette! "And still another couple enter the circle. What wild—what terrible delight! The ecstasy rises to madness; one—two—three of the dancers fall—*bloncoutoum! boum!*—with foam on their lips and are dragged

out by arms and legs from under the tumultuous feet of crowding new-
comers. The musicians know no fatigue; still the dance rages on:

"Quand patate la cuite na va mange li!"

And all to that one nonsense line meaning only,

"When that 'tater's cooked don't you eat it up!"

It was a frightful triumph of body over mind, even in those early days
when the slave was still a genuine pagan; but as his moral education gave
him some hint of its enormity, and it became a forbidden fruit monopolized
by those of reprobate will, it grew everywhere more and more gross. No wonder the police stopped it in Congo Square. Only the music deserved to survive, and does survive—coin snatched out of the mire. The one just given,
Gottschalk first drew from oblivion. I have never heard another to know it as
a bamboula; but Mr. Charles P. Ware, in "Slave Songs of the United States,"
has printed one got from Louisiana, whose characteristics resemble the bamboula reclaimed by Gottschalk in so many points that here is the best place
for it: As much as to say, in English, "Look at that darky,"—we have to lose the
saucy double meaning between *mulet* (mule) and *mulâtre* (mulatto)—

"Look at that darky there, Mr. Banjo,
Doesn't he put on airs!
Hat cocked on one side, Mr. Banjo,
Walking-stick in hand, Mr. Banjo,
Boots that go ' crank, crank,' Mr. Banjo,-
Look at that darky there, Mr. Banjo,
Doesn't he put on airs!"

It is odd that such fantastical comicality of words should have been mated
to such fierce and frantic dancing, but so it was. The reeking faces of the
dancers, moreover, always solemnly grave. So we must picture it now if we
still fancy ourselves spectators on Congo Plains. The bamboula still roars and
rattles, twangs, contorts, and tumbles in terrible earnest, while we stand and
talk. So, on and on. Will they dance nothing else? Ah!—the music changes.

The rhythm stretches out heathenish and ragged. The quick contagion is caught by a few in the crowd, who take it up with spirited smitings of the bare sole upon the ground, and of open hands upon the thighs. From a spot near the musicians a single male voice, heavy and sonorous, rises in improvisation,—the Mandingoes brought that art from Africa,—and in a moment many others have joined in refrain, male voices in rolling, bellowing resonance, female responding in high, piercing unison. Partners are stepping into the ring. How strangely the French language is corrupted on the thick negro tongue, as with waving arms they suit gesture to word and chant (the translation is free, but so is the singing and posturing):

En bas hé, en bas hé, Par en bas yé pé-lé-lé moin, yé pé-lé-lé, Counjaille
'Way yon-der, 'way yon-der, 'Way down there they're call-ing me, they are
    calling, but Coonjye,

A dé-baut-ché. Par en haut yé pé-lé-lé moin, yé pé-lé-lé pou' Mom-selle Su-zette,
has bewitched me. 'Way up there they're call-ing me, They are calling for
    Mom-selle Su-zette,

Par en bas yé pé-lé-lé moin, yé pé-lé-lé, Coun-jaille a é-baut-ché
'Way down there they're call-ing me, they are calling, (but) Coonjye has
    be-witched me

V. The Counjaille

Suddenly the song changes. The rhythm sweeps away long and smooth like a river escaped from its rapids, and in new spirit, with louder drum-beat and more jocund rattle, the voices roll up into the sky and the dancers are at it. Aye, ya, yi!

I could give four verses, but let one suffice; it is from a manuscript copy of the words, probably a hundred years old, that fell into my hands through the courtesy of a Creole lady some two years ago. It is one of the best known of all the old Counjaille songs. The four verses would not complete it. The Counjaille was never complete, and found its end, for the time being, only in the caprice of the improvisator, whose rich, stentorian voice sounded alone between the refrains.

But while we discourse other couples have stepped into the grassy arena, the instrumental din has risen to a fresh height of inspiration, the posing and thigh-beating and breast-patting and chanting and swinging and writhing has risen with it, and the song is changed.

But the dance is not changed, and love is still the theme. Sweat streams from the black brows, down the shining black necks and throats, upon the men's bared chests, and into dark, unstayed bosoms. Time wears, shadows lengthen; but the movement is brisker than ever, and the big feet and bent shanks are as light as thistles on the air. Let one flag, another has his place, and a new song gives new vehemence, new inventions in steps, turns, and attitudes.

More stanzas could be added in the original *patois,* but here is a translation into African English as spoken by the Creole negro:

CHORUS   I done been 'roun' to evvy spot
              Don't foun' nair match fo' sweet Layotte.

SOLO   I done hunt all dis settle*ment*
          All de way 'roun' fum Pierre Soniat';

          Never see yalla gal w'at kin
          'Gin to lay 'longside sweet Layotte.
          I done been, etc.

SOLO   I yeh dey talk 'bout 'Loïse gal—
          Loïse, w'at b'long to Pierre Soniat';
          I see her, but she can't biggin
          Stan' up 'longside my sweet Layotte.
          I done been, etc.

SOLO   I been meet up wid John Bayou,
          Say to him, "John Bayou, my son,
          Yalla gal nevva meet yo' view
          Got a face lak dat chahmin' one! "
          I done been, etc.

The fair Layotte appears not only on the other versions of this *counjaille* but in other song. . . .

Or in English:

> Well I know, young men, I must die,
> Yes, crazy, I must die.
> Well I know, young men, I must crazy die,
> Yes, crazy, I must die. Eh-h-h-h!
> For the fair Layotte, I must crazy die,—Yes, etc.
> Well I know, young men, I must die,—Yes, etc.
> Well I know, young men, I must crazy die,
> I must die for the fair Layotte.

VI. The Calinda

There were other dances. Only a few years ago I was honored with an invitation, which I had to decline, to see danced the Babouille, the Cata (or Chacta), the Counjaille, and the Calinda. Then there were the Voudou, and the Congo, to describe which would not be pleasant. The latter, called Congo also in Cayenne, Chica in San Domingo, and in the Windward Islands confused under one name with the Calinda, was a kind of Fandango, they say, in which the Madras kerchief held by its tip-ends played a graceful part.

The true Calinda was bad enough. In Louisiana, at least, its song was always a grossly personal satirical ballad, and it was the favorite dance all the way from there to Trinidad. To dance it publicly is not allowed this side the West Indies. All this Congo Square business was suppressed at one time; 1843, says tradition.

The Calinda was a dance of multitude, a sort of vehement cotillion. The contortions of the encircling crowd were strange and terrible, the din was hideous. One Calinda is still familiar to all Creole ears; it has long been a vehicle for the white Creole's satire; for generations the man of municipal politics was fortunate who escaped entirely a lampooning set to its air.

In my childhood I used, at one time, to hear, every morning a certain black *marchande des calas*—peddler-woman selling rice croquettes—chanting the song as she moved from street to street at the sunrise hour with her broad, shallow, laden basket balanced on her head.

In other words, a certain Judge Preval gave a ball—not an outdoor Congo dance—and made such Cuffees as could pay three dollars a ticket. It doesn't rhyme, but it was probably true. "Dance, dance the Calinda! Boujoum! Boujoum!"

The number of stanzas has never been counted; here are a few of them.

"Dans l'equirie la 'y' avé grand gala;
Mo cré choual la yé t b'en étonné.

Miché Preval, li té capitaine bal;
So cocher Louis, té maite cérémonie.

Y avé des négresses belle passé maitresses,
Qui volé bel-bel dans l'ormoire momselle.

. . . .

Ala maite la geôle li trouvé si drôle,
Li dit, "moin aussi, mo fé bal ici."

Ouatchman la yé yé tombé la dans;
Yé fé gran' déga dans léquirie la." etc.

"It was in a stable that they had this gala night," says the song; "the horses there were greatly astonished. Preval was captain; his coachman, Louis, was master of ceremonies. There were negresses made prettier than their mistresses by adornments stolen from the ladies' wardrobes (*armoires*). But the jailer found it all so funny that he proposed to himself to take an unexpected part; the watchmen came down"—

No official exaltation bought immunity from the jeer of the Calinda. Preval was a magistrate. Stephen Mazureau, in his attorney-general's office, the song likened to a bull-frog in a bucket of water. A page might be covered by the roll of victims. The masters winked at these gross but harmless liberties and as often as any others, added stanzas of their own invention.

The Calinda ended these dissipations of the summer Sabbath afternoons. They could not run far into the night, for all the fascinations of all the dances could not excuse the slave's tarrying in public places after a certain other *bou-djoum!* (that was not of the Calinda, but of the regular nine-o'clock evening gun) had rolled down Orleans street from the Place d'Armes; and the black man or woman who wanted to keep a whole skin on the back had to keep out of the Calaboose. Times have changed, and there is nothing to be regretted in the change that has come over Congo Square. Still a glamour hangs over its dark past. There is the pathos of slavery, the poetry of the weak oppressed by the strong, and of limbs that danced after toil, and of barbaric love-making. The rags and semi-nakedness, the bamboula drum, the dance, and almost the banjo, are gone; but the *bizarre* melodies and dark lovers' apostrophes live on; and among them the old Counjaille song of Aurore Pradère.

CHORUS   Aurore Pradère, pretty maid,
She's just what I want and her I'll have.

SOLO   Some folks say she's too pretty, quite;
Some folks they say she's not polite;
All this they say—Psha-a-ah!
More fool am I!
For she's what I want and her I'll have.

CHORUS   Aurore Pradère, pretty maid,
She's just what I want and her I'll have.

SOLO   Some say she's going to the bad;
Some say that her mamma went mad;
All this they say—Psha-a-ah!
More fool am I!
For she's what I want and her I'll have.

Mr. Ware and his associate compilers have neither of these stanzas, but one very pretty one; the third in the music and which we translate as follows:

SOLO   A muslin gown she doesn't choose,
She doesn't ask for broidered hose.

She doesn't want prunella shoes,
O she's what I want and her I'll have.

CHORUS   Aurore Pradère, etc.

This article and another on a kindred theme were originally projected as the joint work of Mr. H. E. Krehbiel, musical editor of the "New York Tribune," author of "The History of Choral Music in New York City," etc.; and the present writer. But under the many prior claims of the journalist's profession, Mr. Krehbiel withdrew from the work, though not until he had furnished a number of instrumental accompaniments, as well as the "Quill Song" credited to him, and much valuable coöperation. As may in part be seen by the names attached to the musical scores, the writer is indebted to a number of friends: Mr. Krehbiel; Miss Mary L. Bartlett, of Hartford, Conn.; Madame Louis Lejeune, of New Orleans; Dr. Blodgett, of Smith College, Northampton, Mass.; Mr. C. G. Ware, of Brookline, in the same State; Madame Clara Gottschalk Petersen, of Philadelphia; and in his earlier steps—for the work of collection has been slow—to that skillful French translator and natural adept in research, Mr. Lafcadio Hearn, of New Orleans; the late Isaac N. Philips, Mr. Louis Powers, Miss Clara Cooper Hallaran, the late Professor Alexander Dimitry, all of the same city; Madame Sidonie de la Houssaye, of Franklin, La.; and, through the editors of THE CENTURY, to Mr. W. Macrum, of Pittsburg.—G. W. C.

From *New Orleans As It Was*

HENRY C. CASTELLANOS (1895)

Henry Castellanos was a prominent lawyer, journalist, and educator who lived nearly his whole life in New Orleans. From 1892 to 1895, he published more than a hundred articles on local history in the New Orleans Times-Democrat, *many of which were collected in* New Orleans as It Was *(1895), a volume focused less on notable leaders and political institutions than on the colorful eccentricity of everyday life in the city. Castellanos provides one of the most detailed accounts of Bras-Coupé published in the nineteenth century, drawing from personal recollection, oral tradition, and old newspapers.*

A t a period when the institution of slavery, viewed under its most human-itarian aspect, had become one of the pillars of our prosperity and prog-ress, fostered by a spirit of benevolence and patriarchal affection, a salient feature of the times was the frequency with which our African bondsmen would hie themselves into the deepest recesses of our forests to escape thral-dom for a short space of time, and enjoy a season of comparative rest. While yet a boy, I distinctly remember the proximity of the woods to the sparse hab-itations that fringed the outskirts of the town. Marais street was then deemed the border land lying between *terra firma* and "trembling prairie," an impen-etrable morass, beyond which none but experienced hunters or fugitives ven-tured to enter. In the darkest parts of these thickets and along the margin of some sluggish bayou or *coulée,* a rude hut was occasionally to be found, hast-ily thrown up with willow branches, and securely sheltered from wind and rain by latanier or palmetto leaves, deftly worked into the roof. This was the usual habitation of the runaway negro, until he was driven to seek a new shel-ter by the professional "slave catcher" with his pack of trained bloodhounds.

Even when not pursued, these outlaws were compelled to emerge at night from their solitary haunts in quest of nourishment. Hence it was that New Orleans, despite the efforts of an inadequate police, became the scene of noc-turnal thefts, robberies and assassinations. With the spoils and money thus obtained, a "cabaret" was always ready to supply the hunted-down outcast with powder, shot, whisky and such other articles as were required for his most pressing wants. It was only when, in the course of years, the city had extended its habitable limits beyond Claiborne street that these bold refugees sought new quarters along the borders of Lake Pontchartrain, in the rear of the parishes of St. Bernard and Jefferson.

One of these I well remember, from the terror which he inspired into the stoutest hearts. His reputation for audacity and deeds of ferocity was not in-ferior to that of "Fra Diavolo," the hero of Italian romance, and, if the truth must be told, no one cared to face this bandit in the woods. The account given of him by Cable is pure fiction. His name was Squier. He was owned by General William De Buys, than whom no kinder or more humane master ever lived. The General, in fact, who was greatly attached to him, had petted and completely spoiled the fellow. Fond of field sports, he had made him his huntsman and usual attendant. He indulged him in every one of those *dou-ceurs* which favorite servants were wont to enjoy; but these acts of kindness, instead of generating gratitude and love, only resulted, such was the negro's savage nature, in developing a spirit of revolt and insubordination. To escape from an existence of ease and indolence into one of strife and constant danger became a chronic passion, and although frequently caught and punished he would relapse as often into his inveterate habit. On one occasion, when pursued by a patrol of white planters, headed by Mr. Fleitas, of St. Bernard, he bravely stood at bay and defied capture, until he was laid low by a heavy charge of buckshot. From the effect of the wound his arm was amputated, and hence the origin of the surname of *Bras Coupé*, by which he was known thereafter.

For a series of years his escapes, adroit devices to baffle pursuers, and manifold crimes were the subject of entertainment not only in the public prints, but even in the home circle. He seemed to be endowed with the gift of ubiquity. No hound could follow his scent, no officer keep on his trail. If seen in one place, he was soon to be met miles away, laughing at his would-be captors. Even around the domestic hearth, his name of "Bras Coupé" became a familiar word,pronounced in hushed and subdued tones to frighten children. Rewards were offered for his capture, dead or alive, but no one had as yet been found daring enough to confront the fearless brigand.

On April 7, 1837, the following notice appeared in one of the city prints: "The negro, Squier, notorious for the crimes and cruelties he has committed in the neighborhood of the Bayou St. John, has at last atoned for them. Yesterday two men belonging to the guard of the First Municipality were hunting rabbits on the land of Mr. L. Allard (now the Lower City Park), on the other side of the bayou. Impelled by the ardor of the chase, one of them pushed into the swamp somewhat further than his comrade. What was his surprise to be stopped, not by the game he was pursuing, but by a stout fellow taking aim at him with a gun! The gun was fired at a distance of fifteen paces, and fortunately missed its object. Not entirely a novice in these things, the guardsmen quickly returned the compliment, and with success. Squier, although severely wounded, attempted to escape by running, but was soon overtaken, and died under his blows. We understand that a detachment of the guard will this day be dispatched to find the body."

This announcement was received with satisfaction by some, with incredulity by others. Cunning and desperate as Bras Coupé was known to be, it was generally believed that he had succeeded with his usual luck in effecting his escape, notwithstanding the severe blows which he had been reported to have received. On the following day an armed posse repaired to the spot, accompanied by the police officers, but despite the most diligent search through the devious paths of the *cyprière,* no trace of the criminal could be detected, although the spot was searched where the conflict was said to have taken place. A trail of blood, soon lost in the slimy waters of the marsh, furnished the only evidence of his presumed fate.

This incident was put down as a police *canard,* and for some time the matter remained shrouded in mystery. Scouting parties, formed at intervals with the view of discovering his retreat, had been sent out, but had invariably returned, disappointed and worn out with fatigue. Week followed week without any additional disclosures, until the public mind, engaged in other subjects, had begun to forget the hero and his exploits, when reliable news of his tragic death unexpectedly reached New Orleans.

It would be amusing to describe in detail the excitement which the event produced. Not only on 'change or at Hewlett's, but in the workshops, markets, and even among families was the subject discussed. A stranger to our city and customs, judging from the general commotion, would have believed that some extraordinary event had just occurred. The daring, the insolence and the utter contempt for law which *Bras Coupé* had ever exhibited were freely commented upon. The wound he had once received at the hands of Mr. Fleitas, and the circumstances connected with his former capture, confinement and escape from the hospital were common subjects of gossip. It was remembered how, when lying prostrate after the surgical operation which had bereft him of a limb, and when reduced by an attack of dysentery to the very verge of death, he had eluded the vigilance of the nurses by flinging himself out of an open window. It was also related how, on another occasion, he had captured a negress who, on effecting her escape from his camp, reported an act of ferocity of which she had been made an unwilling witness. The story concerned the fate of an Irish woman whom he had forcibly carried into the woods, detained for several days, tied to a tree and finally shot to death.

It was on a Monday, July 17, 1837, that one Francisco Garcia, while fishing at the mouth of Little river, on Lake Pontchartrain, met the black desperado. The former had got out of his pirogue to reach for a fish car, which he had temporarily left ashore, when, just as he was about to possess himself of the box, he heard the explosion of a fulminating cap. Happening, fortunately, to be holding an iron handspike, to which he was in the habit of fastening his boat, he rushed forward about seven paces, and came upon a man concealed behind the trunk of a fallen tree, in the act of resetting a fresh cap, with his right hand and teeth. Losing no time, the Spanish fisherman struck him three times with his ponderous bar, and felled him dead to the ground.

Such was the account given by Garcia, although there were many persons who, conversant with the character of the slayer, affirmed that *Bras Coupé*'s death was the result of treachery, as Garcia was his usual purveyor and friend. The conviction was that Garcia, seduced by the hope of a large reward, had murdered the man whom he had promised to protect, and whom he had found asleep.

Be this as it may, the Spaniard, on accomplishing the deed, dumped his valuable freight into the boat and proceeded with it to New Orleans. Reaching Milneburg, the body was thence conveyed to the front of the Mayor's office, where Denis Prieur, the then chief executive of the city, ordered it to be exposed to public view on the Place d' Amies, opposite. That thousands and thousands rushed to that historic square to take a look at the ghastly remains is a matter of notoriety. No Mardi Gras procession, no special pageant that I know of, ever attracted such surging crowds as were witnessed under that broiling, solstitial sun. Men, women, children; whites and blacks, freedmen and slaves; professional men and laborers in their working blouses, all seemed to have gathered there to satisfy their morbid curiosity. The body, with its crushed and mangled head, in a state of rapid decomposition, remained in that condition from 1 o'clock in the evening until the darkness of approaching night commanded its removal to Potter's Field. The still unhealed and gaping wounds, alleged to have been inflicted by the city guard, who had reported him dead, made the spectacle still more hideous.

It was generally believed at the time that the different municipalities had offered liberal rewards for *Bras Coupé*'s capture, dead or alive, and Garcia was much congratulated upon his good luck; but, when the day for settling came, it was ascertained that only the section below Esplanade street had made any provision for the event, whereupon the sum of $250 was immediately paid the claimant, as promised in the proclamation.

This is a strange story, and it will read more strangely, perhaps, in the eye of the present and growing generation; but the institution of slavery was one pregnant with constantly recurring changes and new phases. Without entering into any discussion on the abstract right and justice of keeping in bondage a class of people, manifestly designed by the Creator to be "drawers of water and hewers of wood," it is obvious that the form of servitude under which they lived, regarded from the standpoint of practical philanthropy, was a vast improvement on their original condition. It is true that here and there a cruel and barbarous taskmaster was occasionally to be found, but these instances, it must be admitted, formed the exception and not the rule, for every Louisianian positively knows that the planters who thus erred, fell under the ban of social reprobation for that very cause. Whoever attentively reads the old Black Code will observe how stringent were the laws for the protection of the slave. And while I am upon this subject, let me be permitted to say as an historical fact that no master was ever more exacting, despotic, nay, cruel to the negro, than the planter or farmer of African extraction—an anomaly, it is true, but still a fact.

Koanga: Opera in Three Acts

FREDERICK DELIUS AND C. F. KEARY (1899)

Frederick Delius was a classical composer from England. He spent time in Florida from 1884 to 1886, where he tried unsuccessfully to manage an orange plantation. Returning to Europe, he began to compose works, including Koanga, *inspired by the vernacular music he had experienced in Florida. With a libretto by C. F. Keary,* Koanga *is based on the story of Bras-Coupé as it is recounted in* The Grandissimes. *Performed privately in Paris in 1899, Koanga premiered in North Rhine-Westphalia, where it was performed in German. At its premiere and in ensuing performances, characters like Bras-Coupé and Palmyre were depicted by white actors in blackface. Koanga was revived with a multiracial cast for performances in Washington, D.C. in 1970–1971 and in London in 1972. It was subsequently performed in Port-of-Spain, Trinidad in 1995 where it was presented with an all-black cast.*

PROLOGUE.

The verandah of a Southern plantation-house, orange trees on the left; huts in the background. It is evening. Dancing is going on in the house.

(FOUR GIRLS *enter laughing.*)

CHORUS
Ha, ha, ha. Ha, ha, ha. Ha, ha, ha. Ha, ha, ha.

RENÉE *and* HÉLÈNE
Stop! Stop! I am weary of play, and dancing from the early morn.

AURORE
Stop! Stop!

OLIVE
Stop! Stop! For I'll not join again in their never-ending roundelay.

RENÉE
Look, here is Uncle Joe to greet us all! What a store of tales that he can tell!
(RENÉE *goes to meet* UNCLE JOE.)

AURORE
Then join us here, Paulette, Marie, before the day is fully gone!

(JEANNE, MARIE, HORTENSE *and* PAULETTE *now enter and join the others.*)

ALL THE GIRLS
Look, how the shadows of night are falling, falling;
And from the hill the whip-poor-will is calling, calling.
Soon, soon the yellow moon will be shining, shining,
And the mocking bird for his truant mate will be pining.

HÉLÈNE *and* MARIE
Then let us in a ring now rest awhile.

ALL
Sit close and hear!

RENÉE *and* JEANNE
And you, good Uncle Joe, recount a story old of lover's grief and pain!

ALL
And pain! Oh no! Oh no!

UNCLE JOE
Nay! I have nothing fresh that I can tell. You will not care to hear again a tale so many times retold!

RENÉE, JEANNE, HÉLÈNE *and* MARIE
Oh, yes, begin!

ALL
At once, at once, begin!

UNCLE JOE
The story of Koanga and Palmyra.

ALL
Begin, at once, we long to hear!

UNCLE JOE
Koanga and Palmyra.

ALL
We wait, to hear!
(*Clouds descend and cover the scene.*)

(*The clouds clear away gradually and disclose the garden of the plantation with slave-huts to the right.*)

ACT I.

Fields of sugar cane are seen in the distance, and behind them a stretch of the forest. It is quite dark though the full moon watches over the waving cane. PALMYRA *sings:*—

PALMYRA

Ah! grief is mine! How sad and lonely all around!
My country lost! My native land a stranger grown! For evermore!
How far remote my spirit seems from tyrant's hand or humble slave,
And yet no other life I know!
Up, up, for all too soon the sun again will shine.
(*Cowhorn heard from the distance.*)
That note resounding wakes the workers to their toil, (*Somewhat nearer.*)
Commands they shall no longer sleep, however grateful their repose!
(*Again nearer.*)

SIMON PEREZ

Now then, 'tis time, quickly arise! (*Cowhorn now quite near.*) The dawn begins to gild the East;

PALMYRA

Each cabin door opens to greet the strident call.

SIMON P

Get up, 'tis time! The dawn begins to gild the East.

PALMYRA

The world resumes again its old unchanging round,

SIMON P

Another day has now begun.

PALMYRA

And yet no hope shall dawn for me, nothing to ease my aching spirit!

126

SIMON P

Ho, there, get up! get up! Each to his task, and mind you hurry, you lazy, indolent pack of slaves.

(NEGRO MEN *and* WOMEN *appear at the hut doors; they rub their eyes, yawn and gaze stupidly around.*)

NEGRO WOMEN
'Tis dawn, 'tis dawn!

SIMON P
Up, now up! 'Tis dawn, come get to work!

NEGRO MEN
'Tis dawn, 'tis dawn!

SIMON P
Each to his task, the sickle now to test;

NEGRO MEN
Each to his task, the sickle now to test!
Not until the sun is high may we pause for rest!

ALL THE WOMEN
Get up Pete, get up Pete, will you never waken?
And Sal, ne'er so trim or neat,
Since Sambo left you forsaken!

SIMON P
Now then, get up! Time to be working!
The dawn begins to flush the skies.

ALL THE MEN
Ha, ha, ha, ha, ha, ha!
Now haste, you girls, in toil to share,

(SIMON PEREZ *disappears into the slave quarters.*)
The indigo fields are awaiting your care;
So the sickle truly test ere you pause for rest!

WOMEN
Ha, ha, ha, ha, ha, ha!
Why, here's Ned, one shoe off, one shoe on,
They've roused him with the whip,
He sleeps by far too long!

MEN AND WOMEN
Come out, brothers, come out to cut the waving cane;
The moonlight shadows are faded and the day is back again.
The humming bird is waking, good brothers don't complain;
So come once more and hasten to the fields of sugar cane!
To work!

(*They go to their work; it is now full daylight.*)
(*Enter* SIMON PEREZ.)

SIMON P
Soft! 'Tis Palmyra.

PALMYRA (*notices* SIMON PEREZ)
So my trials begin with day!
Once again this hateful wooing!

SIMON P
O lovely Palmyra, wherefore turn aside?

PALMYRA
Shall I never escape him?

SIMON P
You are fair as the dawn.
And as the sun in splendour gleams, so my heart burns for you.

You are like the tender lily growing, by dark gleaming lake,
Like the lonely clouds a'sailing through the radiant vault of heaven.
Pale as moonlight, your brow.

(*The* NEGROES *are heard from the fields.*)

NEGROES (*all*)
Come out, brothers, come out to cut the waving cane;
The moonlight shadows are faded and the day is back again.
The humming bird is waking, no brother dares complain,
When once they please to call us to the fields of sugar-cane!

SIMON P (*He approaches nearer to* PALMYRA.)
Dark as night your hair,
My soul is all on fire,
I shall claim you for my bride,
Oh lovely Palmyra!
(*He tries to embrace her.* PALMYRA *frees herself.*)

PALMYRA
Nay, that shall never be. Leave me! The love you offer, I can never share.

SIMON P
That, time alone will prove! Foolish girl, must I remind you, you are a slave,
I am free!

PALMYRA
Though you call me slave, a secret still I prize: Am I not from Jaloff race
descended!

SIMON P
Oh silly child, to seek your hand is no small honour I pay you! Why try to
rule and govern us, and think we all must yield to a wilful slip of a maid,
instead of our mistress, Lady Clotilda? Remember, here you play with men,
and not with children?

PALMYRA

I hate you, but I am not afraid; my mistress is stronger than you!

SIMON P

And if I did hate my pretty one, you'd find it far more bitter than my love!
But here comes our master!

(*Enter* DON JOSÉ MARTINEZ; PALMYRA *is about to go.*)

NEGROES *in the fields*

Work, brothers, work, with sickle in hand,
We live by our labour and worship the land;
For many a bundle of cane must be bound,
In the meadows a-waving ere master comes round;
For many a bundle of cane must be bound,
Ere the sun sinks low in the forest,
Low in the forest, low in the forest!

DON JOSÉ MARTINEZ

Stay, Palmyra! (*After "Stay, Palmyra!"* PALMYRA *says: "And my lady?"*)
Stay here! And another time ask me first if I wish you to go. (*To* SIMON
PEREZ.) Well, what's the news to-day?

SIMON P

The men are down in the canes.

MARTINEZ

That scoundrel Pete is hardly awake, give him six lashes of the best! And the
women?

SIMON P

They are all in the indigo fields. But the profit will be less than we made last
year.

MARTINEZ

'Tis true, Diego's load of slaves has lately been of poor account, hardly worth the honest whip.

SIMON P

And yet to-day he sends a rare and splendid prize, a noble warrior who comes of ancient race, a Prince of his realm.

MARTINEZ

We must find a way to render him of service.

SIMON P

My orders are to bring him here. See where he comes!

NEGROES *in the fields*

Work, brothers, work, with sickle in hand,
We live by our labour and worship the land;
For many a bundle of cane must be bound,
In the meadows a-waving ere master comes round;
For many a bundle of cane must be bound,
Ere the sun sinks low in the forest,
Low in the forest, low in the forest!

(KOANGA *is brought in, chained, guarded by two Negroes. He looks neither to the left nor to the right, and advances to the front of the stage.*)

KOANGA

O Voodoo Manian, my fathers from your graves revenge me, revenge me on the vile Myangwa. Ye hosts arise again and let the traitors' blood in the rivers flow!

(PALMYRA *suddenly rouses herself and gazes on* KOANGA.)

KOANGA

Let them be nailed unto a thousand piles! Nay more! A heavier curse,—
Send them beyond the sea for white men's slaves!

PALMYRA

The signs only too well I know, a Jaloff Prince, a Voodoo Priest, who scarce will deign to glance on those around.

KOANGA

But I shall never, never see again the slow Inlanga river, nor the wide and shady forest, where the serpent crawls at ease, and great beasts roam in search of prey; nor the azure heights that harbour gods of air, and the woodland glade where the deer would drink at eve. Nor shall I hear again that ever grateful sound of arrow speeding home. For by a traitor's hand I now am captive, yet never tho' my flesh be torn away with whips will I be slave to those that bought me. Voodoo, Koanga vows it, hear his oath!

MARTINEZ

Thy words are bold enough for princes, but one thing must thou learn, the slaves I buy from overseas repay me by their toil. Come, Simon Perez, speak your mind, what is the task he shall perform?

SIMON P

Alas! my master, none such as he can be made to yield. He'll not obey, I know his kind too well.

MARTINEZ

Then we must use the lash, and in a little while restore both peace and happiness.

SIMON P

And even that would be but waste of time. He never would complain, never would murmur, sigh or groan, but laugh even at death! The common Congo slave may be cowed by the whip, not such as he! Over a wild and savage clan, once he was Prince, and Priest. His tribe were evermore ashamed did he but bend the knee, and ancient vows would still arise to grant his soul no hope of heav'n.

MARTINEZ

'Tis idle talk, Perez! There's a way, surely, to tame him, this Prince and

Priest, who's but a common slave, like all the rest. Make him worth the money I have paid, or else the sun shall bleach his bones!

PALMYRA

Ah!

MARTINEZ

Who cried so loud? Is it Palmyra? I had forgotten you were near us. My child, now see if woman's wiles can conquer him!

PALMYRA

Oh hapless fate, to me decreed!

MARTINEZ

A maiden's words may still prevail, where strength of man is idly spent, so speak to him, Palmyra; and if 'tis useless try a soft caress!

PALMYRA

Am I so weak, or is my heart aflame? Am I not stirred with that same pride which renders him a god? Don José, spare me this, I am afraid.

MARTINEZ

Afraid, and why?

PALMYRA

Alas, how can I tell? Myself, I hardly know! Some magic in him dwells!

MARTINEZ

I think the magic lies the other way. Yours is the power to make him know it. Come, show how my servants work!

PALMYRA

The work of slaves! He and I in bondage together, and will not Voodoo arm his Priest with pow'r?

(*She turns to* KOANGA.)

If thou wilt only bow the head, Koanga, thy chosen fate may not prove
too hard to bear. In fancy, picture here Inlanga's water flowing, for thou
must learn to wield the sickle as the sword. It is little they shall ask of thee,
Koanga, Jaloff Prince, Voodoo Priest, in part a god! Thou has heard the
sound of weeping in thy country. Learn how merry here the life that mortals
lead! What charm enfolds my mind, what spell of madness? It wakes
those dim-remembered things, strains half forgotten, once I knew in early
childhood's days, like shadows beyond the grave. Is it the past that binds me
still in chains, or presage of sorrow still to come? Yet, if thou wilt only bow
the head, Koanga, thy chosen fate I will gladly share.

KOANGA

What voice is this now strikes thine ear, Koanga? Soft as the sound of silver
torrent playing on the rocks in summer's mid-day langour? See, I repent
me of my hasty word. Pale grows the vision of the wide Inlanga. Against my
ancient foes let others draw the sword; so soon the words of wrath by love
are chasten'd! I could work with your bondsmen in the fields! For her sake
I will toil, and gladly bear my lot. Give me the maid! I will renounce my
people, my ancient home forget! Bind, if you will my hands, and take my
freedom, I shall not care! She is a slave, let us be slaves together! Be she a
slave, we will be slaves together, and you our master own.

SIMON P

It works too well! And he is all on fire. Well said, Palmyra! Yes, if thou wilt
only bow the head, Koanga, thy chosen fate may not prove too hard to
bear. Inlanga's banks too far away thy call to answer! We are the masters,
thou no longer hast a sword. Drink then! And forget the wide Inlanga, and
learn, merry is the life that niggers lead! Yes, if thou wilt only bow the head,
Koanga, thy chosen fate may not prove too hard to bear.

MARTINEZ

The magic works! She holds him fast! Yes, if thou wilt only bow the head,
Koanga, thy chosen fate may not prove too hard to bear. Inlanga's banks too
far away thy call to answer! Masters are we, thou no longer hast a sword.
Drink then! And forget the wide Inlanga, and learn, merry is the life that

niggers lead! Yes, yes, if thou wilt only bow the head, Koanga, thy chosen
fate may not prove too hard to bear.

CHORUS *in the fields:*
WOMEN
We are pulling, pulling, pulling
Downy seeds as white as snow,
We are culling, culling, culling
Dainty heads of indigo.

But soon we shall put scythe and sickle away,
For the dinner bell will be tolling,
Oh, Oh, Oh!

MEN
Ply the sickle, whet the scythe,
While the day is young and blythe,
Sheaf on sheaf and row on row
Mount before us as we go.
Each one as he passes by,
Will hum a Negro melody.

We are singing, singing, singing,
Through the cane-brake, hid from sight,
Listen how the scythe is ringing,
Bare your arm, nor cease to smite!

But soon we shall put scythe and sickle away,
For the Dinner bell will be tolling,
Oh, Oh, Oh!

MARTINEZ
Agreed then, 'tis a bargain! The girl belongs to him.

SIMON P (*aside*).

My plans have come to nothing, if I must lose Palmyra! (*To* MARTINEZ)
My master, you cannot give the Lady Clotilda's maid away!

MARTINEZ

I cannot? And who will counter my desire? I like his honest ways and will
make of him what I choose.

(*Enter* CLOTILDA, SIMON PEREZ *whispers to her.*)

MARTINEZ

Come Clotilda, for you shall take a part and bring the girl to reason.

CLOTILDA

This thing shall never be, my husband. Well you know, my father placed in
my care Palmyra when still a child.

(MARTINEZ *turns to* NEGROES, *who strike off* KOANGA's *chains.*)
(KOANGA *approaches* PALMYRA, *who stands spellbound.*)

MARTINEZ

Be silent wife, and see how the charm begins to work!

SIMON P

Our good confessor would refuse to sanction such an evil deed.

MARTINEZ

My sanction is enough. I'll hear no more! Our good confessor shall be paid.

PALMYRA (*turns to* CLOTILDA)

My fate approaching leads me to my doom. No longer now I need my lady's
help. I am captive in the toils, yet my pride of race still burns in my heart, in
my brain. I hear my mother's cry, her last wail of bitter grief as in death she
sank to sleep.

KOANGA

Can I hope to win the lovely maid's affection? Oh were she mine! God of my fathers, ancient pow'rs, heed not the vow I made; she bides near, ye are far. Voodoo, temper the force of my oath! Jealous god, be thou not aveng'd on me, for thou art far, while she bides near.

PALMYRA

Oh gentle mistress, how gladly I served you! Kind and so tender, never cruel to the child who though of alien line, her mother lost, to your care was giv'n. Like a net around me thrown, that in vain I strive to rend, pow'rs unseen now hold me fast. Is it love, is it pain? And soon, gentle mistress mine, they will bear me from your side, I am captive in the toils. Yet my pride of race still burns in my heart, still burns in my brain, though never, never more can joy to me return!

CLOTILDA

How my father could I tell what to Palmyra falls? She to my loving care was giv'n, for a reason that I know all too well! My own father's child is she; her unwilling hand bestow'd on a heathen unbeliever, on a wild and pagan Prince! Shall I give a Christian maid, to a heathen for his bride? Her unwilling hand bestowed, who to me was freely giv'n! Palmyra, my father's child, on a cruel pagan Prince! No, I swear it shall never be; I will guard, and will save her from harm!

SIMON P

Never, never had I dreamt of this-that she could now escape me! I thought my victory won, with my mistress well disposed. Curses on this princeling's head! My schemes have come to nought. And curses on the whims of Don José! But the closest bonds e'er tied, may by cunning be unbound.

KOANGA

My bride thou soon shalt be, ere clouds conceal the moon. And yet my spirit fails! Thy magic holds me fast, as in a spell; I tremble, I falter before a maid! I who ne'er did flinch in war, must in love fainthearted prove! Oh ye ancient powers, forgive me the vow I made! She bides near and ye are far.

Once, only once we live. My fathers, oh hear my call! Jealous god, jealous god, be not aveng'd! Thou art near, she is far!

MARTINEZ
Yes, before the moon is full shall our pact be duly seal'd. My own birthday I will fete with him; and my slaves shall feast in idleness; yea, before the moon is full! So heed my word; for, by Heav'n, my command shall be obeyed! Cease then, Clotilda, cease to mourn; let all remember I am firm! Don José is not to be denied, however strict his manner of control! And in truth she's mated well, wedded to a noble warrior Prince. For the brave deserve the fair!
(*A bell rings*).

NEGRO CHORUS *in the fields:*
WOMEN
We are pulling, we are pulling
Downy seeds as soft as snow;
We are culling, we are culling,
Dainty heads of indigo.
Each one, as he passes by,
Will hum a tune or heave a sigh.

But now we may put scythe and sickle away,
For the dinner bell is a-ringing.

MEN
We are singing, we are singing,
Through the cane-brake hid from sight,
Listen how the scythe is ringing,
Bare your arm, nor cease to smite!

But now we may put scythe and sickle away,
For the dinner bell is a-ringing.
(*Curtain.*)

138

ACT II.

(Songs are heard behind the curtain.)

CHORUS
Now once in a way,
Be it but for a day,
We may lay down our shovels and our hoes;
The cane may wave tall,
The sheaves need not fall,
No girls tread the long cotton rows;
Oh! Oh! Come out, come out!
Oh! Oh! Come girls, come out!
Ha, ha, ha, ha! Ha, ha, ha, ha! Ha, ha, ha, ha
(Curtain.)
A view of the terrace before the main entrance to DON JOSÉ's *house. On one side are seen the pillars and steps of the verandah; on the other side, behind orange trees, is an awning, under which* NEGROES *are celebrating their master's birthday and the wedding day of* KOANGA *and* PALMYRA.

NEGROES *(all)*
He will meet her when the sun goes down,
When the whip-poor-will sings to the moon;
When, from magnolia trees, the heavy scent is blown,
And strange lights wander o'er the dark lagoon.

(Enter CLOTILDA *from the house.)*
*(*SIMON PEREZ *enters from the plantation;* CLOTILDA *does not see him.)*

CLOTILDA
Alas! what can I contrive? This marriage must never come to pass!

SIMON P
If my master, Don José, is bent upon it, no words of mine can overrule his will.

CLOTILDA

'Tis you, yourself, far more than my husband, would seek to force the Prince upon her.

SIMON P

Nay! She is all too ready, and longs to greet the fatal day!

CLOTILDA

Oh! had it been some other suitor, to save her from this act of madness!

SIMON P

Who can turn the stubborn mind of woman, tho' may bring disaster?

CLOTILDA

My husband will not help me, I know not where to turn! Must I confess the secret? Palmyra is my own father's child.

SIMON P

By Heav'n, is it so? A double danger! Then all the surer, never can she marry the slave! But if you, alone, are helpless, and I by chance persuade the couple to break the bond that binds them, is it agreed that I myself wed the maiden?

CLOTILDA

Yourself, wed her? But my husband . . .

SIMON P

May I not prove as welcome as Koanga? Your promise give, and I will help you in your trouble.

CLOTILDA

I see her coming, so hear my word: Strive but this marriage to prevent; and if you free Palmyra, gladly I'll give the maid to you.

PALMYRA (*singing behind the scenes*)

How time flows on! Whether 'tis dawn of day or evening, scarce I know!

Some secret pow'rs within me lie, and urge me on, in spite of fear. My life was all so dull and vain, while things to come no brighter promise give. All the past was like a faded leaf;

(*Enter* PALMYRA, *splendidly attired in bright silks, a silk scarf wound round her head.*)

and what the future holds is but a doubtful Spring. In some waking dream I live, recalling to mem'ry half forgotten scenes, and melodies I used to hear, yet ne'er were sung beyond my home!

SIMON P
Come, rouse yourself, PALMYRA, and listen.

PALMYRA
'Tis you? Then I have dreamt the old familiar dream again, and in my restless, troubled sleep, I heard your oft repeated vows, that still offend my ears.

CLOTILDA
Oh, child, what fancies fill your brain! And why so headstrong and proud? One gift to you Koanga brings-the gift of shame!

PALMYRA (*proudly, almost fiercely*)
A Jaloff Prince, a Voodoo Priest! Oh, could you fathom, oh, could you feel the bond of blood, the ties of race, that work to make us one!

CLOTILDA
Madness, and frenzy of folly! Would you renounce your faith and creed?

PALMYRA
Naught to me, faith or creed!

SIMON P
No, lady, no; to try her I've a better way; leave me with her a while! When you return, judge if my words are true!

CHORUS

Be it but for a day,
Ned, the fiddler may play,
And we'll dance while the sky is aglow;
But when night shadows fall,
We will drink in the hall.
And relate all the tales brothers know!
He will meet her where the moon is high,
Where the ancient oak stands alone;
There, where the screech owls hoot and cry,
While the poplar trees wail and moan!

(CLOTILDA *goes out.*)

SIMON P

Listen, Palmyra! Know you the secret of your birth? You are the sister
of Clotilda.

PALMYRA

Our mistress?

SIMON P

Now, you will surely see, you must forget Koanga.

PALMYRA

Forget him, so near to my heart!

SIMON P

A Negro slave, and you a planter's daughter! Mine you shall be! I love you,
and I will promise to make you happy, Palmyra!

PALMYRA

What was I told of faith and creed?

SIMON P

Deny them and you will! But do not reject my love!

PALMYRA
Koanga waits for me!

SIMON P
Palmyra, I know you hate me now, yet there is a time, a time for all!

PALMYRA
The hour I shall not fear!

(*Enter* CLOTILDA.)

(*The* NEGROES *accompany themselves with a rhythmical clapping of hands.*)

(NEGRO CHORUS *behind the scenes*):
WOMEN
Come, leave the work, if it's only for a minute;
When there's frolic about, a brother will be in it!
Dansons la Calinda, Ohé, la Calinda, Ohé, Ohé,
la Calinda! Ohé, la Calinda!
La, la, la, la, la.

MEN
La, la, la, la, la, la, la.

CLOTILDA
Well, have you persuaded her?

SIMON P
No, and never shall. We must use force, if we would win.

(CLOTILDA *and* SIMON PEREZ *go out.*)

PALMYRA
The hour has come, when I to him my soul surrender.
Koanga, beloved, is it a dream?
Kindly warmth of sunlight pouring,

Thy grateful gift I still recall from days gone by!
Africa, land of my fathers!
Glowing in splendour, in radiance gleaming,
Rapture-filled I think of thee.
Koanga, beloved, in cruel captive chains,
From distant country hither brought, a common slave!
And yet, a Prince Palmyra doth worship;
Yea, to serve him with undying faith shall be her vow!
Dark and brave one, in joy or sorrow, whate'er befall us,
Oh hear me promise, I am thine!

CHORUS
La, la, la, la, la, la, la.

MARTINEZ
Here comes the honest bridegroom,
Dress'd as a bridegroom should be;
Koanga greet, Palmyra too;
Such is the will of Don José!

(KOANGA *enters, dressed in bright African robes.*)

CHORUS
Koanga, hail!

(KOANGA *gazes around him. He advances slowly and with great dignity
towards* PALMYRA, *and lays his right hand upon her head.*)

KOANGA
Far, far away, Palmyra, my people mourn for me,
The streams more gently flow bewailing my fate.
The mountains call me, yet I may never listen;
No charms my land could offer, deprived of thy love.
Here will I toil for thee, a patient, humble slave,
And in thy service find the labour sweet!
Far, far away my foes enjoy their triumph,

The false Myangwa jeer and mock at me,
And round their fires at night will run the story,
How in the West, Koanga is a slave!
But vengeance were a poor reward, Palmyra,
If I may linger by thy side, toiling for thee,
And find labour sweet!

NEGRO CHORUS
How firm the ties of homeland and country;
How fast still they bind!
But for him, love is stronger,
And faith more dear than palace of kings.
Ah, Koanga, learn the lesson of strangers,
For we are also vowed to bondage,
And yet may dance and sing beneath the shady trees!

CLOTILDA
Not yet, Koanga, nay, not yet!
First a cup of wine,
And then the priest shall hither come!

(*Wine is served. The white folks gather round the table.* PALMYRA *hands a cup to* KOANGA *and kneels before him.*)

SIMON P
A cup of wine to pledge our noble guest,
Our chieftain of to-morrow!

PALMYRA
Hail to thee mighty Prince!
At thy feet I gladly fall to bless our bond, and grace our love!
Now, behold, for thee alone I'll dance;
Unloose my girdle, my hair untwine, to please my chosen lord.

CHORUS
Dansons la Calinda! Ah!

Ha, ha, ha, ha, ha, ha,
Dansons la Calinda! Ah!
Ha, ha, ha, ha, ha, ha,
La, la, la, la, la.

Koanga, we drink the health of our chieftain that shall be!
For the bride, the lasting wish: may she never live to mourn!
And is there one among us to be found that will not hail the toast?

PALMYRA
Come, take the drink I offer, greet thy bride,
Pledge her in crimson wine!
Drink! Drink, for ere the dawn of day,
Koanga and Palmyra shall be one!

PALMYRA *and* CHORUS
Dansons la Calinda! Ah!
Ha, ha, ha, ha, ha, ha.
(*Ballet of Creole dancers.*)(*During the ballet,* PALMYRA *finds herself swept to the back of the stage.*)

CHORUS
He will win her when the sun goes down,
And the whip-poor-will sings to the moon!
When from magnolia trees, the heavy scent is blown,
And dragon flies disturb the dark lagoon.
Ah! Ah! Ah! Ah!

(SIMON PEREZ *and a few servants seize* PALMYRA *and drag her away by force.* KOANGA, *astonished, does not understand at first.*)

(KOANGA *approaches* DON JOSÉ MARTINEZ *and strikes the table violently with his hand.*)

KOANGA
Where is my bride?
Who dares to steal Koanga's only joy?

MARTINEZ
Who dares in turn to question Don José?

KOANGA
Quick, bring her back, before my curses light on ye!

(KOANGA *holds his hands to Heaven.*)

MARTINEZ
African slave, my whip shall make you tremble!

(THEY *fight.* MARTINEZ *falls.*)
(*Thunder and darkness.* KOANGA *alone on the stage advances, and falls on his knees, with arms outstretched.*)

KOANGA
Hear me, god Voodoo;
I have betrayed my trust,
I have forsworn my faith,
False to my fathers, now on thee do I call.
I know thy secret pow'r,
Reject me not, and grant the gift I crave!
Let all my white companions learn what magic may perform,
That on their heads descend the worst of mortal woes,
The triple curse on land, on air, and flood: From water ling'ring death,
starvation on the earth, and tainted fevers to corrupt the air! Now with this
threefold evil visit them, and let thy thunder wake applause!

(KOANGA *is seen, by occasional flashes of lightning making his way through the dense forest.*)

KOANGA (*in the distance*)
Voodoo Manian, Voodoo Manian,
Thy hand hath set me free!
Atoua, the silent one, protect me from harm!

(*Curtain.*)

ACT III.

A glade in the dense forest, at night-fall. Will-o'-the-wisps shine over the marshes. On the right, the ground rises towards the hills.

VOICES (*heard from afar*)
Ah! Ah! Ah! Ah
(*Curtain rises.*)
Ah! Ah! Ah! Ah!

NEGRO CHORUS
Segami! Segami! Segami!
Inmoua, Segami!
Itu, the Bull? Approach!
Oh, have no fear, oh, have no fear!
Approach, Inmoua, Segami!

(NEGROES *gather on the stage.*)

RANGWAN
The chief, the chief, Koanga, comes.
I hear his heavy tread throughout the glade.
No beast nor bird may safely sleep,
While phantom lights before him wane.

NEGROES
The chief, the chief, Koanga, comes.

(*Enter* KOANGA, *accompanied by* NEGROES *with torches.*)
All hail, Koanga, save us now,
And lead us to our promised home!
Under thee, free shall we live,
Mighty is thy rule.

KOANGA
Is Rangwan here, the holy priest?
Ye know the spell that shall be cast to-night.

RANGWAN
We know it all, the magic spell that shall be cast to-night.

KOANGA
Hast thou the nameless thing for sacrifice?

RANGWAN
The blood is all we need to work the charm.

KOANGA
To-night the moon is full, another phase begins,
Atoua's prophetic night!
Our day of golden freedom soon shall dawn.
Voodoo, now grant thine aid!
Rangwan, the holy priest, prepares the ancient sacrifice we offer.
Gods of the upper air, and the realm of shades, your secret will proclaim!

NEGROES
Koanga is our hero Prince;
No foe we fear when he is nigh.
Now blood shall flow from wounded arms,
And eager fires consume the horrid meal!

(KOANGA *and* RANGWAN *gash their arms with knives. The priest pours blood from a gourd on the fire.*)

149

Look, he performs the ancient rite!
Fear now is fled, Koanga is with us,
And Rangwan of the silver hair repeats the words of sacrifice.

RANGWAN

Voodoo behold! The fire receives the blood!

KOANGA

Voodoo hear! For thee I maim my arms!

NEGROES

Voodoo guard us, now as ever, safety lies in thee alone.

RANGWAN

Atoua, listen, and assemble thy host!

NEGROES

Great Atoua, we call on thee,
Thy thrice ten thousand gifts to prove!

KOANGA

Mayami, hear! thou the last of the holy three!

(KOANGA *ascends the hill.*)

NEGROES

Voodoo guard us, now as ever,
May this blood redeem our shame!
Oh lend thine ear, thou midnight goddess,
Great Atoua, hear the call!

(THE NEGROES *gash themselves with knives and commence a wild dance.*)
(*The fire dies down, a mist covers the scene. Voices are faintly heard through the darkness.*)

NEGROES

See, he prays! Voodoo must hear him! Can he reject a son? Long was our woe! Yet we did bear it! Now is the torment past! Rangwan waits. The fire is dying. Dark is the night. Far over the marsh the voices call. The distant voices call. What bird in dim shadows flew by on troubled wing? Dark is the night. The distant voices call.

(*A vision of* DON JOSÉ MARTINEZ's *plantation.* NEGROES *are lying on the ground, in the last extremity of distress.* KOANGA *is seen on the hill.*)

NEGROES

Pale and wan, the sunlight sinks on the lone and marshy bed; yea, and we are weary too, and would gladly greet the end. Naught can save us now, then why so long delay? Mist enfolds the realm of night, not a star looks down. No deliv'rance, no relief! Hope is fled; and life is vain; death alone can save!

PALMYRA (*plaintively*)

Ah! Ah!

KOANGA

I hear a far off cry, a woman's wail of grief, wafted on the cooling midnight air. Once to me that voice was life itself, and I must follow where it called! Close my ears, O god, let me not listen, or else my newborn kingdom falls to ruin! Naught upon this earth I hold so dear, as my lost country's cause and fame.

PALMYRA

Ah woe is me! Ah woe is me! My only love is far away!

KOANGA

Again the cry, and there is none to answer! She must perish before I reach her side! Let my kingdom sink, and fall to ashes! Wait, I come to thee!

(*The vision fades, and the morning star appears.*)

KOANGA
Kindly morning star, oh light me on my way!

(*The vision fades, and the scene changes to* DON JOSÉ's *plantation.*)

NEGROES
Woe! Woe!

(*Early morning, a lurid light shines through the mist; on the left are seen some cabins with* NEGROES *lying at the doors, or on the grass. On the right, a country chapel with a shrine outside; houses of the white folk behind.* NEGROES *are praying before the shrine;* SIMON PEREZ *is among them.*)

NEGROES
Once again, the weary sun ascends from pallid ocean bed. Now another day begins in this land of living death. In the grave, only, is release!

(*Enter* DON JOSÉ MARTINEZ.)

MARTINEZ
Fools ye are to weep and wail.
Christians, Negroes, all are one,
Short of courage and of heart!
Will lamenting change your fate?
Join your fellows before the shrine
It may be relief is gained in prayer;
Sinners surely have found it so!

(*Pointing to a house.*)

Who lies in there?

NEGRO 1
Palmyra, master.

MARTINEZ

Palmyra, whom once I gave in marriage to a precious foreign Prince? The slave who fled; his name I have forgot.

NEGRO 2

Forgot so soon? But if his anger has brought this curse upon us?

MARTINEZ

Fool! Can you believe the tale?

NEGRO 2

We all believe it.

NEGROES

We all believe it.
Naught can escape the curse of a Voodoo.
Yes, we are dying through Koanga's curse.
Forget him, master!
Let him not return, but rejoice in his freedom lest a worse fate befall us,
Even than we know!

MARTINEZ

Christians, this is naught save heathen chatter, and yet a bargain I will make with you; if I this slave should ever capture, he shall know the ills, he shall suffer pains, that ye yourselves have borne! That is a promise I will keep.

NEGROES

No, master, no, it is Koanga's curse, make peace with him, let him never return again; or else a dreader fate may fall, than even the one we know!

MARTINEZ

Enough! Silence! (*to* SIMON PEREZ) Simon, I would warn you, a troop of horsemen hither ride. They must be entertained with ease and comfort, for in the forest they will hunt all day.

(*He goes out.*)

NEGROES

Alas, our only hope of joy is fled, our days are nearly done.

(PALMYRA *steps out of a house; she is weak and leans against the door.*
The NEGROES *disappear slowly.*)

PALMYRA

Ah, tell me where Koanga bides! Will he return again? For ever lost?
For ever gone? So feeble and worn am I now, there's none to care for me!

SIMON P

There's one who cares, Palmyra sweet! It is foolish thus to grieve; let's be
merry while we may!

(SIMON PEREZ *tries to embrace* PALMYRA.)
You were born for me, and I was meant for you!

PALMYRA

No, never! Let me go! Come, Koanga, and help me! Koanga!

SIMON P

In vain to call Koanga; he is a thousand miles away.

PALMYRA

Nay, it is false; a shameful lie!

SIMON P

And yet, I will not leave your side! 'Tis foolish thus to moan and grieve!
Let us be merry, while we may! You and I, Palmyra sweet!

PALMYRA

Oh coward! To face him you would never dare!

SIMON P

What! Is it still of him you think? All in vain, for Koanga never will return.

PALMYRA
Ah!

(SIMON PEREZ *takes her in his arms.*)

SIMON P
And I shall gain your love! Great God in Heav'n! What sight is this?
He comes!

(*Enter* KOANGA.)

KOANGA
Now, by the seven times seven plagues, in Atoua's deepest realm; it was time
Koanga came!
(He *approaches* PEREZ.)

SIMON P
Touch me not, spare me! She is free, if I go unharmed.

PALMYRA
Slay him, O great Koanga, slay him! Kill him like a dog, O grant me that!

KOANGA
It shall be granted! One, one at least, my weapon strikes!

(SIMON PEREZ *flees,* KOANGA *follows and kills* SIMON PEREZ *with his spear.*)

PALMYRA
Alas, he too is lost! Yes, they are upon him! Away, away, and leave the
coward where he lies! The horsemen are nearing; quick, Koanga, fly!
(*Horsemen behind the scenes.*) They overtake him! Ah! too late!
(*A wild shout.*)

PALMYRA
How can I bear the sight! Would he were killed at once! But they are not so
kind! They scourge him to death with their whips! O spare him, God!

(KOANGA *is brought in on a litter and set down beside* PALMYRA. *She falls on her knees.*)

KOANGA (*faintly*)
My spear, where is my spear? Palmyra, is it thou? Oh Voodoo, I have forsaken thee, but now I do repent, and wait thy sentence, god! Defend my people, upon the wide Inlanga, under the oak tree stem that proudly stands, those budding leaves that bless our father's graves! Where every moon my clan would gather round; (*half raising himself*) I see them all, the priesthood, singers too, they dance, they dance; Oh Voodoo, they call on thee, arm them with secret pow'r, their ways prepare! The day shall come, oh sunlight send it soon, when on my white companions Koanga's vengeance falls! And then, then all is over! (*He dies.*)

PALMYRA
Alas, Koanga, dead! Dead, my hero consort, Prince and Prophet! The hour of reck'ning shall it be delayed too long? He has passed beyond your anger, white companions, tribe accurst! Double tyrants, hatred fill'd, for ever false! He has passed beyond your anger! Mighty Prince of Jaloff's house; brave in war, in love supreme! Thou and I one kindred shared; to thy estate Palmyra rose, Prince of Jaloff race! And therefore I belong to thee. Christian faith, a phantom wild! Receive the blood of both, Voodoo; and remember thou the day! (*She stabs herself.*)
(*Clouds cover the scene.*)

EPILOGUE.

(*The verandah steps of the plantation house [as in the Prologue]; the* GIRLS *are grouped on the steps listening intently to* UNCLE JOE.)

JEANNE
Alas, alas, Uncle Joe, we all must weep;
Mournful is the ancient story.

156

RENÉE
Alas, alas, I'll never lay me down,
But I shall hear Palmyra's dying wail!

JEANNE, HÉLÈNE, AURORE, OLIVE, PAULETTE
Alas, alas!

RENÉE
Let us wait and watch the coming dawn of day;
For the weary stars begin to pale.
No fear, no troubled thought shall grieve our mind;
When once again, the grateful sunlight streaming falls!
(*Day breaks.*)

RENÉE, JEANNE, HÉLÈNE, AURORE, OLIVE, PAULETTE.
Once more the fields are all aglow,
The warmth of Springtime greeting;
May God to parted lovers pity show,
And bless their meeting!
(*Sunlight floods the scene.*)

THE END.

From *History of New Orleans*

JOHN SMITH KENDALL (1922)

John Smith Kendall worked as a foreign correspondent and editor for the New Orleans Picayune *and as a Spanish professor at Tulane University in New Orleans. Kendall's* History of New Orleans, *his best-known work, was published in three volumes. In contrast to Cable, Hearn, and Castellanos—all of whom were amateur polymaths—Kendall was an academic specialist, and accordingly,* History of New Orleans *concentrates on matters, like the mechanics of local government, favored in his time by professional historians. Kendall's short account of Bras-Coupé focuses on the facts of the case, with particular reference to how it speaks to political tensions during Mayor Denis Prieur's administration.*

Connected with the matter of police regulation, was, of course, the question of the slaves. In 1828 the city, in obedience to a mandate from the legislature, enacted regulations governing the traffic in slaves, especially forbidding the exposing of negroes for sale in the more frequented parts of the city. Two years later the community was greatly excited over the possibilities of a slave rising. It was, as Martin observes, "a time of vigilance." The first promise of trouble came from persons from other parts of the United States, presumably abolition agents, who were detected traveling around in the parishes, trying to incite the blacks to insurrection. Had these individuals been apprehended, the white population would probably have summarily disposed of them. They made their escape, however, but the legislature was led thereby to pass laws making it a capital crime to incite the slaves against the whites in any way, whether by word, deed, or merely by importing into the state pamphlets composed elsewhere which tended to that end. In fact, the danger being apparently apprehended chiefly from free men of color, a very severe law was enacted expelling all persons of this description from the state. Within a twelvemonth the excitement seems to have been allayed, as some of the harsher provisions in these laws were then modified, and the decree of banishment was limited to those half-breeds who were known to be "worthless."

On the whole, the relations between the races in New Orleans appear to have been friendly, the masters kindly and considerate, the slaves loyal and devoted. Cases like . . . Bras Coupé were exceptional. . . . [Bras Coupé] seems to have been a wild, untamable soul, probably less the Robin Hood that he has been represented to be, than a natural criminal. His real name was Squier. His sobriquet was earned by the loss of an arm, amputated as the result of a gunshot wound. He belonged to Gen. William DeBuys, known as a humane and considerate master. He was DeBuys' hunting companion and personal attendant. But nothing could keep him at home. His frequent disappearances, the pursuits by the sheriff or a posse of citizens, his recapture—these were topics of constant discussion in the city. Finally, several serious crimes caused a price to be set on his head. He sought refuge in the swamps. In July, 1837, he was killed by a Spanish fisherman, in his hiding place on Lake Pontchartrain. Just how Bras Coupé came to his end was never clearly established. His slayer claimed to have been attacked while at work in his boat. Seeing Bras Coupé about to shoot at him, he seized an iron bar and beat him to death. On the other hand, there were not lacking those who said that the fisherman was in reality a confederate of the negro's, and murdered him treacherously in sleep. At any rate, the body was brought to the city and exposed to the public view in the Place d'Armes where it was viewed by thousands.

Bras Coupé's adventures had interest for his generation because he was the type of negro runaway from whom the whites felt they had most to apprehend. The newspapers of Prieur's time are full of notices of fugitive slaves, and of rewards offered for their capture and return. Sometimes these negroes turned bandit, like Bras Coupé, and from their hiding places in the swamps near the city issued at night to perpetrate the robberies so often chronicled in the press of that day. They were usually arrested through the efforts of the law officers; sometimes they returned voluntarily after a vacation more or less protracted. But always over the white population hung the threat of danger, which was slavery's menace to the slave-holding class.

From *The French Quarter*

HERBERT ASBURY (1936)

Herbert Asbury worked as a journalist before he began writing true crime books like The Gangs of New York *(1928) and* The Barbary Coast *(1933). In* The French Quarter *(1936), Asbury tackles the New Orleans criminal underworld in a historical survey of violence, prostitution, gambling, street crime, con artistry, and political corruption in the city. Asbury provides evidence and cites his sources, but he has also been criticized for exaggerating and sensationalizing the colorful stories he tells. Asbury describes Bras-Coupé in a section of the book on Congo Square, blending Cable's ethnography seamlessly with material from* The Grandissimes, *generating in the process a new comprehensive description of Congo Square that would be cited as historical fact in later influential studies of history, culture, music, and dance.*

Throughout the hundred or more years in which the French and Spanish dominated Louisiana, there was little if any relaxing of the rigid discipline by which the Negro slaves of the province were kept under control. In New Orleans it was the unusual practice among slave-owners to lock the black chattels in their quarters soon after sunset, with armed sentinels posted about the building to see that none attempted to leave before daybreak. On many plantations the slaves commonly worked in the fields laden with chains and guarded by overseers with guns and whips, the latter of which were used freely to punish laziness, malingering, or any of a score of other faults, real and imaginary, while packs of hounds were kept in readiness to pursue runaways. The lot of the slave on some of the large French and Spanish estates, particularly those in the back country away from the protection afforded by settlements, was scarcely more pleasant than it had been in the slave camp which the French government established in a swamp near New Orleans soon after Bienville proved that the new town would be permanent. To this camp the early cargoes of *Africains bruts* were brought directly from the slave ships, and there they were either tamed or killed. If the former, the men were taught to use the hoe, the ax, the plow, and other tools and implements, and the women were trained in the rudiments of housekeeping. Manacled in groups to a long, heavy chain and frequently burdened with the additional weight of an iron collar, the men labored in the fields from dawn to dark under the watchful eyes of soldiers, who drove them to and from their quarters like cattle. Except for an occasional fine specimen who was kept at stud, their rations were meager to the point of scarcity, and their clothing likewise; in the summer months they were clad only in cotton trousers, and during the damp, biting Louisiana winters they wore thin blanket robes with hoods, and shoes called "quantiers," pieces of rawhide cut to lace over toes and ankle somewhat in the manner of the modern snowshoe harness.

Since the fear of a Negro uprising was omnipresent in early New Orleans and Louisiana, many laws were promulgated by the French governors to prevent both the free colored people and the Negro slaves from assembling in large or small groups and to limit as much as possible the black man's intercourse with his kind. The thirteenth article of Bienville's Black Code forbade slaves belonging to different masters "to gather in crowds either by day or by night, under the pretext of a wedding, or for any other cause, either at the dwelling or on the grounds of one of their masters, and much less on the highways or in secluded places." Slaves who thus transgressed were whipped, and for frequent offenses of this nature the Code provided that "the offenders shall be branded with the mark of the flower de luce, and should there be aggravating circumstances, capital punishment may be applied at the discretion of our judges." The Marquis de Vaudreuil also called attention to the perils inherent in assemblages of slaves, and thus dealt with the subject in the police regulations which he issued in 1751:

> We forbid all the inhabitants of citizens of this colony to permit on their plantations, or at their places of residence, or elsewhere, any assembly of Negroes or Negresses, either under pretext of dancing, or for any other cause; that is to say, excepting the Negroes whom they may own themselves. We forbid them to allow their slaves to go out of their plantations or premises for similar purposes, because His Majesty has prohibited all assemblies of the kind. . . . We also forbid the town or country. Negroes to assemble in the town of New Orleans, or in its vicinity, or elsewhere, under any pretext whatever, under the penalty, for said Negroes, of being imprisoned and whipped. . . . Should any inhabitant or citizen of the province permit on his plantation or premises an assembly of Negroes other than his own, under any pretext whatever, he shall, for the first offense, pay one hundred crowns to the treasury of the church, and for the next offense of this kind, be sentenced to work for life on King's galleys.

Various laws of a similar character, all designed to insure as far as practicable the isolation of the individual Negro, were enacted and rigidly enforced by the Spanish governors and the Cabildo. The slaves in Louisiana had no freedom of movement whatsoever until the coming of the Americans, who brought to bear upon the whole question of slavery a new viewpoint, entirely different from that of the French and Spanish, which gradually compelled the liberalization of the laws and customs regulating the life of the black man. Recognizing the value of recreation and a measure of social intercourse in keeping the Negro contented with his lot, the American authorities, soon after the Louisiana Purchase, began to allow the slaves to gather for dancing. These assemblies appear to have begun about 1805 and at first were held in various places in and near the city, among them an abandoned brickyard in Dumaine Street. The most celebrated of all the slave rendezvous, however, was a large open space at Rampart and Orleans Streets, part of which had been indicated on the maps of Bienville's engineers as a public square. In early times the field was used by the Oumas Indians as the place of celebrating their corn feasts, and consequently, in the eyes of the red man, was holy ground. When the slaves began to use the site for dancing, the whole area was popularly known as the Place des Nègres, and later as the Congo Plains; and the square itself, to which slaves were restricted when the Plains were divided into building lots, was called Congo Square, and is still so known among the Negroes of New Orleans. Its official name, however, was never anything but Circus Square until after the Civil War, when it was changed to Beauregard Square in honor of General P. G. T. Beauregard of the Confederate Army, who was born near New Orleans. Until the latter part of 1820, when grass, shrubs, and sycamore-trees were planted by order of Mayor Louis Phillipe Roffignac, the square was merely an expanse of barren, dusty ground, rutted and pitted by the shuffling of hundreds of black feet.

During the first decade or so after the American occupation of Louisiana, the slaves of New Orleans were allowed to congregate every Saturday and Sunday afternoon at whatever place they chose to assemble, and frequently were permitted to continue their merriment far into the night. The result was that often a dozen dances were in progress in as many vacant lots in different parts of the city, and the authorities received many complaints from householders who had been kept awake, and from slave-owners whose Negroes had failed to return home at seemly hours. On October 15, 1817, the Municipal Council adopted an ordinance directing that "the assemblies of slaves for the purpose of dancing or other merriment, shall take place only on Sundays, and solely in such open or public places as shall be appointed by the Mayor." Congo Square was designated by the Mayor as the only place to which the slaves might resort, and thereafter all such gatherings were held under strict police supervision. The dancing was stopped at sunset, and all slaves were driven out of the square and sent home. Under these and other regulations, the custom of permitting slave dancing in Congo Square continued for more than twenty years, when it was abolished for reasons which the old city records do not make clear. It was resumed in 1845, when this ordinance was adopted:

"Whereas, numerous citizens have requested the Council of Municipality No. One, to grant permission to slaves to assemble on Sundays on Circus Square, for the purpose of dancing.

"Whereas, when such a merriment takes place before sunset and is not offensive to public decency, it can be tolerated; provided, it being under police inspection.

"Resolved that from the 1st of May to the 31st of August of each year, the slaves, provided with a written consent of their master, be permitted to assemble Sundays on the Circus Square for the purpose of dancing from 4 to 6 ½ o'clock, p.m.

"Resolved that it shall be the duty of the commissionaires of police of the 3rd and 5th wards, of the commanding officer at the Post Trémé and five men of the day police, to watch that no police ordinance be violated during the time allowed to Negroes to dance on Circus Square."

The weekly concourse of slaves in Congo Square reached the height of its popularity and renown during the fifteen years which preceded the Civil War; sometimes there were almost as many white spectators surrounding the square to watch the slaves "dance Congo" as there were black dancers weaving and stamping under the sycamore-trees. Even in earlier days a Congo dance was considered one of the unique attractions of New Orleans; visitors were always taken to see the slaves at play, and in their eyes the spectacle ranked second only to a Quadroon Ball as a colorful, exotic display. "The Circus public square," wrote the editor of New Orleans' first directory, published in 1822, "is very noted on account of its being the place where the Congo and other Negroes dance, carouse and debauch on the Sabbath, to the great injury of the morals of the rising generation; it is a foolish custom, that elicits the ridicule of most respectable persons who visit the city; but if it is not considered good policy to abolish the practice entirely, surely they could be ordered to assemble at some place more distant from the houses, by which means the evil would be measurably remedied." Not many contemporary observers agreed with this estimate of the slave gatherings; practically all of them, and a vast majority of the people of New Orleans, appear to have looked upon the Sunday afternoon dancing as innocent merriment and as a beneficial outlet for the energies and repressions acquired during a week of hard labor. And if the police supervision was as strict as the old records indicate, it is difficult to see how any considerable degree of debauchery could have crept in.

The slaves usually began to assemble in Congo Square an hour or so before the time fixed for the dancing, the men strutting proudly in the cast-off finery of their masters, and the women in dotted calicoes, with bright-colored Madras kerchiefs tied about their hair to form the popular head-dress which the Creoles called *tignon*. With them were their children, in nondescript garments relieved by bright feathers or bits of gay ribbon. On the outskirts of the chattering crowd were the hawkers of refreshments, some with great trays slung around their necks and others with deal tables screened from the sun by cotton awnings, and all offering ginger beer, pies, lemonade, and little ginger cakes called "mulatto's belly." At a signal from a police official, the slaves were summoned to the center of the square by the prolonged rattling of two huge beef bones upon the head of a cask, out of which had been fashioned a sort of drum or tambourine called the bamboula. As the dancers took their places, the rattling settled into a steady drumming, which the Negro who wielded the bones maintained, without a pause and with no break in the rhythm, until sunset put an end to the festivities. The favorite dances of the slaves were the Calinda, a variation of which was also used in the Voodoo ceremonies, and the Dance of the Bamboula, both of which were primarily based on the primitive dances of the African jungle, but with copious borrowing from the *contre-danses* of the French. The movements of the Calinda and the Dance of the Bamboula were very similar, but for the evolutions of the latter the male dancers attached bits of tin or other metal to ribbons tied about their ankles. Thus accoutered, they pranced back and forth, leaping into the air and stamping in unison, occasionally shouting "Dansez Bamboula! Badoum! Badoum!" while the women, scarcely lifting their feet from the ground, swayed their bodies from side to side and chanted an ancient song as monotonous as a dirge. Beyond the groups of dancers were the children, leaping and cavorting in imitation of their elders, so that the entire square was an almost solid mass of black bodies stamping and swaying to the rhythmic beat of the bones upon the cask, the frenzied chanting of the women, and the clanging of the pieces of metal which dangled from the ankles of the men.

The Congo Plains must have presented an extraordinary spectacle on these festive occasions, but the picturesqueness of the scene was lost on at least one European traveler who recorded his impressions of the dancing.

J. G. Flugel, the German trader already quoted, saw the slaves "dance Congo" in February 1817 and was content to record in his journal that "their dances certainly are curious, particularly to a European." He saw them again in April of the same year, and thus described them:

"Their postures and movements somewhat resembled those of monkeys. One might by a little imagination take them for a group of baboons. Yet as these poor wretches are entirely ignorant of anything like civilization (for their masters withhold everything from them that in the least might add to the cultivation of their minds) one must not be surprised at their actions. The recreation is at least natural and they are free in comparison with those poor wretches, slaves of their passions. I saw today among the crowd Gildemeister of Bremen, clerk or partner of Teetzmann. He told me that three of the negroes in the group closest to us were formerly kings or chiefs in Congo. I perceive in them a more genteel address. They are richly ornamented and dance extremely well."

One of the famous Bamboula dancers of the early days, and also an expert wielder of the beef bones, was a gigantic Negro owned by General William de Buys, who is said to have been the first to attach little bells to his ankles instead of the customary bits of metal. He could leap higher and shout louder than any of the other slaves who stamped and cavorted in the dance; his stamping, indeed, shook the ground, and when he cried: "Badoum! Badoum!" the tops of the sycamore-trees trembled and swayed in the wind caused by his mighty bellowings. And in his ham-like fists the beef bones rattled upon the head of the Bamboula drum with a crashing roar that resembled nothing less than a salvo of artillery fire. His name during the period of his fame as a Bamboula artist was Squier; a few years later, as Bras Coupé and the Brigand of the Swamp, he acquired a different sort of renown.

General de Buys was well known in New Orleans as a remarkably kind and indulgent master; he petted, coddled, and spoiled the Negro Squier, taught him to shoot, and permitted him to go alone on hunting expeditions in the forests adjacent to the city. And Squier practiced assiduously with the General's rifle; premonition, he said afterwards, warned him that he would eventually lose an arm, and so he became an expert marksman with either hand alone. The taste of freedom which Squier experienced on his journeys into the woods after game was too much for him. He began running away, and received only slight punishment when he was captured and returned to General de Buys. Early in 1834 Squire was shot by a patrol of planters searching the swamps for runaway slaves, and his right arm was amputated, whence the sobriquet Bras Coupé, by which he was thereafter known. As soon as his injury had healed, Bras Coupé fled into the swamps and organized a gang of escaped blacks and a few renegade white men, whom he led on frequent robbing and murdering forays on the outskirts of the city, with an occasional venture into the thickly settled residential districts. He was New Orleans' most feared outlaw for nearly three years, and the successor of the *Kaintock* as the hobgoblin with which nurses and mothers frightened the Creole children. Reviewing his career, the *Picayune* after his death described him as a "semi-devil and a fiend in human shape," and said that his life had been "one of crime and depravity."

Among the slaves Bras Coupé soon became a legendary figure endowed with superhuman powers; in the folklore of the New Orleans Negroes he was installed alongside the redoubtable Annie Christmas and in many respects was accounted her superior. He was, of course, fireproof and invulnerable to wounds, for he was familiar with the miraculous herbs described by the French travelers Bossu, Perrin du Lac, and Baudry des Lozières, and with many others which these avid searchers after botanical wonders had not discovered. Hunters returned to New Orleans from the swamps and told how, having encountered Bras Coupé, they fired at him, only to see their bullets flatten against his chest; some even said that the missiles had bounced off the iron-like body of the outlaw and whizzed dangerously close to their own heads, while Bras Coupé laughed derisively and strode grandly into the farthest reaches of the swamps. And according to the slave tradition, detachments of soldiers sent after him vanished in a cloud of mist. Moreover, his very glance paralyzed, if he so wished, and he fed on human flesh.

The popular belief in Bras Coupé's invulnerability received a rude shock when, on April 6th, 1837, he was wounded by two hunters who braved his magical powers and shot him near the Bayou St. John. And it was dissipated entirely on July 19 of the same year. On that day a Spanish fisherman named Francisco Garcia, who was known to the slaves as a friend of Bras Coupé's, drove slowly through the streets of New Orleans a cart drawn by a decrepit mule, and watched with tender solicitude an ungainly bundle, wrapped in old sacks, which jounced in the bed of the vehicle. Garcia stopped in front of the Cabildo and carried his bundle into the office of Mayor Denis Prieur, where he unwrapped it and disclosed the body of Bras Coupé. The fisherman told the authorities that on the day before, the 18th, he was fishing in the Bayou St. John when Bras Coupé fired at him and missed, whereupon the indignant fisherman went ashore and beat out the brigand's brains with a club. The truth, however, appears to have been that Bras Coupé was slain as he slept in the fisherman's hut. Garcia demanded the immediate payment of the two-thousand-dollar reward which he had heard had been offered for Bras Coupé dead or alive, but he received only two hundred and fifty dollars. The body of the outlaw was exposed in the Place d'Armes for two days, and several thousand slaves were compelled to march past and look at it, as a warning.

The Sunday afternoon dances of the Negroes in Congo Square were abandoned during the troublous days that followed the capture and occupation of New Orleans by Union forces during the Civil War, and while an occasional gathering of the sort was held in reconstruction times, they were never again a regular feature of the black man's life. As late as the middle 1880's, however, a considerable number of Negroes, most of whom had been slaves, frequently assembled on Sunday afternoons in the back yard of an abandoned property far out on Dumaine Street, where they trod the measures of the Bamboula and other Congo dances, which appear to have changed little since slavery times. A correspondent of the New York *World* thus described the dancing:

> "A dry-goods box and an old pork barrel formed the orchestra. These were beaten with sticks or bones, used like drumsticks so as to keep up a continuous rattle, while some old men and women chanted a song that appeared to me to be purely African in its many vowelled syllabification. . . . Owing to the noise I could not even attempt to catch the words. I asked several old women to recite them to me, but they only laughed and shook their heads. In their patois they told me—'no use, you could never understand it. *C'est le Congo!*—it is the Congo!' The dance was certainly peculiar, and I observed that only a few old persons, who had probably all been slaves, knew how to dance it. The women did not move their feet from the ground. They

only writhed their bodies and swayed in the undulatory motions from ankles to waist. . . . The men leaped and performed feats of gymnastic dancing which reminded me of some steps in the *jota Aragonesa*. Small bells were attached to their ankles. '*Vous ne comprenez pas cette danse-la?*' an old woman asked me. I did not altogether understand it, but it appeared to be more or less lascivious as I saw it. I offered the woman some money to recite the words of the Congo song. She consulted with another and both went off shaking their heads. I could obtain no satisfaction."

From *Gumbo Ya-Ya*

LOUISIANA WRITERS' PROJECT (1945)

A collection of anecdotes, folktales, songs, and sayings combined with descriptions of local customs, Gumbo Ya-Ya *was edited by Lyle Saxon, Robert Tallant, and Edward Dreyer for the Louisiana Writers' Project, one of the state agencies created in the 1930s by the Works Progress Administration to assist unemployed authors, musicians, artists, and teachers. With its main office in the Canal Bank Building in New Orleans, the Louisiana Writers' Project directed its employees in ethnographic observation, folklore collection, and archival research, combining the results into three volumes, the last of which was* Gumbo Ya-Ya, *a book that was remarkable for its consistent voice and lyrical exposition, qualities that resulted from the heavy editing by Saxon, Tallant, and Dreyer.* Gumbo Ya-Ya *offers a composite version of the legend, drawing from historical newspapers, government records, vernacular tradition, and literary fiction.*

The most famous of all runaways in Louisiana history was a gigantic mulatto renowned as the greatest Bamboula dancer ever to shake the earth of the Congo Square in New Orleans, and whose stentorian shouts of 'Bamboula! Bamboula! Bamboula!' thundered through the bloodstreams of the voodooists assembled in the Square.

His name is said to have been Squire—or Squier—and it is believed he was the personal slave of General William de Buys, though the only newspaper account of his ownership mentions him as the property of a John Berry West, living somewhere between Plaquimine and Baton Rouge. However, it is generally accepted that he was the property of de Buys, and that he was accorded the most lenient of treatment, accompanying the General on hunting expeditions, was even allowed to carry arms and go on hunts alone. Despite this, Squier ran away again and again. After one such escapade he was shot and suffered the amputation of an arm. Almost immediately he received the appellation of *Bras Coupé,* by which his notoriety spread throughout the balance of his long and hectic career. He quickly became a legendary figure among both the white and colored races and his reputation for daring and infamy spread. Little children were for years frightened into instant silence and obedience at the mere mention of the name of *Bras Coupé.*

The day after the amputation of his arm hospital attendants found his bed empty. He had vanished into the near-by cypress swamps, where, it is said, he gathered a band of renegade slaves and led them in nocturnal raids on the plantations in the neighborhood. Becoming known as the 'Brigand of the Swamp,' tales of his prowess and immunity to death grew. Terrified hunters returned to tell of having shot him, having seen their bullets go through his body, without apparent harm. No plantation was safe from the nocturnal raids of *Bras Coupé* and his henchmen. Female slaves were sometimes carried off, and it is reported that at least one white woman fell into his hands.

On April 6, 1837, a New Orleans city guard brought in a report of having killed the Negro. He said he had met *Bras Coupé,* shot and wounded him seriously. Then, after being certain he was seriously wounded and helpless, he had beat him to death with the butt of his rifle. When returning officers located the spot where the incident had occurred, however, there was no body, only a perfectly perceptible trail of blood where the "dead man" had escaped into the swamp.

But an attack on a white man finally cost *Bras Coupé* his life. This occurred on July 7, 1837, and *The Bee* of July 20, the same year, published the details of his end, in a story headed *Death of Squier,* telling how a fisherman, leaving his boat, had turned at the detonation of a gun, and had seen a giant Negro fitting another cap into his weapon. The fisherman had then rushed the brigand and killed him with a kind of crowbar, having to bring it down on his skull three times.

The body of *Bras Coupé* was then brought to New Orleans and "exposed for inspection on the public square. The marks of the wounds given by one of the city guards who had left the brigand for dead, were very visible and completely corroborated the story told by him, against which some discredit had been thrown."

"Tiger of the Bayous"

J. ANDREW GAULDEN (1946)

J. Andrew Gaulden's "Tiger of the Bayous" was published in December 1946 in Negro Digest, *a popular magazine that featured a range of articles on art, politics, culture, and history directed at a predominantly African American audience. Gaulden served as principal for several schools in Louisiana while working as a lobbyist and advocate for equal rights and equal pay for black school teachers in the state. He later took a position working at Grambling University. Gaulden published fiction and nonfiction in magazines and newspapers, from the* Shreveport Sun *to the* Los Angeles Sentinel, *and in the 1950s he was the editor of a magazine called* Negro Louisiana. *Gaulden's creative adaptation of the legend appeared in* Negro Digest *as a short story.*

"I Was Raised with Alligators and Weaned on Panther's Milk!"
"I Can Outrun, Outjump, Outshoot, Throw Down,
Drag Out, and Lick Any Man in the Country!"
"I'm a Roaring, Rip-Snorter and Chock-Full of Fight!"
"I'm the Pizen Wolf from Bitter Creek and This Is My Night to Howl!"

Such were the flamboyant challenges the rough and tumble flatboat bullies on the Mississippi used to hurl at each other when making ready for a fight. Brutal battling was one of their three standard occupations, the other two being working the steamboats and getting drunk. And what with kicking, biting, stabbing, and clubbing (all regulation tactics), the river gladiators were admittedly the most ferocious of all the stalwart Americans who carved a republic out of a wilderness.

Whenever two or more boats stopped for a night in the same settlement, the champion from each, with red turkey feathers in their caps, would saunter forth, issue an always-accepted challenge, and the riotous fight was on. It never ended until one of the Samsons yelled "Enough!" Provided he still had a tongue to yell with.

Naturally enough these husky bullies became legendary. Mike Fink, according to the tales which grew with each telling, could whip any man alive with one of his hands tied behind his back, outshoot anyone blindfolded, outrun anybody hopping on one foot and lift more with his little finger than the average man using both hands.

Old New Orleans often played unwilling host to dozens of these reckless Titans, who recognized no law except that established by bludgeon, knife, pistol, murderous fists, stamping feet, and a set of sharp teeth. For a number of years all of these huskies were whites of various extractions, but one morning in March, 1834, a new champion took over.

In the fringe of trees at the edge of a swamp just outside of New Orleans, two giant men stood face to face. Their fists were doubled, arms crooked, their taut bodies ready to spring. Each was nearly seven feet high and weighed over 250 pounds. Each sported a long shiny knife rammed down in his belt. Each looked as rough and tough and rusty as pig iron. When one claimed he was the devil's son and ate stewed barbed wire for breakfast, the other declared that he was the devil's father and slept on broken bottles every night.

The only difference was that one was white, the other black.

After the last swaggering challenge had been hurled, the two men met, in a clash that sounded like the impact of two maddened bull elephants. It was a good fight, the outcome of which was that the successor to all the legendary giants along the mighty Mississippi was Bras Coupé—*Cut Arm*—the Tiger of the Bayous. A burly, broad-shouldered Negro, he could carry a barrel of flour under his arm with another balanced on top of his head.

Bras Coupé wasn't his original name, however, and he didn't enter adulthood as a legendary desperado. Except for his impressive physique, he was just an ordinary Negro. In fact, he was a slave, the property of General William de Buys. And at first the husky black giant answered to the name of Squier.

Bras Coupé, as Squier, first attracted attention as a rip-snorting *Bamboula* dancer. Every Saturday and Sunday during the years just before the Civil War, a great many slaves were allowed to assemble in the place called Congo Square. There, to the extended rattling of two big beef bones on the head of a drum called the bamboula, men, women, boys and girls did the Dance of the Bamboula. The men pranced back and forth, leaped into the air, stamped their feet in unison, tinkling bits of tin attached to ribbons around their ankles. The women swayed their bodies rhythmically from side to side, barely lifting their feet from the ground, and chanted a monotonous and ancient dirge. The drum rattled on until nightfall ended the ceremony.

Everyone could tell when Bras Coupé was on the Square. His thundering of the beef bones on the bamboulas was like the crash of a salvo of artillery. His stamping seemed to shake the ground. He could leap higher and yell louder than any other man in the dance. And when he yelled, "Dancez Bamboula! Badoum! Badoum!" his booming voice seemed to rip out over the surrounding trees.

General de Buys was extremely kind and considerate to all his slaves, especially Bras Coupé. Instead of doing the usual dreary slave work, the brawny black used to ride and hunt with his master, and became in every way his ubiquitous sidekick.

Thus Bras Coupé came to know and love easy-going freedom more than anything else, even more than dancing the Bamboula. It began to annoy him even when the General gently ordered him to fetch his favorite horse. But alas, he was a slave, and there was only one way to attain his freedom.

In 1834 Bras Coupé started running away, and each time when they went to hustle him back he put up a tougher fight. Leaping gullies, bounding over underbrush, and jogging through the swamps, he would go crashing and bellowing like some giant beast. He was a brilliant woodsman, and never lost his bearings.

One moment they'd think they saw him over there in front of them, but suddenly they'd hear a thundering laugh and there he was behind them. As soon as they turned he was gone again. Sometimes he made a noise like stampeding cattle, then he moved without snapping a twig. Once more they caught him, but not before a large posse cornered him and put two warning shots in his right arm. Bound like a bear, he was brought back.

His badly injured arm had to be amputated. Hence the name, Bras Coupé. Immediately his arm healed, he was gone. He had walked into his master's study late one night with the white man's shiny rifle in his one hand. He was smiling.

"I'm leaving," he announced firmly. His smile vanished and his eyes flashed. "And you can tell 'em they ain't going to get me no more, not while there's a quiver left in one of my fingers."

So he took to the bayous and swamps. Precisely where he went and how he lived nobody knew until strange tales started pouring into the city about the amazing strength and prodigious fighting feats of a massive, one-armed black, the Tiger of the Bayous.

It came to pass that anyone with business in the bayous—slaves seeking freedom, criminals avoiding the law, cutthroats pirating on the river—all had to deal with Bras Coupé. For three years following 1834 he prowled in the swamps, organizer and grand master of a gang of runaway slaves and renegade whites, reigning supreme as the chief terror of then-rowdy New Orleans.

Life was bloody in the bayous, dog had to eat dog, and one could hold the position of Big Boss only by beating and battering all challengers into submission. But it was always man for man. If one licked Bras Coupé, the Tiger's men and authority were his, and the only regulations were that nobody interfere and that one of the contestants be decisively put out of action.

The loss of an eye or ear, or a broken arm, or a stab wound in a vital spot usually decided the outcome, but in other instances nothing except converting one's adversary into a hump on the ground would do. It was among such men that big black Bras Coupé became undisputed champion.

Easily enough, therefore, the Tiger of the Bayous became a legendary character. To the admiring Negroes he was fireproof, bulletproof, and otherwise endowed with superhuman powers. No wounds bothered him because he had intimate knowledge of the miraculous herbs which cured him almost instantly.

White hunters returning from the bayous swore that when they encountered Bras Coupé and fired dead at him, bullets merely flattened against his mighty chest, bounced off and boomeranged back, sizzling perilously close to their own heads. When a detachment of soldiers was sent after him, according to a traditional slave account, it vanished forever in a cloud of mist.

But Bras Coupé was flesh and blood. He and his men consumed great quantities of whiskey and food and they had no objection to frequent contact with women. Thus the Tiger and his gang frequently swooped into the city to replenish their stores. Whenever and wherever Bras Coupé hit town he took over, and became the temporary owner of any place which suited his fancy.

At first these reckless forays were laughed about. Mothers with wakeful children to put to bed found that the simple statement, "Bras Coupé is going to get you if you don't watch out!" would do the job immediately. But the rampaging Tiger started going deeper into the city's thickly settled residential districts. Soon not only the kids were afraid of Bras Coupé. Once a kind of hero, he was now declared a menace. A $2000 reward was placed on his head, alive or dead.

But who could capture the mighty Bras Coupé? So they asked in the drinking places up and down the New Orleans streets. Hadn't the soldiers tried it several times already? Even while they talked, Bras Coupé swept into the city and left unscathed.

Thus for a whole year after the offering of the reward, the Tiger remained at large. Indeed, everyone believed that he would die none but a natural death, or just vanish away into thin air.

But, alas, Bras Coupé had a friend. Francisco Garcia, a hobo-like Spanish fisherman, maintained a hut on the banks of Bayou St. John, and there in the evening quiet the two would sit for hours, drinking and exchanging news and products of the city for those of the bayous. They had a close friendship, Bras Coupé making it possible for Garcia to fish anywhere he desired in the bayous and the latter enabling the Tiger to keep tabs on doings in the city. Garcia was known as the only person Bras Coupé would permit behind his back.

On July 18, 1837, Garcia pulled his boat through the marshes, clambered ashore, and entered his hut. There, stretched out on his moss bed, was Bras

Coupé, peacefully asleep. Garcia smiled benignly, but then he thought of $2000. That reward would be a lot of cash for a struggling fisherman. Looking down at the Tiger of the Bayous, Garcia frowned, took off his battered hat, and ran his fingers slowly through his big mop of silken black hair.

This is my best friend, he thought, my best friend. How could I have made it out here without him? Well, at least I will give him a chance.

"Bras Coupé," he called softly. "Bras Coupé, it is Francisco; wake up!" But the sleeping giant didn't stir. "Two thousand dollars," Garcia said in a long whisper, and shrugged. Then he yanked his knotty club from the corner, raised it high with both hands and brought it down hard, one time, two times, three times. . . .

Early next morning Francisco Garcia drove his decrepit old mule and ramshackle cart through the streets of New Orleans. Few noticed that he kept taking quick glances at the unsightly bundle wrapped in old sacks which bounced in the bed of the cart. Finally he came to a halt in front of the Cabildo. He struggled with his bloody bundle and finally dropped it on the floor in the office of Mayor Dennis Prieur.

"Bras Coupé is dead," he muttered.

Everybody had to see for himself. For the next two days the body of the giant lay exposed in the Place d'Armes for everyone to see. It was the Tiger of the Bayous all right. However, Francisco Garcia didn't get the plaudits he expected. Even the authorities were cold about his deed and all he ever got was two hundred and fifty dollars.

Somehow everybody, especially the thousands of slaves in the city, felt that life was going to be different now. Bras Coupé, the Tiger of the Bayous, was dead.

From *Band of Angels*

ROBERT PENN WARREN (1955)

Robert Penn Warren was a poet, novelist, and literary critic. He was awarded the Pulitzer Prize for All the King's Men *(1946), a novel about a populist Louisiana governor. Warren adapts the Bras-Coupé legend in his novel,* Band of Angels, *which was made into a feature film starring Sidney Poitier as Bras-Coupé. The novel is narrated by Amantha Starr, the daughter of a Kentucky plantation owner, who learns her mother was a slave. After her father's death, Amantha is enslaved and transported to New Orleans where she is bought by Hamish Bond. She meets Bond's favorite slave, Rau-Ru, a character based on Bras-Coupé, a fact the novel confirms through several allusions to the legend.* Band of Angels *extends the legend past its usual endpoint. Rau-Ru escapes to the swamp to lead the maroons, but when the Civil War arrives in Louisiana, he leads the maroons out of the swamp to join the cause as guerilla fighters. Rau-Ru takes a new name, Oliver Cromwell Jones, as he rises in the Union Army ranks, and he works as a government official during Reconstruction. This excerpt starts after a constitutional convention is attacked by a white supremacist mob, a sequence in the novel based on historical events from 1866. Rau-Ru is injured in the violence, and he is enraged that supposed moderates in the city, including his former master, Hamish Bond, failed to provide support during the riot. After Amantha and Rau-Ru are reunited, they travel with Jimmee and other maroons through the swamp to Hamish Bond's plantation at Point de Loup.*

The beam of the lantern, on the first instant, found nothing but the trodden earth, the sloping wall, boards, tin, palmetto. Then I swung the light left, and there he was. He was propped on a sway backed military cot, wearing a white shirt split open to allow for bandages on right arm and shoulder, sweat standing on his face, blinking slow as he stared at me, or rather, at that focus of light which would have obscured me behind it. Not thinking, I kept the light on him, my gaze fixed on him.

Then he said: "So you waited."

"Yes," I said.

"Get that light out of my eyes," he said.

I obeyed, swinging it to one side. An up-ended cartridge box served as a table, I saw. A tin cup was on it.

"They near ruined us," he said.

"How do you feel?" I asked.

"They gave it to us," he said.

"How bad are you hurt?" I asked.

"The troops didn't come," he said.

"How bad are you hurt?"

"It's always the ones on your own side," he said, "the sweet talk and the lie."

"Are you hurt bad?"

"It is always the sweet-talking ones that promise you, then fix it so you get ruint," he said.

"Won't you tell me how bad you are hurt?"

"What do you want to know for?"

"I've got to know!" I cried out.

"So you got to know," he said.

I found I was passing my tongue over my dry lips.

"Come a little closer," he commanded.

I moved slowly toward him, a step or two.

"Stop there," he said.

I stopped.

"Turn that light on your face," he said.

I did it.

"Hold it out farther."

I did it.

"Look right into it," he said.

"What do you want?" I said. I was, I suppose, afraid, suddenly.

"Nothing," he said. "Except just to look at you."

The beam was on my face, but after a moment, I let the light waver.

"I said hold it," he said, sharply.

I held the light and stared into the beam. I could hear the rustle of his breath over in the dark beyond.

"How does it feel?" he demanded, almost whispering. "How does it feel with the light on your face, and not seeing anything but the light and the dark around the light, and knowing I'm over here, in the dark, and you can't see me, but I'm looking at you, I am looking at you all the time?"

"Oh, I can't stand it!" I cried out, and jerked the light from my face, flinging the beam wildly about.

"You couldn't stand it?" he questioned, softly.

"No," I said, "no!"

"Put the lantern on the box," he said.

I set it down.

"What are you going to do?" I asked.

He looked meditatively at me. "Something," he said, "something that just came over me I got to do. I got to do it now."

"What?"

"It came over me, me over here in the dark, looking at you."

"But you're sick," I said, my words pouring desperately out, "yes, you're sick, you've got fever, you ought to be quiet."

"I'll be quiet later," he said.

"But you're sick, you—"

He had drawn a cord from inside his shirt, on the cord a whistle, and the blast cut across my words.

I stood there in absolute silence, looking at him, he not seeming to notice me any more, till the sack-curtain was lifted.

"What you want?" Jimmee demanded.

"Pack up," Rau-Ru commanded.

"But we just come, we—" Jimmee began, but Rau-Ru cut him short, with a quick, violent gesture.

"Pack up!" he said.

"But what—"

And very quietly, leaning forward on the cot, Rau-Ru asked, "Do I have to start getting your permission for what I'm going to do?"

By day the swamp was a twilight. The moss hung down like twilight from the high cypresses. We moved, as before, by some secret channel among the cypress stools, Rau-Ru and two men in the pirogue ahead, then Jimmee and another man and I, then two more pirogues behind. The cottonmouth, not bothering to array its cumbrousness, would drop fatly off the cypress root, an overripe plop into the water. Once, on a hummock, a white heron leaned forward on the improbable ricketiness of its legs, thrust the neck jabbingly forward with the wing-beat, and rose. It moved ahead of us, white over the black water, under the gloom of moss, far off.

We stopped twice to eat. We ate in the pirogues, munching the cold corn pones, the cold side meat, washing it down with water from the canteens that were passed around. During this process the pirogues were drawn up together. There was no conversation. Rau-Ru was propped in the middle of his pirogue, sweat beading his face, and sweat coming through the white shirt to make it stick to his skin. Once I asked him how he felt. He looked at me from some meditative distance, then shrugged his good shoulder. "I'll make it," he said.

Then he turned from me, ignoring me.

I slept most of the afternoon, on the bottom of the pirogue, my face down, hidden in my bent arms.

Just at dusk, we stopped again, ate, drank some of the tepid water. The paddlers lay back and rested for a half-hour or so. Then Rau-Ru looked at his watch. Without a word spoken, the paddles began their motion.

The swamp was thinning here, the trees smaller, less moss, more land visible, and some underbrush, sycamores and other trees now, the sycamores very white in the dusk.

It was not really swamp now, rather a marshy forest threaded here and there by bayous. Looking up I could see the sky now. Stars were coming out.

Very late, they made a camp, with smudge fires. When broad day came, we went on.

In the middle of the afternoon we stopped again. Long since, the bayou had given place to swamp, then swamp again to forest. We were in forest now.

They drew up the pirogues, and tied them to trees. Then, with Jimmee leading, Rau-Ru next, me next, we took a faint trail into the trees. After a while we heard dogs barking. We had entered a sort of clearing now on high ground. Jimmee stopped, turned his head over his shoulder. "Here 'tis," he said.

Rau-Ru nodded. He walked away from the trail, across the little clearing, some twenty feet, and sat down, propping himself against a tree. The group edged over toward him. They disposed themselves, some simply dropping down, head on arms, asleep by the time they hit ground. I propped against a tree. Rau-Ru's eyes were closed, but I did not think he was sleeping.

There was not a word spoken until near dusk, when we ate again. It was the last of the food. There was no talk now, now and then the shifting of a body, the slapping of a hand against bare flesh where an insect had struck. At length one of the men got up, and began to gather bits of stick and wood for a smudge fire. He arranged the material, and struck a match.

"You light that fire," Rau-Ru's voice said from his shadow, "and I'll shoot you between the eyes."

Not looking up, very carefully, the man blew the match out and dropped the stub. Night had come on very dark now, and cloudy.

I went over and away from the others, and covered my face with my skirt again.

It must have been an hour later when Rau-Ru rose, and wordlessly moved down the trail. We followed him. A half mile or so on, he stopped. We were, I suddenly realized, on the edge of the open, just a fringe of brush screening us. But it was very dark. I could make out nothing.

Rau-Ru turned. "Blue-Tobe," he said, "you stay here. You stay here and keep her." He nodded toward me, paying me no other heed.

He moved out into the open beyond the brush, the other men following. "I'll send back when I'm done," he said, over his shoulder, not even to me I felt, to Blue-Tobe.

The men had moved off into the darkness of the field. "What's he going to do?" I asked Blue-Tobe.

"Ain't said," Blue-Tobe said.

"Do you know where we are?" I asked him.

"Ain't knowin'," he said.

So I stood there, for a little. Then I crouched down and covered my face again. I could hear the man moving about, now over here, now there. I could hear the owls, then the wail of some other night-crier. I crouched there and didn't know where I was.

Not for some forty minutes, I suppose, when I stood up. A little after I had stood up, the moon broke through the clouds. It was just a rift, rather a kind of sluggish dividing of that low-hanging swollenness of dark, then the mass drew together, coalesced oilily again, and the light was cut off. It had, however, been long enough.

I knew now.

But I had not made a sound. I stood there, hearing my heart beat, and said very casually: "I'm just going to step over here a minute."

"Ev'ybody do," the voice in the dark said, and sniggered.

I moved into the brush, made some deliberate noise shuffling it, then moved as silently as possible into the open. I moved up the edge of the field, crouching, each step a calculation. I proceeded this way for some fifty yards, still at the margin of the woods, for shadow in case the moon broke. But it did not break.

I looked back once, saw nothing in the dark, then plunged away from the woods. It was a cotton field. I was running between the rows, stumbling on the clods, hearing my skirts swish against the dew-heavy leaves. I heard Blue-Tobe calling in the dark, far back. I fell two or three times. Several times I had to stop for breath, my chest hurt so. When you run that way, your chest can hurt you till you want to die. But it's funny, it is like it is hurting some-body else.

As I approached the hummock, that darker mass in the dark beyond the field, I kept thinking maybe just the oaks cut off any light there might be in the house. Then I had managed up the incline, using my last breath, it seemed, and there was the house, not a light showing.

The house was shadowed by the absoluteness of the oakdarkness. I stood there at the foot of the steps to the gallery, clinging to the rail, staring up at the house.

For a moment, clinging there, I had the thought that maybe he was lying inside there, asleep in the dark, not knowing I had risen and run out into the dark fields, and run and run, falling in the dirt, all breathless and sick, and had now come back, now here I was, and I would go in now, and lie down, and he wouldn't wake up, but he would shift a little and take my hand. It was just a flash of that kind of craziness.

Then I heard a sound, what I didn't know, distant beyond the house. I had some breath back now. I ran around the house, under the darkness of the live oaks, around the kitchen porch, and there I saw down the hill.

I saw light flickering on the high boughs of pine trees beyond the barn and granary, above the bulk of the buildings, toward the quar ters. I ran down the slope. A dog was barking off down there.

I ran around the corner of the granary, and stopped stock-still.

Two men held fat-pine torches. The other men stood around, with rifles. Beyond, ringing round, were forms, shadowy forms, people from the quarters no doubt, eyes staring. There in the space was Rau-Ru. I could see his white shirt. He was near the old pine tree. He was looking up at something. I saw something, then knew it was a wagon, something big on it. A man stood at the head of one of the mules to the wagon.

I came closer, not running now, stepping up slow and quiet. The dog was barking near the wagon, barking at something up there. Now I could see it was a cotton bale on the wagon. But I knew the dog was not barking at a cotton bale. I felt I couldn't bear to go closer. I just couldn't bear.

But I went closer. And there it was, but it hadn't happened.

I cried out, and I ran toward Rau-Ru, and I grabbed him, crying out, no, no. I shook him, and I beat at his chest with my fists. I called his name, and said, no, no. But he didn't even look down at me. He just grabbed me by the arm with his good hand, and held me in that grip, and kept on looking up, with some sort of intent, rapt look on his sweat-beaded black face, as though my hitting him on the chest were nothing.

So I quit hitting him, and quit calling out, no, no. It was as though his fixed look up there, which seemed to draw him out of himself and just leave his body standing there like a post or the trunk of a dead tree, fire-black out in an empty field, and my hitting his chest did as much good as hitting on that dead tree trunk. It was as though that look involved me, somehow, too, and drew me out of myself. As I said, I stopped striking his chest. I just stared up there, too.

Hamish Bond was standing there on top of the cotton bale. He did not have his blackthorn stick, balancing up there without it. He wore a nightshirt stuck into trousers. His hands were tied behind his back. A rope was around his neck, disappearing up into the shadow of the pine boughs, which wavered with the flickering of the torch flames. It was Hamish Bond, but if I hadn't known it was Hamish Bond, I might not have guessed, he had changed so much. He looked so old.

Hamish Bond did not seem to notice that his hands were tied, or that there was a rope around his neck. He was peering down directly at me, a slow, studious, sadly inquiring look.

"You," he said then, looking right at me, across the distance.

"Oh, Hamish, "I cried, "it's me!"

"Yes—you," he said, from that sad, speculative distance.

"Oh, Hamish," I cried, "I'll save you!"

And I swung toward Rau-Ru, clutching his shirt, jerking at it, calling his name, pleading.

It was the crazy laughing up there that broke across my pleading, that jerked my gaze back up there to the top of the cotton bale, and the shadow-swaying pine boughs.

Hamish Bond, his head thrown back, uttered that laughter up there that seemed to blow the whole world away in a gay, demoniac gust.

Then, all at once, the laughter stopped, and he looked square down at me, square at me, as though discovering me for the first time.

"All niggers," he said then, and his lip curled.

"You, too," he said, and laughed.

"Ass-deep in niggers," he said.

And jumped.

It was strange, the way he had jumped, not like a crippled man, but with a force and lightness, as in the old days when he would put the foot of his good leg on the step of the barouche, and swing up, laughing, swinging up above me with the lightness of youth, crying gaily, "And did I skeer you, Manty? Did I skeer you, little Manty?"

It was that light motion now, like a young man leaping, but the leap was an old man's leap, out from the old angers, the old selftorturing kindness, the contempt and self-contempt, into the stunning blaze of release, into the apocalyptic pain, into quietness.

The dog, down below the bale, began barking again.

* * *

After the event, several things happened. Rau-Ru's hand had released my arm, and in the silence he had moved away to go and sit on the chopping block by the woodpile. For a time he kept staring up there, but then he began looking down at the ground, between his feet. He simply seemed outside of what was going on now.

Some of the men had gone to the smokehouse and broken open the door. Then they broke open the granary. Then they went into the stables. After a time, Jimmee led out a horse harnessed to the old high-wheeled gig I had used to know. Jimmee hitched the horse to a tree and came over to stand in front of Rau-Ru, very quiet, as though waiting for further instructions. By this time, some of the men had worked the bale off the wagon, and were leading the wagon toward the meat-house.

Meanwhile, the people from the quarters—whoever they were now, new ones, some of the old ones from slave-time who had stayed on—stood very quiet, in the background, in the shadows, watching.

I was standing there in the middle of the space. I simply hadn't moved. It was as though all my life were over, as though I were dead and the only thing alive in the whole world were the suffocating pain in my chest.

Jimmee touched Rau-Ru on the shoulder. Rau-Ru looked up at him with a slow, dazed look, then rose. He went to the gig. Jimmee started to help him up, but it wasn't necessary. It wasn't as though Rau-Ru were weak. It was, rather, as though he moved in some heaviness of sleep.

Jimmee came over to me. "Come on," he said.

I followed to the gig. I felt that I, too, was moving in that same, dazed heaviness of sleep. I simply didn't feel a thing now, just a sad heaviness, beyond everything.

Jimmee helped me up, then motioned to another man, the sick looking mulatto. "You get 'em loaded up," Jimmee ordered, "and come on down thar." Then Jimmee climbed up, shoved me over, and took the reins. Jimmee was a skinny man, so he didn't crowd too much.

After we had moved beyond the hummock where the house was and had gained the track between the west fields and the woods, I cast a sidewise glance into the darkness. I really can't be sure that, in my numbness, I had the notion of trying to leap from the gig and run off in the dark. Perhaps I did have the notion, or the possibility was there in me without being even a notion. Anyway, at that moment, I felt the sudden grip of Rau-Ru's hand on my arm. In alarm, as though he had read that notion, or possibility, I looked at him. He was paying me no attention. His face was fixed up the track, into the darkness. But his grip on my arm did not relax.

We had reached the spot where the track branched off through the woods to the Boyd place, the spot where Hamish Bond, accompanying Charles Prieur-Denis and me, would always turn back with the gig and let us ride on. I recognized the spot, even in the dark, the heavier, higher massing of the darkness of the forest. We entered it, the road felt more even, Jimmee touched up the horse, we bowled along in the dark.

After a time the moon broke again. By now we had turned off, again between fields. But I could see that they were uncultivated, water standing here and there. "Levee," Jimmee said. "Levee done cut long back, and nobody keer."

We moved on, and Jimmee spoke again: "Ole Boyd, he doan keer. He done daid."

Then: "Git on his hoss and ride off to kill Yankees."

Then: "Done daid."

There was the darkness of a grove ahead. We entered it; the moonlight showed what had been lawn, or garden, part under wa ter. Over yonder was a broken statue, white and headless in the moonlight. There was the mass of the house. Half had fallen in, just the chimney of that wing standing.

Jimmee nodded toward the ruin. "Yankees," he said.

We drew up the drive, stopped in front of the undamaged sec tion of the house, and got down. Jimmee lighted the lantern and led us in. The rays of the lantern showed that some of the furniture was yet about, much abused and broken. The windows were broken out. Part of the hall showed the marks of fire. I wondered, numbly, how the fire had been put out. Had it broken out while the Yankees themselves were here and they had put it out? Had the Negroes put it out, stirred by some old fidelity? Had it merely rained opportunely, a Louisiana torrent?

Jimmee led us into a room off the hall, what must have been a back sitting room. There was a kind of couch there, Empire, the scrolling off, the upholstery much faded and ripped. Rau-Ru stood in the middle of the floor. Jimmee went up to him, and pointed at the couch. "Lay down," he said. And Rau-Ru propped himself there.

Jimmee provided a candle, lighted it, and set it in its own grease on the marble of a tabletop. "Dey's a crick back de house," he said to Rau-Ru. "Done tole 'um to bring the p'rogues up de crick, we load 'em here. Doan have to tote so far."

Rau-Ru wasn't paying attention, not really.

"Done sent two of 'um, and dey's Blue-Tobe down thar."

Rau-Ru looked at him. "Get out," he said.

Jimmee went out into the hall.

Rau-Ru motioned me to sit down. I sat down on the floor, and leaned against a carved and scrolled leg of the table. I stared across the room at a big pier glass. There were holes plugged in the glass, as though by pistol slugs. The flame of the candle was reflected murkily in the glass. The glass was dirty and much cracked, and it was as though I looked through that webby impediment to vision into a farther room. In that room yonder beyond the glass there was a candle, and two human forms. It was as though this room here did not exist, just the room yonder, and I was one of those motionless, shadowy forms beyond the webbed and dusty glass.

"You killed him," I said.

His face turned soberly at me, but he said nothing.

"You killed him," I said.

For a long time he looked at me, over the distance.

"You were the *k'la*," I said, and waited.

"Yeah," he said, and stirred heavily on the couch. "Yeah, I was the *k'la*."

Then: "I reckon it was because I was the *k'la*."

He kept on looking at me from that sober distance. There was no air moving, and the candle-flame was steady.

"No," he said, then, "no," and sort of shook his head.

"You were the *k'la*," I said.

"It wasn't just because I was the *k'la*," he said. "It was because of what happened."

He waited, collected himself. "Because of what happened day before yesterday," he said. "Yeah, it's always the same, "he said, "those on your side, they give the sweet talk and the promise, and we got shot in the street. Yeah," he said, "and the soldiers never came."

He sank into his meditation. Looking into that farther room of the mirror, where the candle and the two shadowy forms were, I saw his head sink a little on his breast. Then he lifted his head.

"No," he said.

I looked at him.

"No," he said, "not just because of that, either."

"What?" I demanded.

He stared heavily at me. "You," he said.

He heaved himself up a little. "Yeah, because of you," he said. "If you hadn't come and stood there in front of me, I never would have remembered how at night I used to squat in the brush down by the barn, near those God-damned mimosas, and wonder about you up there with Old Bond. If you hadn't come and stood, I never would have done it."

He sank back. "But you came," he said.

"I didn't make you do it!" I cried out.

He seemed to think about that, then pushed up, and said: "You didn't make that Charles do what he did, either."

Then said: "Or did you?"

Then said: "Or make me do what I did to Charles then, and they ran me in the woods and they whipped me?"

He stared slowly at me. "You're just the way you are," he said, and sank back.

The way you are, the way you are; the words were in my head, and I wanted to scramble up and cry out that I wasn't that way, no, I wasn't. But what way was it? But you are the way you are, that is only logical and can't be otherwise, whatever way that is and you don't know what it is, oh, you never know what it is.

From *Where the World Ends*

VERNON LOGGINS (1958)

Vernon Loggins's Where the World Ends *(1958) was the first book-length biography of nineteenth-century classical musician Louis Moreau Gottschalk. Gottschalk was best known for his work integrating creole melodies from Louisiana and the Caribbean into his compositions. Loggins was an English professor at Columbia University whose previous scholarship included an important early survey of African American literature,* The Negro Author: His Development in America *(1931). Loggins describes Bras-Coupé as the most famous performer at Congo Square. According to Loggins, it was Bras-Coupé's singing, dancing, and drumming that inspired Gottschalk's most famous work,* La Bamboula *(1849).*

Of the many games he played by himself the one which excited him most was to go up to the third-floor gallery on Saturday afternoons and dance and sing to the beat of the drums coming from the Place Congo. This great open square of tramped earth was on the opposite side of the rue des Remparts beyond the neighborhood where the quadroons lived. It provided a drill field for the New Orleans unit of the Louisiana militia, and it was also a gathering place where hundreds of New Orleans slaves made merry on the one afternoon of the week they were not on duty to serve their masters. Moreau seemed to know by instinct when noon came on Saturday. Always at that hour he was up on the third-floor gallery listening for the first sounds of the drums. As soon as the beats fell into a steady rhythm he began to march.

Louder and faster the beats grew, and the boy's march turned into a dance. The three slave women were always on the Place Congo for the weekly gaiety, and when shouts began to accompany the drums Moreau sometimes thought he could hear [his nursemaid] Sally. But there was one shout about which he could be sure, that of the best known of all the slaves of New Orleans, a one-armed giant of an African called Bras Coupé. There was no mistaking his voice when he thundered, "Dansez bamboula! Badoun, badoun! Dansez bamboula, badoun!" As the hundreds of dancing slaves sang this snatch of the song, the dancing boy sang it too. Over and over he would repeat the melody, until his mother would come, pick him up, carry him into the nursery, and lay him on his bed. . . .

Moreau . . . was still a little boy on those evenings when his grandmother would come to spend the night. Holding Célestine in her lap as she had held Thérèse, she would sit before the fire in the nursery, with Moreau once more stretched out on the floor at her feet. Again at his insistence she would tell the story of the insurrection of the blacks on the island of Haiti.

When the narrative was well under way, Sally would come in, bringing an apronful of yams. She would place them on the hearth one by one, shovel hot ashes over them, and then settle down on a stool to listen while she waited for them to roast. When finally the grandmother would end her story account of her flight to Jamaica, Sally, always wearing her blue calico head scarf, would follow with the hundredth telling of her tales of the clown Compé Bouqui and the knave Compé Lapin. Sometimes in the middle of a sentence she would stop, shake her finger at the portrait of Napoleon above the mantel, and mutter an incantation. "That man's eyes are trying to bewitch me," she would say.

"They follow me about this room when I dust." Then, sitting up straight and looking angry, she would make the sign of the cross, spit in the fire, and say, "But they're casting no spell on me!" Her face again calm, she would take up her tale where she had left off.

When she had told all the stories she knew, she would carefully turn the yams. It was then that Moreau would look up to his grandmother and ask about Bras Coupé, the big-voiced gigantic African whom he had heard on hundreds of Saturdays shouting "Dansez bamboula!" while leading slaves in their revels on the Place Congo. Madame Bruslé would then repeat a tale which was being told in one form or another throughout Louisiana.

No, Bras Coupé wasn't the kind of Negro to remain the property of the New Orleans doctor who paid two thousand dollars for him in the St. Louis Hotel slave market. One Saturday afternoon, after shouting himself hoarse on the Place Congo, Bras Coupé made his break for freedom, and he didn't stop until he was in the swamps of the Bayou Sarah country. He was still there, living a charmed life, fattening himself on the flesh of the men sent to capture him. Every day he rubbed his skin with an herb which made it so hard that no bullet, however powerful, could penetrate it. A rifle ball on hitting it would flatten and drop at his feet. All he had to do to kill a man was look at him straight. A detachment of troops was sent into the Bayou Sarah swamps to get him, dead or alive. The soldiers never came back, and not a trace of a single one of them was ever found. Bras Coupé of course had got them under the control of his spells and then had devoured every last one of them, bones and all. God only knew what other depredations he'd work before he was captured and brought to the justice of a hangman's rope.

As Moreau listened to the cannibalistic details of this story and realized that Bras Coupé was still alive, he would press close against his grandmother's knees.

From *Treat It Gentle*

SIDNEY BECHET (1960)

A prodigy who began playing with Bunk Johnson's group at the age of eleven, Bechet adopted the cornet, and then the clarinet, before moving primarily to the soprano saxophone. He was one of the most celebrated improvisers in the decades when jazz was getting started in New Orleans, along with legendary figures like Louis Armstrong, Jelly Roll Morton, and King Oliver. Renowned for his wide vibrato and carefully formed but rhapsodic improvisation, Bechet began touring in his early twenties, living between Chicago and New York, before moving to France in 1950. It was in these later years that Bechet had the idea for Treat It Gentle. *Bechet began dictating his memories into a tape recorder, and hired a collaborator, Joan Williams, to transcribe his life story. After a set at the Vieux Colombier, Bechet met the poet John Ciardi, now best known for his standard translation of Dante's* Divine Comedy, *and they began to collaborate on the manuscript. Ciardi edited the text, removing the passages added by Williams, recorded a new set of interviews, integrated the new material, and presented the book to Twayne, where he was working as an editor. When Twayne announced the book, Williams threatened to sue. Twayne shelved the project only to sell it years later to Desmond Flower, an editor who interviewed Bechet again and then revised the manuscript. In 1960,* Treat It Gentle *was finally published by Cassell in England and Hill and Wang in the United States. Bechet changes Bras-Coupé's name for the purpose of his book. He is called Omar. Bechet identifies Omar as his grandfather.*

My grandfather—that's about the furthest I can remember back. My grandfather was a slave. But he was a man that could do anything. He could sing; he danced, he was a leader. It was natural to him; and everyone followed him.

Sundays when the slaves would meet—that was their free day—he beat out rhythms on drums at the Square—Congo Square they called it—and they'd all be gathered there around him. Everyone loved him. They waited for him to start things: dances, shouts, moods even. Anything he wanted to do, he'd lead them. He had a power. He was a strong man. His name was Omar.

Omar, he'd have these dreams about things. There was one time he had a dream about his right arm, about losing it at the elbow. After that, he'd only practice shooting with his left hand.

But maybe that don't belong here. What I'm saying is that he was a musician. No one had to explain notes or rhythm or feeling to him. It was all there inside him, something he was always sure of. All the things that was happening to him outside, they had to get there to be measured—there inside him where the music was.

He made his own drums out of skins of a pig or a horse hide. He knew horns. And when he wasn't working or hunting, he'd be trying them out. His master, he loved Omar. He thought so much of him that he kind of left him alone; and Omar did things his own way. He'd go hunting back in the bayous. Bayou St. John or Bayou Pontchartrain. He'd go fishing back there. My grandfather, he was a free slave long before Emancipation. And he had his music and he could play it whenever he wanted.

Back in those days, it was like I said: Sundays was free for the slaves. They'd be sleeping and they'd never know the time, but there was a clock for them in the dawn when it would come, and the dawn it woke them natural like. All they felt, all that struggled to wake them up was knowing there was work all day until night. Sometimes, if they dreamed, things would come to them out of Africa, things they'd heard about or had seen. And in all that recollecting, somehow there wasn't any of it that didn't have part of a music-form in it. Maybe they'd hear someone from some tribe signalling to another, beating the drums for a feast maybe. They'd sleep, and it would come to them out of the bottom of that dream. They'd hear the drums of it, all sizes and all kinds of drums. They'd hear the chants and the dance calls. And always they'd hear that voice from the other tribe calling, talking across the air from somewhere else.

That was how the Negro communicated when he was back in Africa. He had no house, he had no telegram, no newspaper. But he had a drum, and he had a rhythm he could speak into the drum, and he could send it out through all the air to the rest of his people, and he could bring them to him. And when he got to the South, when he was a slave, just before he was waking, before the sun rode out in the sky, when there was just that morning silence over the fields with maybe a few birds in it—then, at that time, he was back there again, in Africa. Part of him was always there, standing still with his head turned to hear it, listening to someone from a distance, hearing something that was kind of a promise, even then. . . .

And when he awoke and remembered where he was—that chant, that memory, got mixed up in a kind of melody that had a crying inside itself. The part of him that was the tribe and the drums—that part moved on and became a spiritual. And the part of him that was where he was now, in the South, a slave—that part was the melody, the part of him that was different from his ancestors. That melody was what he had to live, every day, working, waiting for rest and joy, trying to understand that the distance he had to reach was not his own people, but white people. Day after day, like there was no end to it.

But Sunday mornings it was different. He'd wake up and start to be a slave and then maybe someone would tell him: 'Hell, no. Today's Sunday, man. It ain't Monday and it ain't Tuesday. Today's free day.' And then he'd hear drums from the square. First one drum, then another one answering it. Then a lot of drums. Then a voice, one voice. And then a refrain, a lot of voices joining and coming into each other. And all of it having to be heard. The music being born right inside itself, not knowing how it was getting to be music, one thing being responsible for another. Improvisation . . . that's what it was. It was primitive and it was crude, but down at the bottom of it—inside it, where it starts and gets into itself—down there it had the same thing there is at the bottom of ragtime. It was already born and making in the music they played at Congo Square.

And that square, in a way of speaking, it was my grandfather's square. He never had to hear it from a distance, because he was always ahead of the music there. It was there in his mind even before he got to the square and began performing it. It was *his* drum, *his* voice, *his* dancing. And people had to come, they couldn't move away from it. It was *all* the people, the masters too.

197

My grandfather was a young man then. He was young and he was strong and he hadn't any bowing to do to anybody. The only thing was, there was some who didn't want their slaves mixing with him, because he was so free and was treated so well by his master.

Another thing about this Congo Square—sometimes it was used for a selling-block. The masters would come there to buy and sell their slaves. My grandfather, though, never had anything like that. You know, someone was telling me once, from a book about Lincoln, something he said when he saw a mulatto girl being sold, how she was being treated, how she was all chained and pinched, and handled by the men what was thinking maybe of buying her. Lincoln, he was with two friends and he was watching, and he said, 'By God, boys, let's get away from this. If ever I get a chance to hit that thing, I'll hit it hard.'

Well, this one Sunday my father told me about, my grandfather was playing at this Congo Square. Everybody was mixing, just mixing as much as there could be. Some was dancing, if there was a feeling in them that way. Others, they were just hollering. But everybody, *everybody* was tapping their feet. Well, on this Sunday, in the midst of all this singing and dancing and drumming, my grandfather saw this girl.

She was standing sort of off by herself, just standing, and well . . . it come over him, it was one of those things. She was standing there, a little off by herself, and he just fell in love with her. Suddenly, everything he was doing, he was doing it for her. The girl, she must have been about thirteen or fourteen, all full of a kind of dream, like in the morning when no one's seen it. My grandfather came over to where she was and he danced and sang. Then he made her dance with him. The more there was of this dancing, the more happy he felt. What he was expressing—the language his feet and voice were making to tell her about himself—it was so rich inside him.

The girl was a slave, a maid for a young girl about her own age; they grew up together. But she didn't have any master like my grandfather had. Hers was mean to his people, watching them all the time. He wouldn't let them mix. It was like he had a fear of him; and mostly he watched this girl, noticing all what she did, all where she went; he wouldn't let anyone come around her.

That Sunday there—standing back some from the crowd, by the square, watching her dance—it came to him. He realized he wanted her for himself. Seeing her hesitate before dancing with my grandfather, that master, he wanted her. It seemed like everything she did sent itself inside him—her voice, soft, almost a hum, her arms, her body moving so strong in the rhythm. When the master saw my grandfather near to this girl, all with a power, dancing for her, and her responding, not being able to help herself, not wanting to . . . all at once the master, he got up to them and took her away.

My grandfather saw it all, saw what it was. He knew he wasn't supposed to talk to this girl or come to see her. And the girl was shy; she'd be frightened. He saw her being taken away. He'd seen her such a short time; it was such a short time he'd known all what he was singing and feeling and what it was leading up to in itself, inside him—to a kind of freedom, to a kind of time catching up to itself to where it was just itself and at peace. That feeling, it got too strong for him. He stopped the singing. He had to stop.

And people about him, they saw it. They'd seen what had happened. And so they started to moan, to let him know. They were moaning because something like that had happened to all of them.

There was an old woman come up to him then, some old hag. She was one of those witch women making brews. She made her living that way, by potions. She would sing into this potion, and bless it, and placate it, you know, and there would be a whole crowd around her when she did it back in the bayous, and they'd all be waiting to see what was going to happen to it; waiting to see if it was going to explode, waiting for it to show if things were going to work out, or if maybe there was an evil coming. The old woman came up to him and told him to come to her cabin the next day. She told it to him secret because it wasn't liked, that voodoo business. She said she was going to fix a potion for him, a love potion so that he could win this girl. She promised him to sing into it, and to praise over it, and to throw out the devils and bring down powers into it to work for him. And that way he would know, she said. If the powers said yes, then he would have the girl, and she would be his.

That old woman came up to him and she danced around him a little, moving in different directions around him, but always coming back to him, making a chain around him, moaning some as she danced. She was all dried-up and skinny, but maybe she thought she'd be this girl if she made the potion right—she could have a part in all the loving. Some women are funny when they get old—they got to hear about everything, they got to know *all* what's going on; they can't bear to miss out on anything. That's how this old woman was about my grandfather. She touched him and she made him promise to come the next night, back there in the bayou where she made those brews. She danced around him and she was laughing and crying to herself. She was singing a love chant. Only it was more a wail. And then everybody in the square took to beating it out on drums, and she was wailing on, and they were all climbing up in the music like it was a tree and they wanting to shake it down and talk to the moon.

My grandfather left the square in the middle of all this. He went off alone, waiting for the next day. No one stopped him. There wasn't no one to bother him. The carts and flies and dogs, the slaves and the masters, they didn't need him.

All he thought about was this girl. He wanted to drop everything at her feet, like he had just come from somewhere far and was bringing it all to her, all that distance. He wanted to stop and listen, like there was a call from the bayous or the woods and he had heard it. She rode around with him all day like a wild bird on his shoulder.

The next day he was busy around the house and the fields, singing to himself—leaving to go watch the river and see how it had no need of the banks, how it carried itself along, not knowing how to do otherwise—moving because that was all it knew, like it was some tongue tasting off the earth and not wanting it.

And that evening he took off for this bayou where the old hag kept herself. There are lots of bayous in that country, and my grandfather knew them all. He knew them so well he could hide in them where no one could ever find him, all in that wild swamp like a jungle. If you've never been down in those bayous that's something to see. It's so even and calm there. There's big dark trees dripping in the water, funny lilies, things rotting, strange birds flying and swooping, bats, snakes—lots of snakes—and when the night come it's just like some burglar coming to steal what little light there is. There's such funny sounds, sounds like you never heard before. You're one place and you think you hear yourself away in another place. And that bayou—it's got to trust you and it's got to know you're trusting it, or it'll get you where you can't find yourself.

This night, when he went to get the potion, there wasn't much light. At that time of night a mist had got into the air. He went back into this one bayou, Bayou LeFourg, and the memory of this girl was following him. And when he got to this witch woman's place, there was a whole lot of slaves there, some free, some runaway—they was all chanting and moaning and beating on drums around this woman who had a big cast-iron pot she was boiling this potion in. They was all waiting to see what was going to happen, if this potion, it would give a sign—what all those roots and herbs and powders, they were going to do when the fire got them hot enough to throw out the devils.

Back there, outside her cabin with all the trees and no light and just the outline of that hut, this old woman started to sing. She bowed to the potion and started in waving her hands and moving her feet, and the rest of the people, soon they was waving and bowing too, cursing at the Evil, telling God where He could find them.

There was just the little light of the fire under the pot, burning just enough so you could see some of the legs moving and bowing and the hands reaching down, and the bottom of the witch woman's dress.

The whole thing there kept building and building up, and those people, they were telling themselves about things that were inside them. They were telling it out to the fire and the dark and the mist, and the only way they knew to tell it was by singing about a place where they all used to be happy once—how they used to stand listening in that place hearing sounds, like hooves when they ran over the ground, a sound of something running. They were trying to bring down some kind of witness to help them, and this love my grandfather felt for the girl started it all. Love was so important to these people, love was the only way to get close to someone. Sometimes it was the only way you could forget.

That's why there was this music in them; music was all they had to forget with. Or they could use it for a way of remembering that was as good as forgetting, a way that was another kind of forgetting. This music was their need, their want. But it had to have a pride too . . . they *needed* my grandfather to love this girl just like he needed her himself so they could bring themselves together and hope.

Then this potion exploded and it was a sign to them, and they set to clapping and shouting. Everyone came up to my grandfather and wanted to touch him to get a hold of some of the Power that was going to work for him. And then they started singing a praise.

The hag, she got some of this potion, put it in a little sack and tied it around his neck. He was to wear it there always for the potion to work. And my grandfather left there knowing that the girl was waiting for him, and that it was all going to be all right. He could hear what all the voices were doing behind him. Way off in the bayou he could still hear the voices where he left them, more quiet now, so deep—some real strain of love, some melody offering itself far back in the night.

The next few days there was to be a big ball for the white people at this girl's master's place. There was to be white musicians and lots of food and important people and everybody all dressed up. The girl was sent to town to get some things for it, but the master went along and the mistress too. The master, he wasn't letting her alone for a minute. But my grandfather followed him and he got a message to this girl that he would come around the evening of the ball. He knew she would be coming to town to buy goods for the ball and he had a friend who worked for his own master tell her. My grandfather, he was feeling the Love and the Power working in him and he was feeling strong. He had a confidence in him.

The day of the ball the whole place was busy, everybody fixing for the big doings, food being prepared, rooms being cleaned, furniture being arranged, the owners having their special clothes made ready. The girl was busy helping her mistress, ironing her things and helping her to pretty up, talking to her, listening to all the excitement and knowing that that evening my grandfather was coming to her. She was scared some, too. She could feel the master thinking about her, watching her. There wasn't none of that confidence in her, but there was an excitement. It was a song too, but it was a different song.

She was too inexperienced to know what my grandfather was out to do. But she had an instinct in her that had been born in her, it came as part of her heritage . . . there was so many girls before her, all having the same thing happening to them. She could sense it; she had an understanding for it. She'd never loved anyone or wanted to understand it for herself because she didn't want to be afraid. But this was all different inside her. It just seemed so much change was happening, but, you know, deep down inside herself, knowing my grandfather, she felt him like a safety inside herself, like he was a place you could rest in and be sure, like some of that confidence that was in him made a place for her too.

She had all this inside her but she kept it quiet—just went on doing her work like nothing was happening. The girl she worked for, her mistress, was so excited about the ball she didn't notice anything. But the master, his desire had kind of put him where he could feel her thoughts; he sensed something. I don't think that he had a hold of it, but there was some instinct in him too, and he was so jealous of my grandfather anyway that this girl was on his mind all the time. You understand, I think he enjoyed all this jealousy. He had a relish for it; he was a kind of sadist to himself, and this jealousy gave him a chance to work it out on other people.

The ball finally started. The musicianers were there playing their music, the kind of music that could fit indoors, the kind of music people would let inside their houses. It was quadrilles mostly and some reels, with maybe a tune like *Tiger Rag,* only different from what we know it today.

The guests started arriving. All the food and drinks was ready. There was the music inside and a whole lot of noise outside—the dogs barking, the carriages drawing up, a lot of voices talking and calling out. Bit by bit, things really got started. All the white people were inside dancing and talking, and all the slaves who had brought their people were outside talking to themselves and carrying on as much as they could, making jokes, gossiping.

And this girl, she slipped out of the house and went away back into the dark. She left the plantation hoping the lights from the big rooms wouldn't catch her when she passed them by, and she went running off into the woods at the edge of the bayous.

She was to meet him off there in the dark. They had made a meeting place near one of the bayous. And he wanted her. He was wanting her so bad, he hadn't waited where the meeting place was, but he had come most of the way she would have to come. He had been waiting on her all day and into the evening, walking around through the bayous in some kind of a spell. And the bayou seemed to know it. All the leaves were thick around one another, all the birds seemed to be going towards one another, and when the moon finally came out it wasn't full, but the light from it was inside him too. It was like that moon had too much light for itself to hold and had to get some of it inside him.

While he was waiting, he sang a little. It wasn't much of a song, not what we'd call a song. There wasn't much rhythm to it, but just pieces of melodies. It was moods he was making up out of himself. There wasn't anyone there to tell it to, but it was like he told it to her. He was finding the way of humming that feeling that the trees and the air were trying to give him, as if they wanted to be part of the power too. He was trying to say how he needed all this quiet of the bayou because so much of it was happening right inside himself. That's the way his song was; it was quiet and far off, but it was everywhere inside him.

So when it got near the time when the girl was to come, he couldn't stand it any longer. He got up and went to where she was coming. He went on almost clear to the house instead of waiting at the meeting place. And that's how he met her.

You know how to imagine the two of them seeing each other, coming close. There's no describing it. It's just for two people. And right there where they were, right by the road she had come, they had each other. Right there where the night was to cool them and with all the trees dancing around them and over them like they was a tribe.

What they didn't know was that the master had followed her. He'd come after her, not so quick as she'd come because he didn't know the beginning of the bayou like she did, but guessing it, leading himself on by some craziness from want of her. And he came up on them where they was lying together. He swore at them and went to grab them, only he was so crazy he didn't know which one he wanted to grab, him or her. Her because she'd done murder inside him (all that kind of picture he had inside himself of the way she moved, all slow, all full, like some day in the middle of summer when it's got no hurry, of the way her eyes got when she was thinking of something, of her dancing there in Congo Square)—like I say he didn't know whether to grab her, or my grandfather (crazy mad at him because the girl had given herself). He stood there thinking all this at once until it exploded inside him, and then all at once he swung up with his gun and he made a grab at the girl, yanking her out of the way, and all in one motion he fired at my grandfather. And that ball, it hit in the arm my grandfather had had that dream about.

Maybe you won't believe it, but that's how it happened. My grandfather knew there was only one thing to do. He had to get away. He was trying to get the girl, get her so they could both run, but the master had a hold of her and he was trying to fix where my grandfather was so he could shoot at him again.

204

The girl was crying, wailing, telling my grandfather to go, moaning out, trying to free herself, scratching at the master, but just not being able to get free. My grandfather ran—ducking under the brush, holding his arm, and running off through the swamp with the master following. The girl ran too, not knowing where, wanting to go where my grandfather was going but not finding him in all that dark, feeling if she were to find the way the master would catch up with them both. She just ran around, hurt like some animal and wanting to hide. She could hear all the noise of the twigs and the branches, everything there had been between them breaking and crashing, becoming just a noise in the dark.

My grandfather kept on running. It was safe for him now; this bayou was so much a part of him. His arm was giving him trouble and it must have been all kinds of hell, pursued that way, not by something he could beat, but by that gun and by the colour jf the hand that held it. He went running on like that, hating, worried over the girl, feeling guilty—all that love torn up just like that, hating all of a sudden even the bayou that was making it safe for him. But he kept on. I think it must be that he was proving out that thing, that survival of the fittest—not out of any book, but out of himself, out of a need he had of knowing he was able, knowing his way in the night. He was meaning to get away, to get strong and to come back. He was going to come back.

When he knew there was no finding him, he stopped and got his breath. He tied up his arm in some way and he took off for the hiding place of the runaway slaves, the ones who had been around when the witch woman was making her brew.

Oh, was he angry. He tore off that potion from himself and flung it into the water. He threw it off as far as he could with his left arm, but it didn't go far. It struck the water and something moved under the water . . . a 'gator disturbed by the splash and disturbing the water, and the ripples of it spread across the bayou moving like snakes in the moonlight and lay at his feet.

All that night he trekked through the bayou, feeling the night as if it was a breath that's wasted itself. At dawn he came upon these slaves that was hiding back there. He didn't explain nothing. Everybody back there, he had his own reason for being there, and every reason it explained every other somehow. There was no need of explanation. He just showed them his arm, and everyone understood everything he needed to.

They'd been hiding out in the bayou for all kinds of time, some of them just recent, but all of them meaning never to go back. They were going to stay there the rest of their lives. They had to stay back there anyhow, because about that time there were a lot of bandits, pirates who'd come in off the coast. The pirates were stealing and raiding off the towns and plantations, and these runaway slaves, they were taking the blame for it. There were posters up for them all around, offering rewards if someone were to catch any of them. Once in a while, these slaves would slip into town to some friend's house. But not often; mostly they stayed back in the bayou and made themselves hard to catch.

Well, my grandfather got to them. He knew most of them anyway. They fixed him up, but there wasn't much they could do for his arm: they had to cut it off later. It was just the way he had had the dream about it—you know, he had had the feeling right along, right from the time he had the dream. He lost his arm, but somehow he had been ready for it. He had a power in him, my grandfather, and he had a wish and a hate and it made him strong. He handled himself just as good not having that arm as when he did have it. There's some can be stopped by a scratch and there's some who just can't be stopped so long as they're living; and my grandfather, he wouldn't be stopped.

But I'm ahead of myself here. After this master had come upon my grandfather and this girl, and my grandfather had run off and the girl had run off too, stumbling around, cowering all crazy-like, he was trying to get another shot at my grandfather, and he was trying to find the girl. He was tumbling around too, not knowing what to do, and so he cried out.

That cry, it wasn't to say anything. The master knew my grandfather and the girl wouldn't answer. It was like another voice crying, like it was his own vexation crying out at the night. But there was people not too far off. They'd heard the shot and all the commotion, and they'd been coming out to see, and when the master cried out they heard him and they came up, breaking through the shrubs in all this dark. The three of them—my grandfather, the girl, her master—they hadn't been far back in the bayou, more or less just at the edge of it, and these people who'd heard the noise came trampling through and they found the master.

'What's happened?' they all wanted to know. 'Are you hurt?' 'What's going on?'

The master was mad, in a frenzy—my grandfather gone, the girl gone, everything he'd thought about himself happening between them happening right there and him coming on it, finished before he had a chance to do anything, and all that lust he'd had for the girl, someone else turning it all bitter—not the lust, but all that pleasure from thinking about it, all that pleasure he'd had warming inside himself all these weeks.

Maybe it's hard to blame him, even. People can't help feeling something when a pretty woman or someone passionate passes by right in front of them; maybe you try to tell yourself something different, but you know that's the truth. If you're a human person, it's just a natural thing to feel something that way.

Well, standing there that way with all those thoughts inside him, all mad, vain, and vexed and foolish, he cried out:

'Rape! One of my girls has been raped!'

Naturally no one would think he'd refer to a coloured girl as one of 'his' girls. They all thought right away he meant his *own* girl, his daughter. A white girl, she had been raped by a Negro—that's the way they got it. And right away it's the same old thing. Right away they are all out for a lynching. They set out after my grandfather right there. They was meaning to have their revenge.

It was too late then for the master to say anything. What he'd said satisfied him anyway. It was so that he was almost feeling good, and he got to believe it, and he followed after them, only he was trying to find this girl before they did so he could hide her.

All those trees there, they was standing like skeletons after the hide of the animal has disappeared. There was moonlight on their tops like blossoming, and there was the darkness under them, the light and the darkness somehow part of one thing that was darker than just plain dark, and all so still. And all that bayou—you could hear the white men's voices sounding from far off where they were chasing my grandfather, a noise way off disturbing the birds somewhere on the other side of the stillness.

Well, the master stumbled around, poking and feeling in the dark, and finally he came upon the girl. She hadn't gotten far. She was all cut up, her face bleeding, her hair all bunched up in some places and falling loose in others.

She didn't know if she was some distance back in the bayou, or how far she was. She was dazed. She was just feeling lost. There was some evil happening, something bigger than she knew how to do with.

The man, her master, found her. He wasn't so sure if it was my grandfather or the girl. He swore and he yelled out: 'Stay where you are, nigger: I've got you!' And he pointed that gun, and the girl, paralysed like, just sitting there. Then all of a sudden she goes to move and the master saw it wasn't my grandfather. He came up to where she was crouching, sobbing to herself, and he hit her across the face to shock her, to quiet her so she wouldn't betray him and he took off his coat and wrapped her in it so her face wouldn't show.

Some of the men was still scattered around there poking about in the brush for my grandfather and they saw the master with the girl in his arms. He picked her up and he was carrying her like that in his arms, and when he crossed a patch of moonlight some of the men saw him and they came running up, wanting to help, all of them having this big excitement to put together, and all of them somehow feeling better about their excitement when they could talk about it, when they were together.

'Is she all right?' they said. 'We'll take her to a doctor.'

'We'll lynch that devil nigger as high as to . . .'

'We'll get him, don't you worry none.'

'We'll get the dogs after him.'

All that excitement, everyone talking, thinking if their own daughters were safe. But more than that, every man hearing a piece of his own excitement in what the other men were saying, feeling his excitement get bigger as he listened to it, every voice full of that excitement and a kind of righteousness; and when you listen to voices like that, what they're saying, you can't tell the righteousness from the excitement: they're the same thing.

The master wrapped the coat around her closer so they wouldn't see. She wasn't one of those real dark girls anyway, and it was dark enough so the men couldn't tell. The master made out to pretend he was too ashamed for them to see, to help him bring her back. He acted it stubborn like, like it was the only right way. Wasn't it his own daughter?

The men got kind of humble and they let him go. They was trying to encourage him, trying to be all together in this thing. They wanted to understand this one thing about themselves, about having this thing, this excitement and righteousness, in common. Maybe then they each one of them would understand about his own self. They was going to see to it that my grandfather, his neck would be fixed good.

Well, the master carried this girl back through the swamps, stumbling over a piece of wood that had gone bad, almost tripping on a bush, not seeing his way too well. And walking along that way there was this feeling, this conviction growing inside him from the weight and the trouble and all the excitement behind him—he had this conviction he had been betrayed. He was feeling it was right and natural for the girl to be cut up and hit. She hadn't had any right going with my grandfather, a black man. That's how he thought of it: my grandfather was black. His lust had made him forget all about what colour *she* was. All he could remember was her eyes, all warm, all melody like when she was dancing—her hips, like sides to a moon, moving, swaying; her body, all about to topple over because of that love feeling she'd had when she was dancing. The master had that picture in his mind and he had that weight in his arms and they got to being the same thing inside him. He had the feeling that something that was his had been hurt and he'd had to go out and rescue it. It was right what he'd done.

He got back to his place, to the plantation, and all the lights and dancing and music, they were still carrying on. A couple of dogs set to barking, but he hushed them up. He cursed at all the voices and the laughter. Through the windows he could see his guests and he cursed them. They were going about flirting, amusing themselves, complimenting themselves on their importance and he could feel himself hating them. He was like some crazy man who was sick and had gotten away. He even rocked this girl in his arms, forgetting who she was, remembering only who he wanted her to be.

'We'll get him, honey,' he told her. 'We'll get even. Don't you worry; we'll strap him up good.'

He walked through the yard and into the kitchen. The slaves out in the yard fell away from him, not speaking, looking after him then looking at each other and shaking their heads. His face the way it was, the slaves didn't dare say anything. He took her into the kitchen and up the back stairs to a little room they kept for storing things—things they didn't use any more but weren't meaning to throw away.

He laid her down there and he wanted to forget about her now. Things, they became sharp to him now. He was beginning to have a danger for himself, what it was he had to do to put back this trouble he was feeling, all of it mixed up with the picture he had in him from the memory of what he had done—the bayou, her and my grandfather mating, the shot, the noise of brush being trampled, and all the people running. He didn't know what to do, what thing to go after first. He stood there thinking, trying to arrange everything in his mind.

It was quiet up there, he could hardly hear the music from downstairs. He looked at the dummies that his wife and his daughter used for modelling dresses. They were just standing there like something left over from a thing that was done. It was scaring him. Even the dummies were a reminding to him. There was always something left over. There was always something that could be put away only so far and no further. He would have to find his wife. He would have to send his wife to find her daughter and bring her upstairs, get her out of the way. He would have to talk to his wife.

When a man gets to feel a panic he acts in a quick way—things, they have to be cut away from him sharp, in a hurry, like he's got a knife. The master went down the stairs again fast. There was one of the slaves there cutting up fruit, not showing her face, only paring up a bowl full of fruit. He told the slave to hurry out and find his wife and tell her it was important, she had to come right back to the kitchen to talk to him.

The wife was worried; this didn't seem natural. She pardoned herself from her company, trying to be graceful in leaving so all in a hurry. She came back to the kitchen and her eyes were asking everything she didn't say. The master sent the slave outside and went over to the wife, up close. He's talking low and kind of fast.

'Where's Eveline?' he said.

'Why, she's inside,' the wife said. 'She's been dancing. She's been having a nice time. I believe she's . . .'

'Hush,' he said, 'that isn't it. Go get her. Bring her back here right away.'

The wife asked what had happened. She was wanting to know what it was, why he was sending for them both right then with all this ball on their hands and all these neighbours in the house. But the master, he was a man with his own made-up mind; he wasn't for no discussion of it just then.

'This isn't something you know about.' He said, 'Just do as I say.'

His wife, she had reason enough to know his ways. He was so often abrupt and she knew it only made it worse when she tried to bring her reason into it. She picked up her skirts, smoothing them a little, and she went. Everything had been going so nicely, all the furniture polished so well, the music kind of laughing and sighing so nice, the lights doing so well by her antiques, Eveline behaving so good—that part of things she knew about real well, the mistress things of making a house right. But this other, this was a thing she didn't understand. It was the thing in him she had never been able to understand, the thing she hadn't been brought up to understand.

When the three of them was back there in the kitchen, he ordered his wife to take Eveline to her room and keep her there, to lock her in. His wife wasn't liking the way this was turning out. He made it so easy for her to resent him, never making up to her for what her parents had done, giving her away to him, not having been fair, knowing she hadn't wanted to marry him. But there was nothing she could do. And she had a feeling things were going to be said that it was better Eveline didn't hear, things it wasn't right for her to hear. So she did like she was told. She took Eveline upstairs and put her to bed thinking her own thoughts, and when she came out of the room she turned the key in the lock and turned around and found her husband waiting for her in the hall.

He took her aside and he told her how it was. He told her that out there in the bayous, this girl, Eveline's maid, she had been raped. He'd come upon her and tried to save her, he said, but he'd been too late and the buck had gotten away. But he knew who it was and the whole countryside was out searching for him. He told her that the girl had been hurt, all cut up and crying and wounded and that in all that excitement when he'd tried to get this nigger after he'd shot at him, people had come running up and he'd cried out 'Rape!'

His wife interrupted him then, asking him how he was sure it was rape.

'The girl,' he said. He claimed the girl had told him that. And he told his wife not to interrupt any more, that the story wasn't finished.

So he went on. He told her how he cared for this girl, she was so close to Eveline, how he had always treated her like she was a daughter. And how it had shocked him when he found out what had been done to her, he was so mad with it, and how it was then he had cried out, not thinking, forgetting it was the girl who had been so close to the daughter and as if she had become the daughter for that instant. How it was then he had cried out: 'One of my girls has been raped!' and how people, they'd taken it for his daughter, for

Eveline, and he had been so confused and mad still that he hadn't said anything, hadn't known what to say. . . .

And so that's how people were thinking it, he told her. That's why he had to talk to her. People, they were thinking now that Eveline, she had been raped.

And now all those people, he told her, they'd be coming around the house soon wanting to know was Eveline all right, or if there was any danger. And how could he tell them it was all a mistake? A man like him, he couldn't afford to lose face that way. He didn't dare tell them; it was frightening him. What if they refused to hunt for the black? It was important: he had to be caught. What if that nigger might want to avenge him . . . come back there and really try to get the daughter, or the wife, even try to shoot *him*. New Orleans and the country around it wouldn't be safe. And it wasn't much matter anyhow, one nigger more or less—wouldn't make much difference. You needed to put the terror in them once in a while, keep them where they knew they ought to be, else there might be ideas getting started in their heads— ideas you didn't want them to have.

Well, you know, he talked. He kept talking on and arguing with his wife. She got to pleading at times but he cut her off, getting sharper and sharper with her. And last of all he began threatening—wives, they had to help out their men, they had no place deciding things, thinking they knew better. 'You keep Eveline in there,' he told her. It was an order. There'd be so much confusion no one would know exactly when she had disappeared. 'I'll handle it all,' he told her, 'you just do as I say.'

So when the man who was acting as a kind of sheriff come up with some of the other men, the master was ready. There was some of the men who had been out by the bayou, and there was some others had come out from town with the sheriff, and there was some guests from the ball had heard something about it. They all come round, and the master met them and told them his daughter was upstairs and that a doctor was sent for. They could understand, he said, how no one was to see her. Her mother was with her, comforting her, trying to take away some of the shame. And he asked them please, not to say anything to the rest of the guests, the ones who hadn't heard anything already. They'd hear about it soon enough, he said. And he was so troubled . . . he felt he had to have a little time to collect himself. But right off he announced he was offering a reward for that nigger. Anyone who was to catch him or find out where he was keeping himself, he would get a nice piece.

The men left him then, and he went back to look for his wife. All this time the wife, she'd been thinking about all what was happening, trying to figure it out. She didn't trust his story. She felt there was too many places where it didn't hang together, all entire.

She got to wondering where the girl was, what he'd done with her, what it was the girl would have to say to her. But at the same time she wasn't trusting herself to decide anything. She wasn't daring to think, not even to herself, on any way of crossing her husband. Women in those days, they had no tradition that way. Maybe in other ways they got around it, but speaking up—that didn't happen. But this thing, it would be found out. She had that feeling for certain—that if the evil was big enough it couldn't stay hidden. She wasn't all that kind of an outside woman, but she knew that.

So she went hunting through the rooms and hallways up there, wondering where he had put the girl. And he came up while she was searching. He found her there and demanded to know what she was doing, and the wife told him she was looking for the girl. Where had he put her? That girl, she might be hurt and need looking after.

The master was beginning to worry about the girl too. He wouldn't know what to do to fix her. So he brought the wife to the store-room and he unlocked the door and both of them stood there in the doorway, looking in out of the hallway light that picked its way from behind them among the clutter of things inside, falling between the dressmaker's dummies and some old furniture and not finding anything, seeming just to sink into that darkness, a frightening thing.

It scared them both when they found the girl there, she was lying so quiet and still, almost as if she wasn't breathing. It was hot in that room and it smelled like a piece of goods you pull out of a trunk that's been sealed a long time. They stood over the girl, looking at one another, and they could hear the slaves outside, out by the trees, singing to themselves, a soft singing, almost a hum. It was one of their spirituals: *Trouble time's come, pick up my burden, white man's riding out.*

The man picked up the girl and the woman led the way. They brought her to a small room they had, put her on the bed. The wife got some water and washed the girl's face and hands. She undressed her and put her to bed and sat by her. The man stood by the window, looking out, thinking.

It's the way of things sometimes. A man will go ten miles out of his way to spread harm to someone. He'll talk twelve hours and he won't spend one minute saying a good word. This master was like that. Here was this girl lying two steps away from him and downstairs there were all those people. He could tell the simple truth so easy like—how she wasn't sick from no rape, but she'd just been with a man she wanted. But the master knew he couldn't do that, and he knew he didn't want to. A man spends so much effort, so damn' much of his time doing all the *bad* he can, that when the times comes when there's some good he can do, he'd just as soon rope himself up to his own front door.

And when you start one of those lies, there's nothing you can do but go about getting it finished. It gets all out of your hands, and you're trying to catch at it every which way. But there's nothing you can do once it has got started. All the mending and repairing you do to it, trying to keep it where it started, trying to keep that one lie from becoming a thousand lies. But you can't do anything about it. You're just like a dog that's chasing rabbits when there's so many of them he doesn't know which one he's after.

So the master went downstairs. He went downstairs and he stopped the music and he called all his guests and said how sorry he was but something had come up in the family, an accident, it was terrible, his daughter had . . . a Negro had been there and done this thing . . . and they would excuse him, they would understand, but he needed the house quiet . . . there was this sorrow upon it . . . and how his wife was not feeling able . . . they would know how it was. . . .

The next day there were posters up all over town and around the plantations. There was a big reward offered and the posses were working out in all directions. You could hear the dogs working the bayou all day long trying to pick up a trail.

The slaves worked quiet, working hard, singing maybe, some plaint like *I'm worried,* waiting it out, wondering what really *had* happened, and not understanding. They all knew my grandfather and they couldn't understand. They all knew he had no business for a white girl. He just didn't have a need for a thing like that. It was a thing they couldn't understand except to fear it. There was a fear of it in the air.

214

You see, this master would have realized that he *had* to say my grandfather raped his daughter or else no one would hunt after him. They all loved him too much. His own master would never allow it. But as it was, that master was in a spot: there was nothing he could do. The law was against him.

My grandfather's master tried to stop all that tracking down, the dogs and the posses. He knew my grandfather, knew he wouldn't do a thing like that. But all the people living there came up to him and showed him he had no right. The girl's master went over to the plantation and *he* told him he had no right; and so there was nothing my grandfather's master could do. My grandfather, he wasn't property any more; he couldn't be protected. It was all over, his being a free slave.

And the girl's master, it was just what he wanted. It was because of that he had to say it had been his daughter. Because there was still that hate in him. He had to see my grandfather brought down for what he had done, for what he had spoiled out of that dream the master had been storing up inside himself. He didn't care for the truth and he'd didn't care even for the girl any more. It was that thing he had felt die in himself out there in the bayou. He had felt it die out of him, like it was himself was being killed. And there was no resisting it any more. He had to have my grandfather; he had to see him dead if he was to ruin himself doing it.

And somehow the wife understood this. She stayed back at the plantation taking care of the girl, fixing things the best she could to make her comfortable. Sitting and waiting for the girl to come out of her shock. She never left the girl. She sat there through one night and into the day and feeling the next night settling in, waiting, letting the night say what it had to say when it hit all the buildings, the slaves in their cabins, and her even. Waiting and being half afraid what the girl would say when she got relaxed enough to talk.

She sat there thinking about her life, about the kind of child she had raised, about all the things she had done in the years that made up her life. And underneath all that she was feeling what kind of a man her husband was. Beginning to know for certain, and wishing life could give you a time to be young all over again so you could have it different.

And when the girl came to, when she stopped rambling inside herself from the shock and began to cry and to call my grandfather's name—not hateful like but in a kind of pain, crying his name like she was saying she had lost something, like everything had become unbearable . . . it was then the mistress knew she couldn't doubt any more. She sat in the night hearing the girl call my grandfather's name and she knew for certain. She heard it all in a kind of tenderness for the girl. This feeling she had, that they were losing something together, it filled her with a softness, a pity. That feeling, it's got no touch with how things are in the day. It was a night kind of knowing, like when you wake up in the dark and hear your own name, your own voice— and then when you get beyond that, when you get to calling a name that's not your own, but that's got even more of what's you in it, more of what's got your heart. . . .

'You love him?'

That was what the women asked. And the girl, she didn't answer outright. She cried. She clutched the covers and she cried as if the crying was far away inside her. And the woman left her then. She stopped watching out the nights with her.

All this time the search parties were fanning out through the bayous, dogs wailing and yelping, one calling to another. They'd find a part of his track and then it would lose itself in some swamp, and they'd find another and lose it again. Night and day, you could hear the pack calling from the bayous. And everyone living around there, they couldn't talk about nothing else, all of them waiting to hear what was happening, wondering if they'd found him yet, waiting to see how it would be.

The slaves felt a trouble on them. Nights, they was talking low to themselves, trying superstitions to keep away more evil, keeping under cover, trying to stay out of the white man's way. And days, they had their trouble on them. The overseers were being more cruel; the meals had less food to them; the work, they made it harder and there was more and more whip behind it. There was a whole lot more slaves getting beatings those days.

The only thing they had that couldn't be taken from them was their music. Their song, it was coming right up from the fields, settling itself in their feet and working right up, right up into their stomachs, their spirit, into their fear, into their longing. It was bewildered, this part in them. It was like it had no end, nowhere even to wait for an end, nowhere to hope for a change in things. But it had a beginning, and that much they understood . . . it was a feeling in them, a memory that came from a long way back. It was like they were trying to work the music back to its beginning and then start it over again, start it over and build it to a place where it could stop somehow, to a place where the music could put an end to itself and become another music, a new beginning that could begin *them* over again. There were chants and drums and voices—you could hear all that in it—and there was love and work and worry and waiting; there was being tired, and the sun, and the overseers following behind them so they didn't dare stop and look back. It was all in the music.

And back in the bayou where my grandfather was with the runaway slaves, there was music back there too. Those runaway slaves sensed the bayou warning them . . . *trouble, trouble* . . . the moon and the shadows and that heavy air, it was telling them an evil. And little by little they began to sing it.

Some of them had been at the square when my grandfather had sung for his girl. They'd seen him dance. They remembered that, and they took the melody and the music he'd had then; they took it and they sang it for him, beating out the time on their drums. It was just like they were in Africa again, like they was calling to one another, to another tribe, like they was trying to be with their people who was back there in the cabins, waiting all night to another dawn, working all day to another sunrest, working and waiting. Back there in the bayou, those runaway slaves took that glad song my grandfather had made and they sent it away into the night, sending it back to my grandfather, trying to give him the gladness and the power of it again.

My grandfather couldn't sing, though. They tried to bring him to where that place inside him had been, to the things a man promises himself, to the things that maybe happen just once. But all this worry he had, all this torment over the girl—there was all that in him blocking him from the place he meant to get to once. There was this terrible change in him; and the song just couldn't reach him.

Pretty soon word got around to them about the posters, about the reward, about how he had raped a white girl and how the whole countryside was after him. My grandfather couldn't understand it. He hadn't raped no white girl . . . what was happening back there? The girl, *his* girl . . . she hadn't told them to say that.

His mind jumped over one thing to another that was haunting him all the time . . . that memory of her and him, the way they had been together there at the beginning of the bayou . . . that calm place in the night before the night blew open on them. He looked up from that memory and he saw the bayou around him there where he was . . . the birds still meeting and flying over to one another, mosquitoes making their sounds as they swam around in the air, leaves and vines not letting one another go.

He'd look up from that memory and see all this living around him, all busy with itself, and he'd feel a question in him big as the whole earth: what was a man, what was he here for anyway? He'd sit there hitting at a bug, breaking a branch, running the soil through his hand. Everyone, they'd be silent watching him, wondering at him, not trying to get to him any more. They could feel the trouble of it in the air like big black wings, like a buzzard circling and circling over all the air, and they were waiting there to see where it would settle.

My grandfather could feel how they were, how they were waiting, and after a while he couldn't stand it no more. He'd get up and disappear off into the bayou where no one could see him. And it was like going into himself, walking through himself, waiting to see where it would all lead.

One day he was walking around that way, feeling all this misery tightening inside him. It was like a rusty wheel when it gets so tight it can't turn no more. He was feeling it lock inside him and he couldn't get it moving. He was wanting to see the girl, yearning for her, not living except for that. There was that part of him that was still free from all the torment, all the fear . . . it made that longing in him. And all at once it swelled up in him: he was walking around by himself and all at once he stopped where he was and he felt it change. It was like he'd gotten that wheel loose and turning at last. It was almost like he was free . . . and he knew he had a thing to do. He had to see her and talk to her. He had to take his chance and he had to hear her telling him she didn't have any part in all this, that nothing had changed inside her. He had to find her and take her away, or if she was safer where she was he had to let her be, but he had to talk to her, he had to feel her holding him.

He came back to the camp where those runaway slaves were, and he told them how it was . . . there was no helping it, he couldn't choose. One or two of them tried to keep him from going, but it didn't take no effect. They seemed to know it couldn't take no effect even as they was trying to stop him. So they watched him go and they sat there singing, knowing he'd be hearing them a long way gone. It was like they were following him, sending the song along with him to be a strength to him the way he had to go.

My grandfather could hear the song behind him, and it was like he could hear the silence ahead of him. He kept going through the bayou and bit by bit he felt the song fading out of the air and the silence taking it. He got to the place where he had to stop and strain to hear it . . . where he wasn't quite sure he *was* hearing it, but somehow still feeling the rhythm of it on the air. He felt it fade away and he felt the silence coming, and all at once he was strong again.

He went on fast as he could then, moving ahead, dodging the places where there might be some kind of a trail, breaking his way into swamps so he wouldn't leave much trace. It was dark in there. He'd look at things and it seemed like everything was inside some tunnel, a dark the trees made. The going wasn't very good in the dark and with all that tangled footing. And his arm was giving him trouble. But somehow he trusted that too—it was kind of like a sign—a place where all the trouble could catch itself and stop. So long as he could feel the hurt of it he had a thing to hold on to, a way of knowing what was real. Sometimes he thought he could hear things—the sound of a dog, a voice shouting. Maybe a bird would wake up and fly funny; he'd have the feeling when he was running about that something was pacing him. He'd watched rabbits when he had hunted for them, how they flattened back their ears and made their whole bodies slick-like, making less of themselves by tightening up so that nothing could get at them, not stone or bullet. My grandfather had that feeling on him, a thing hunting him.

Bit by bit, then, he was nearing the outskirts of the bayou. After that there'd be empty land, land that's got nothing mated to it, just dry-seeming grass; and behind that there'd be the plantations. New Orleans was off to the right. He knew that if he hit all that dry land there wouldn't be many trees for cover. He guessed they'd probably have that watched. It would be hell getting over all those fences. Even at night there'd be enough moon to make him seen. And day or night, there'd be dogs about.

Finally he hit out towards New Orleans, figuring on going to a plantation that was pretty close to town, to a cabin of a friend of his. If he was to mix with a lot of slaves it would give things a better chance to work for him. For a minute he was almost forgetting about that arm, how being a one-armed man would make him seen no matter how many he mingled with. For that minute, planning ahead, all eager, the fact slipped him. Then, just standing there, he felt it come back. He knew all over again who he was, what a dark there was for him. But he had to go on. There was no stopping there now.

* * *

He made it to his friend's place and woke him up. The fellow couldn't believe it. Surprise, it takes away liking a thing or disliking it; this fellow, he was supposed to feel good seeing my grandfather again. But even after the first shock, it was easier just to keep acting that surprise.

My grandfather woke him up and they just sat there, talking low. That fellow was talking up all about how worried he'd been—talking up to let my grandfather know what a friend he was, wanting my grandfather to share some of the bed. But all the while he was figuring something—a thing moving, taking shape in his mind, bending like all those black branches do when a rain is hitting the trees. That reward, that chance maybe a slave would have to get himself a little more freedom, if he was to bring in my grandfather. But this fellow didn't know how to go about it.

That fellow knew my grandfather. It wouldn't be easy. My grandfather wasn't too awful tired out, and even with just one arm, he was strong. And that fellow wasn't sure yet. It hadn't really come to him inside what he was out to do. He went on talking low, hearing the slaves in the other cabins just recent turned to sleep, seeing the lines of cabins like chicken coops outside his window, listening to my grandfather's voice in the dark.

My grandfather noticed how his friend was funny-acting, but he guessed it was because he was scared. He didn't worry about it any; there were too many questions he had to ask. Those questions didn't leave much room for other things. *Were they watching her plantation? People around, what were they thinking? How come this story about raping a white girl, how did it get started?* He sat there in the dark asking his friend and feeling the scaredness in the friend and breathing in the thick dark air. That air, it was like something pasted up and closed, thick and heavy; it was like it had been in a shoe a long time, there was something spoiled in it.

After a while there's no more to ask, and not much answer given. This friend made like he was turning in to sleep and he offered to share the bed, but my grandfather thanked him and sat up. Suddenly he was feeling like an old man who's lived too long and is scared awake by the noise of a clock falling. He felt a fear working into him from the night, a dark thing.

But he was a man and there was his woman out there and he didn't have time to worry out about what's wrong with the rest of everything. There was just that one thing that had to be done. He sat there in that dark, knowing that was the only thing. Then suddenly, there was no more thing to it: he got up from there and he took off, leaving his friend asleep. He skirted around the cabins and the fields, keeping clear of the big house, staying back in the shadows. There was a comfort to being on the move again; he could hear the night crooning to him like it was trying to rock him. Being out that way, finding his road in the dark, it was a comfort to him after that waiting. And when he reached that place where it was just grassland there between the bayous and the plantation, when he got there and was able to feel the wet of the grass touching him, feeling himself mighty now that he was on his way—when he got there he wanted to press that whole black night down on the ground like it was a towel. He felt a strength in him, a kind of knowing where he was going and how he was to get there. He got near to her plantation and stopped, wondering how he was to signal her, how he was to make himself known.

And while my grandfather was waiting, his friend was up there. He hadn't been sleeping at all and he'd known for sure where my grandfather was going; he'd gotten out of bed and raced ahead by the road and he was up there pounding at the big door at the front of the house where the girl was, banging on the knocker, trying to bring the master to open it, pounding away all in a fear, his hand beating against the door until suddenly without his ever knowing it, the door's not there and his hand is beating on nothing and he's pushing against a servant what had opened the door, the servant holding him back, amazed to see him there, telling him he must be crazy thinking to come to the front door that way. 'You crazy, man? Git around to the back door. You crazy?'

But he told the servant he had a right, there was something he had to tell the master, and he was sure going to stand right where he was when he told it.

But the master wasn't at home. His wife, the lady of the house, heard the noise and she came, moving slow through the hall, dressed all in some kind of dark lace, making her own shadows with her candle as she came. She asked him what it was he wanted: the master wasn't in, he was out in a searching party: she couldn't tell him more. She didn't say out in words what she felt seeing a Negro at her front door; she guessed it was all part of this thing. So many changes were happening. She felt tired. Everything she touched or saw seemed tired. She felt like she'd been breathing tired air—the way it was when she did things, climbed stairs or arranged for dinner or just went off to sit, wondering what her thoughts were working up to. This slave went mad like, all crazy with eagerness and fearing it would go wrong. He had to hurry, he had to find out where the master was, he had to push down everything and take what was his to take—because if you don't take something when it's given to you, it comes back mean at you. You have to act quick, especially when there's a fear behind it, especially when you know a man might be learning what you're fixing to do to him.

That fellow ran off to try a whole lot of places where he might find the master. And this woman, the master's wife, went back into the library they had off their main room and played a piece on a piano they had, some ballad she'd learned when she was a girl. She touched the piano and she was thinking how pleasant the room wanted to be, how it wanted to put back all that dark that gathered to it. She sat there touching the piano with her fingers and let the piece play itself out, but in her mind she was thinking about the girl. Marie, her daughter's maid.

She sat there playing to herself, playing back the dark, and almost as if she was talking to the music she was whispering: *Those are Marie's thoughts. Every day, it's like this. Every day we know.* Where will it stop? she asked herself. Where can it stop? The hunting parties, the posters, the trouble building wider and wider; back there in the storeroom with her husband, with the girl lying there, she might have done something, it might have been different. But he had just told her to be quiet, commanded her, talked of marrying Eveline into a family down Florida way. It was to be done as he said, and he wasn't aiming to stop anything.

And now it had widened and it was beyond them. She sat touching the piano in that big room, and felt it about her: that girl's eyes, Marie, looking at her; Negroes pounding the front door almost before morning; the men gone on searching parties behind their dogs, tired and mad and hating. And a lie inside it all, waiting to break, insisting on being made known. She let her hand fall away from the piano and listened to the strings dying out of the air in that big room.

All this time my grandfather was waiting back there wondering how he was to do, trying to make out if there was any stirring, thinking how to reach the girl; he had come so far; there was that sickness of love tied to him like a ring when it won't come off because your finger's grown too tight. He didn't know how to do, but he couldn't wait any longer, he had to take his chance.

He ran then and crept up to the back of the house. There was no one about. Everything was like it was drowned in quiet. He crept up to the kitchen window and he looked in. He saw a servant come into the kitchen and he rapped on the window, gentle and fast. It frightened that servant plenty, his appearing that way, being who he was with half the country out hunting him. The servant began to moan a little prayer; she was scared this was a bad omen, that things was going to be worse still. But my grandfather spoke to her; he told her to go find the girl, Marie, he had to see her and he didn't have much time. The servant stopped her moaning some, but it was like she was afraid to move and my grandfather had to tell her all over again. He was beginning to get desperate now; he didn't know whether that servant woman was going off to betray him or if she was going off to call Marie, but she left him at last and he stood there waiting. It was like he was drowning. He couldn't tell what was coming to him out of the air, whether it would be Marie coming to answer that feeling in him or men suddenly jumping out of the night.

And then he heard a step inside the house and he saw the kitchen door turning, and it was over. It was Marie, her eyes as big as the night looking at him, her hands trembling when she touched him. For a minute then he took her to him, held her against him, feeling her arms go around him, feeling their bodies meet and soften and the bad feeling wearing itself out of them. There wasn't anything said, there wasn't anything to say.

After a while he led her away, back from the house and the side porch, back to a kind of spot that was dug up a bit from dogs scratching to make a hole. They lay there together in the dark, pressed into the ground, and at last they could talk out what they had to say. The girl told him all what the master had done, how it had happened, how there was a guard around the house; he'd been lucky, they'd gone off for a rest. They lay there talking the need out of themselves. He told Marie about the runaway slaves back there, how it had been with him. It hadn't made itself all clear to him yet, what she had told. It wasn't until he had been talking to her a while that he began to know it, feel it inside himself, all what the master had done to them, all the evil piling up from that one thing. He began to curse it. It came up like a thing from far off inside him, small at first, small and bitter, but building inside him, swelling and coming, making a feeling that when all that bitterness burst it would sour the world; thinking one lifetime, it wasn't enough to get rid of this story, to make it right.

The girl tried to soothe him. She told him about the mistress, how she'd been kind, how she knew what had really happened, knew they hadn't done nothing wrong; she'd help them. She touched his arm and she wanted to weep. But she was learning. She had no strength of her own, but somehow she had a strength to give. Almost it was a way of making things right, a hope. And he could feel it now, too. An answer, a part of an answer: or else it was a real answer, if only it could be made long enough. They were touching now, reaching. They had to have each other. And for that time, it *was* an answer. They had that to give, they were free inside themselves.

All this while the friend was out, going everywhere to find the master, asking everyone he saw where it would be best to look for him. Someone finally told him he'd gone to New Orleans and the fellow took off running as though to split, running till his breath got to be just one big pump inside him, pumping a need he had, that big feeling that he was changing himself, feeling he was becoming one of the master's kind. Soon now he could forget all about the fields, that sun that leaves a man with a tongue growing clear up from his stomach, the weed-chopping that takes a man's arms clear off his body, the cotton-picking that makes your fingers want to break. The reward, all that money, it would be coming to him. He found the master, told him my grandfather was back there at the house, with the girl; it would be easy getting him—he could be surrounded like nothing. The reward, it would be his. . . .

The master didn't even talk to him, just looked at him like he wasn't there. He left him just standing there. He walked past him like he didn't exist.

This fellow's master, he was there too. He passed the fellow. 'You, git home,' he said. 'Git!' And he left him standing there like the other master had done. Not even looking at him.

They didn't waste any time. They had the whole country around there strung around like a rope. Where the bayous began, they got men to lay in cover. The whole land there, lying empty, like a freight yard without any trains. The quiet, it was almost shrill like, everyone so tense. Some people took to indoors; others got together, talking, laying bets, remembering stories they'd heard growing up or maybe that had happened a year ago, about a man being hunted, maybe escaping, maybe getting caught. Everyone had his own theory about what makes a Negro like that, making sure of their reasons for keeping him where he was. 'They haven't got enough with their own people,' they was saying. 'They want to come over to ours too.' And that something, it was something alien; they had no way of understanding; they didn't want to understand, anyway. It was a kind of assuring—assuring themselves *against* the black man, assuring for himself, or maybe *in*suring for himself.

That sort of conflict—you know, when you're not secure—like as a white man he'd feel inside himself, kept him from the Negro's music too. He didn't want it unless he could do it, too, do it better. But I don't want to get away from my story. There's so much books and speeches made about it, there's not much use talking about it all. I just play my music.

My grandfather, he was leaving the girl, holding her, telling her to wait out; God wouldn't just let them drop, as if they gave too much pain. 'You're mine,' he told her, 'and that makes it mine too, what I say. I can do anything I want in all the world when you're with me. And I'll get out of this. We'll have our time. . . .'

He left then, hunching himself over, running over the grounds. But the farther he got away from the plantation and got to where it started to be a little wilder, the more he felt like the weeds and grass somehow were trying to make a grab at him. And then he heard a shot, and he guessed what it was, there was an ambush for him, and he ran another way. He kept running and running and running: everyone after him, every way he went to go, getting cut off. He just had no way of getting safe, back into the bayous. Well, he kept on till he got to a clearing, right before the plantation of his friend. It was late and he was getting tired. Just an hour or two, some little rest he wanted, it was all—so he could figure something out. He crept up to his friend's cabin, went to him, shook him a little. And his friend there, he sprang up like, all quick; he hadn't been sleeping, but his eyes were closed; he was wondering what next move he was to take, lying there thinking, feeling positive about that reward, hearing the shot and thinking it was beginning then, they were after him, the reward would be coming.

'Who's that?' he said. My grandfather, he told him it was him—could he rest there a bit? . . . not much, just a little rest. The fellow, would he watch out for him? The whole country was after him; just give him an hour. . . .

So my grandfather, he couldn't help it, he started to sleep—not heavy like, but his eyes were closed, and he was forgetting some. And his friend there, lying on the cot, couldn't find anything to say to my grandfather, he was so shocked, having him appear like that. So he tried to lie quiet and let my grandfather sleep, remembering the master not saying anything to him when he'd told them where my grandfather was. It made him nervous, like he wasn't to be noticed; it kind of put him in a frenzy, how they weren't saying anything to him, like the only thing for him to do was get my grandfather himself—then they'd have to give him the reward.

My grandfather looked a hell of a lot different to his friend, lying there. There wasn't much to fear in him asleep, a one-armed man, wore out. He didn't have much to rejoice about now; he hadn't no right going with a girl that hadn't no approval, singing songs about it, getting everybody stirred up, everyone having to take a lot of misery just because of him and this girl.

And hearing that shot before, knowing it was shooting for my grandfather, it didn't make him so much alive somehow. As if that bullet was his death, and it had already been let loose, a thing that was already in the air. Somehow, even without hitting him, that shot had made a dead man of him. This friend sat there in the dark thinking, *He's dead . . . as good as dead . . . that shot already killed him.* Suddenly he heard himself saying it out loud and it frightened him. The whole night was frightening him.

He killed my grandfather. He killed him and he stood over him, looking at him. It hadn't even made a sound. He was still warm, even. There's not much to a man, the fellow thought; when he's through, there's not much to him.

He wiped up the blood and dragged and carried my grandfather out over the fields, sweat coming off him, to the master's house. He could hear lots of noise now. People were still out, hiding, waiting to catch my grandfather. Someone stopped him, and this friend told him he had my grandfather, they could all come in, he'd killed him. So the men that was around there, that one place, not too many, they started to follow; they couldn't believe it. They all come up to the master's place and this fellow took my grandfather off his shoulders and threw him on the ground. 'There he is. I got him. Where's the master? There's a reward to me who's got Omar.'

Well, the master came up. He'd left New Orleans by that time and the people he was talking to, trying to get everything together so my grandfather couldn't get away; and then when he came, having him dead right there that way, he didn't know what to do next . . . it was all so quick. A reward for a man, you know, at the time you set it up, it's all kind of far away. The reward and the man . . . then the man when he's dumped dead at your feet, nothing left to him, it's two different things.

His wife came up to him, angry; after what had happened, she wasn't able to stay outside of it any more. She wanted to know if he was going to tell them.

'Tell them,' she said, 'or I'll tell them myself.'

There had been too much night-waiting inside her. Marriage, duty—they'd gotten smaller inside the things she'd had to think about. She'd lived beyond herself and found a power inside herself; it had changed her.

'You tell them,' she said, 'now.'

And the master sensed it. He knew he couldn't command now. Somehow, even, he was wanting to say it himself, as if he had always meant to, as if saying it was part of what he'd been planning all along.

He stood there looking out at all those people, some with their guns still: a whole lot of faces circled around the dead man, and the girl lying by him calling to him. And back of them the slaves . . . that damn' singing . . . *how* they was singing . . . something he could never set foot on. The whole place around was so busy—all that shouting, all the lights on in the house, the yard so crowded. All these things were giving him a pressure.

So he explained how, when it had all happened, he'd called out, 'one of my girls'—this coloured girl, she had been like a daughter. He hadn't meant his own daughter, Eveline. Later, when all the confusion came, he'd been too scared and con fused, it had all gotten so he didn't know what to do; and he'd been so angry that Marie the coloured girl might have been hurt, he'd thought she *had* been raped. He hadn't known his wife had taken care of her . . . please try to understand him. It had been so dark in the bayou. He couldn't have seen who it was, just someone who needed some help. He'd left the girl as soon as he'd brought her to the house. He hadn't known.

He told it all, humbled himself as much as he could, said it all out of himself. And all the time he talked his eyes were on the girl, never looking up, staring hard at her as if every word he said was making her disappear, changing her into a mist and blowing her away. As if he were having done with her.

The people felt sick. They wanted to do something, but there was nothing they could. They just stood there—some arguing, some calling all kinds of things to the master, but by law, they couldn't get at him. Some didn't think it was too important, not enough to get people to taking sides, causing a lot of bad blood. So they cleared away finally. The man who was some kind of sheriff came back then; he asked questions, moved around a lot and kept people talking. But what was there to say?

And this fellow who'd killed my grandfather, he didn't get the reward. He was left there. They couldn't get him to leave, and finally they had to threaten him to make him clear out.

Some people who had got a love for Omar, they stayed wanting to fix up a funeral for him. They wanted to help out, a lot of them sorry, even before they knew that the girl hadn't been raped by Omar. But the master there told them no, he had to do it; he wanted to; it was the only way he had for making up for it some. It was a tragedy, he said; he wished it had never come around to him, no part of it. And so after a while there was only his wife and this girl. Everyone had left, and you could hear the mourning all the slaves were singing, trying to tell my grandfather to prepare a place for them, trying to give him some of their religion in case he'd got a need for it. They were singing, chanting again, beating themselves with their hands, beating on the ground, finding a way to let my grandfather go.

You know, things like that, they stay with you, more than if things happened natural like. In a way, it's what comes when people, they're living outside of themselves; maybe, living too much of everything at the same time, finding all kinds of laws instead of just the one there is.

My grandfather, he never tried to plan anything. Anything he did or tried happened because he couldn't help it, like he was trying to find things the same outside, as they were inside himself. And it wasn't weak things that happened. He just had a way of being happy or sad. He was like a piece of rhythm. Thinking about it, you see all kinds of things, ways to look at a life. Maybe in him things just hurried up to happen. Things what's dragged out a long time in most people, happened to him all in a little time.

And you know, he was a leader, he led the music. But still, as an idea, the way he played his horns, the way he beat on his drums, he was still a background music. It was still a music that hadn't broken loose, it hadn't stopped being scared. It was irresponsible in a way to all its worries.

It was an awful early beginning.

BIBLIOGRAPHY

WORKS IN THIS EDITION

Herbert Asbury, *The French Quarter: An Informal History of the New Orleans Under-world* (New York: Knopf, 1936), 237–253.

Sidney Bechet, *Treat It Gentle: An Autobiography* (New York: Hill and Wang, 1960), 6–44.

"Bras Coupe," *Ouachita Telegraph* (19 November 1880), 1.

George Washington Cable, "The Dance in Place Congo," *Century Magazine* 31 (1886): 517–532.

George Washington Cable, *The Grandissimes: A Story of Creole Life* (New York: Charles Scribner's Sons, 1880), 219–253.

Henry C. Castellanos, *New Orleans as It Was: Episodes of Louisiana Life* (New Orleans: L. Graham, 1895), 209–215.

"Death of Squier," *New Orleans Bee* (20 July 1837), 2.

Frederick Delius and Charles F. Keary, *Koanga, Opera in Three Acts,* rev. by Sir Thomas Beecham and Edward Agate (1897; rev. London: Boosey and Hawkes, 1935).

Louis-Armand Garreau, "Bras Coupé," trans. Sarah Jessica Johnson, *Transition* 117 (1856; trans. 2015): 23–39.

J. Andrew Gaulden, "Tiger of the Bayous," *Negro Digest* 5 (1946), 23–27.

Louis Moreau Gottschalk, *Notes of a Pianist,* ed. Clara Gottschalk (Philadelphia: J. B. Lippincott, 1881), 104–105.

Lafcadio Hearn, "The Original Bras-Coupe," *New Orleans Daily City Item* (27 October 1880), 2.

John Smith Kendall, *History of New Orleans* (Chicago: Lewis Publishing, 1922), 131–132.

Vernon Loggins, *Where the World Ends: The Life of Louis Moreau Gottschalk* (Baton Rouge: Louisiana State Univ. Press, 1958), 27–28.

"Squire—the Outlaw!" *New Orleans Picayune* (19 July 1837), 2.

Lyle Saxon, Edward Dreyer, and Robert Tallant, eds., *Gumbo Ya-Ya: A Collection of Louisiana Folk Tales* (Boston: Houghton Mifflin, 1945), 253–254.

Robert Penn Warren, *Band of Angels* (1955; reprint, Baton Rouge: Louisiana State Univ. Press, 1983), 102, 106–108, 118–120, 141–145, 154–157, 199–200.

SOURCES FOR MAPS

The maps were designed by Mary Lee Eggart. The Vieux Carré map is adapted from S. Pinistri's *New Orleans General Guide and Land Intelligence* (1841), and the map including the swamp is adapted from the inset sketch on Francis Ogden's *City of New Orleans* (1829). The locations on the maps are based on the sources listed below. For locations in the city, note that the house numbering system has changed twice since the 1830s, first in 1852 and again in 1894, when the city converted to the decimal system still in place today. Many street names in New Orleans have also changed. Several locations on the maps were identified with help from Richard Campanella.

Henry L. Abbot, *Approaches to New Orleans.* Color Line Block, 1863, Williams Research Center, Historic New Orleans Collection, New Orleans, Louisiana.

Charles André Boraud, *Les Origines, La Vie et Les Oeuvres de Louis-Armand Garreau, Publiciste, Romancier, et Pamphlétaire Angoumoisin-Saintongeais* (Saint-Hilaire de Barbezieux: Charles André Boraud, 1940), 30–32.

"Bras Coupe," *Ouachita Telegraph* (19 November 1880), 1.

H. A. Cohen and Bennet Dowler, *Cohen's New Orleans and Lafayette Directory* (New Orleans: Printed at the Office of the Picayune, 1855), 66.

"Council of the Third Municipality," *New Orleans Bee* (1 July 1836), 2.

"[The Cypress Swamp]," *New Orleans Bee* (6 June 1836), 2.

"Death of Gen. DeBuys," *New Orleans Picayune* (25 May 1856), 2.

"Death of Squier," *New Orleans Bee* (20 July 1837), 2.

Henry Didimus, "L. M. Gottschalk," *Graham's Magazine* 42 (1853): 61–69.

A Digest of the Ordinances, Resolutions, By-Laws and Regulations of the Corporation of New Orleans: And a Collection of the Laws of the Legislature Relative to the Said City (New Orleans: Gaston Brusle, 1836), 459–460.

Louis-Armand Garreau, "Bras Coupé," *Les Cinq Centimes Illustrés* 2 (29 March 1856), 122–126.

Louis-Armand Garreau, *Louisiana*, ed. D. A. Kress (Shreveport, La.: Éditions Tintamarre, 2003), 10–11.

Gibson's Guide and Directory of the State of Louisiana and the Cities of New Orleans and Lafayette (New Orleans: J. Gibson, 1838), 54, 58, 304–307, 355.

Dianne Guenin-Lelle, *The Story of French New Orleans: History of a Creole City* (Jackson: Univ. Press of Mississippi, 2016), 152.

Thomas Sydenham Hardee, *Topographical and Drainage Map of New Orleans and Surroundings*. Lithograph with Watercolor, ca. 1877, Williams Research Center, Historic New Orleans Collection, New Orleans, Louisiana.

Lafcadio Hearn, "The Original Bras-Coupe," *New Orleans Daily City Item* (27 October 1880), 2.

Laws for the Government of the District of Louisiana Passed by the Governor and Judges of the Indiana Territory (New Orleans: Jerome Bayon, 1835), 68–69.

"[The Negro Squier]," *New Orleans Bee* (7 April 1837), 2.

New-Orleans Annual and Commercial Directory for 1843, Containing the Names and Residences of All the Inhabitants of the City and Suburbs of New-Orleans (New Orleans: J. L. Sollée, 1842), 132.

New Orleans City Guard, Reports of the Captain of the Guard 1826–1836, 16–17 Août 1835, City Archives, Louisiana Division, New Orleans Public Library, New Orleans, Louisiana.

New Orleans City Guard, Reports of the Captain of the Guard 1826–1836, 21–22 Janvier 1836, City Archives, Louisiana Division, New Orleans Public Library, New Orleans, Louisiana.

The New Orleans Directory; Containing the Names, Professions and Residences of All the Heads of Families, and Persons in Business, of the City and Suburbs, with Other Useful Information (New Orleans: Stephen E. Percy, 1832), 54.

"New Orleans—Drainage and Sewerage: Uprising of the People for Sanitary Improvement and Financial Success," *Sanitarian* 359 (1899): 300–301.

The New-Orleans Guide; or, General Directory for 1837, Embracing the Three Municipalities, and Containing the Names, Professions and Residences of All the Heads of Families and Persons in Business, Together with Other Useful Information (New Orleans: Gaux and Meynier, 1837), 15.

Francis B. Ogden, *City of New Orleans*. Engraving, 1829, Williams Research Center, Historic New Orleans Collection, New Orleans, Louisiana.

Ordinances and Resolutions, Third Municipality, vol. 1, Seance du 29 Juin 1836, City Archives, Louisiana Division, New Orleans Public Library, New Orleans, Louisiana.

S. Pinistri, *New Orleans General Guide and Land Intelligence*. Hand-colored engraving, 1841, Williams Research Center, Historic New Orleans Collection, New Orleans, Louisiana.

Von Reizenstein, *Diagram Showing the Inundated District: Sauve's Crevasse May 3rd, 1849*, lithograph, 1900, Williams Research Center, Historic New Orleans Collection, New Orleans, Louisiana.

"[Robberies are Still Committed]," *New Orleans Picayune* (25 January 1837), 2.

"Runaway Negroes in the Cypress Swamp," *Liberator* (2 July 1836), 107.

Soards' New Orleans City Directory (New Orleans: Soards Company, 1875), 141.

"Squire—the Outlaw!" *New Orleans Picayune* (19 July 1837), 2.

"[Squire and James Outlawed]," *New Orleans Bee* (30 June 1836), 2.

S. Frederick Starr, *Bamboula!: The Life and Times of Louis Moreau Gottschalk* (New York: Oxford Univ. Press, 1995), 24.

Roulhac Toledano and Mary Louise Christovich. *New Orleans Architecture*, vol. 6, *Faubourg Tremé and the Bayou Road: North Rampart Street to North Broad Street, Canal Street to St. Bernard Avenue* (Gretna, La.: Pelican, 1980), 63–66.

Robert Penn Warren, *Band of Angels* (1955; reprint, Baton Rouge: Louisiana State Univ. Press, 1983), 304–307.

Charles F. Zimpel, T*opographical Map of New Orleans and Its Vicinity*. Hand-colored engraving, ca. 1833, Williams Research Center, Historic New Orleans Collection, New Orleans, Louisiana.

ARCHIVES AND MANUSCRIPT COLLECTIONS

The following collections were consulted during the research for this critical edition. Documents in facsimile appear courtesy of the New Orleans Public Library.

Jason Berry Papers, Amistad Research Center, Tulane University, New Orleans, Louisiana.

George W. Cable Collection, Manuscripts Department, Special Collections, Howard Tilton Memorial Library, Tulane University, New Orleans, Louisiana.

Marcus Christian Papers, Archives and Manuscripts Division, Earl K. Long Library, University of New Orleans, New Orleans, Louisiana.

Conseil de Ville, Official Proceedings 1803–1836, Records of the City Councils, City Archives, Louisiana Division, New Orleans Public Library, New Orleans, Louisiana.

Financial Records of the Municipality 1836–1852, Third Municipality Treasurer's Office, Records of Financial Administration, City Archives, Louisiana Division, New Orleans Public Library, New Orleans, Louisiana.

Henry Kmen Papers, Hogan Jazz Archive, Howard Tilton Memorial Library, Tulane University, New Orleans, Louisiana.

Letter Books 1811–1920, Records of the Office of the Mayor, City Archives, Louisiana Division, New Orleans Public Library, New Orleans, Louisiana.

Louisiana Image Collection, Louisiana Research Collection, Howard-Tilton Memorial Library, Tulane University, New Orleans, Louisiana.

Louisiana and Lower Mississippi Valley Collections, Hill Memorial Library, Louisiana State University, Baton Rouge, Louisiana.

Messages to the Council 1836–1852, Records of the Mayor's Office, City Archives, Louisiana Division, New Orleans Public Library, New Orleans, Louisiana.

Notarial Archives of the Office of the Clerk of Civil District Court for Orleans Parish, New Orleans, Louisiana.

Official Proceedings 1836–1852, Third Municipality Council, Records of the City Councils, City Archives, Louisiana Division, New Orleans Public Library, New Orleans, Louisiana.

Ordinances and Resolutions 1836–1852, Third Municipality Council, Records of the City Councils, City Archives, Louisiana Division, New Orleans Public Library, New Orleans, Louisiana.

Reports of the Captain of the Guard 1826–1836, Records of the Police Departments, City Archives, Louisiana Division, New Orleans Public Library, New Orleans, Louisiana.

Sainte-Gême Papers, Williams Research Center, Historic New Orleans Collection, New Orleans, Louisiana.

Slave Manifests of Vessels at New Orleans, Louisiana, 1807–1860, Records of the US Customs Service, National Archives and Records Administration, Washington, D.C.

PUBLISHED WORKS

Aaron, *The Light and Truth of Slavery: Aaron's History* (Worcester, Mass.: Published by the Author, 1845).

"Abolition Papers," *New Orleans Picayune* (28 September 1837), 2.

Roger D. Abrahams, "Phantoms of Romantic Nationalism in Folkloristics," *Journal of American Folklore* 106 (1993): 3–37.

William Francis Allen, Charles Pickard Ware, and Lucy Mckim Garrison, *Slave Songs of the United States* (Chapel Hill, N.C.: Courier Corporation, 1867).

American Anti-Slavery Society, *American Anti-Slavery Almanac, for 1839* (New York: S. W. Benedict, 1839).

"Anti-Slavery," *Liberator* (31 May 1839), 1.

Herbert Aptheker, "Maroons within the Present Limits of the United States," *Journal of Negro History* 24 (1939): 167–184.

Louis Armstrong, *Satchmo: My Life in New Orleans* (New York: Prentice Hall, 1954).

Herbert Asbury, *The French Quarter: An Informal History of the New Orleans Underworld* (New York: Knopf, 1936).

Francis Baily, *Journal of a Tour in Unsettled Parts of North America* (Carbondale: Southern Illinois Univ. Press, 1969).

Whitney Balliett, *Jelly Roll, Jabbo, and Fats* (New York: Oxford Univ. Press, 1983).

Amiri Baraka [Leroi Jones], *Blues People: Negro Music in White America* (New York: William Morrow, 1963).

Sidney Bechet, *Treat It Gentle: An Autobiography* (New York: Hill and Wang, 1960).

Aphra Behn, *The History of Oroonoko: or, The Royal Slave,* 9th ed. (Doncaster, UK: C. Plummer, 1770).

Gonzalo Aguirre Beltrán and Deward E. Walker, *Regions of Refuge* (Washington, D.C.: Society for Applied Anthropology, 1979).

Jason Berry, "African Cultural Memory in New Orleans Music," *Black Music Research Journal* 8 (1988): 3–12.

———, "Jazz Literature: Through a Rhythm Joyously," *Village Voice* (8 May 1978), 61–82.

Mark Frederick Bigney, *Poetical History of Louisiana, to Which Is Attached Columbia, a Centennial Poem, Respectfully Dedicated to Exposition Visitors* (New Orleans: E. A. Brandao, 1885).

Rudi Blesh, *Combo U.S.A.: Eight Lives in Jazz* (Philadelphia: Chilton Book Company, 1971).

———, *Shining Trumpets: A History of Jazz* (New York: Knopf, 1946).

Charles André Boraud, *Les Origines, La Vie et Les Oeuvres de Louis-Armand Garreau, Publiciste, Romancier, et Pamphlétaire Angoumoisin-Saintongeais* (Saint-Hilaire de Barbezieux: Charles André Boraud, 1940).

Benjamin Albert Botkin, ed., *A Treasury of Southern Folklore: Stories, Ballads, Traditions, and Folkways of the People of the South* (New York: Crown Publishers, 1949).

Frances Botkin, *Thieving Three-Fingered Jack: Transatlantic Tales of a Jamaican Outlaw* (New Brunswick, N.J.: Rutgers Univ. Press, 2017).

"Bras Coupe," *Ouachita Telegraph* (19 November 1880), 1.

Van Wyck Brooks, *The Times of Melville and Whitman* (Boston: Dutton, 1947).

Catharine Savage Brosman, *Louisiana Creole Literature: A Historical Study* (Jackson: Univ. Press of Mississippi, 2013).

William Cullen Bryant, *Poems* (New York: Harper and Brothers, 1836).

George Washington Cable, "After-Thoughts of a Story-Teller," *North American Review* 158 (1894): 16–23.

———, "The Convict Lease System in the Southern States," *Century Magazine* 27 (1884): 582–599.

———, "Creole Slave Songs," *Century Magazine* 23 (1886), 807–828.

———, "The Dance in Place Congo," *Century Magazine* 31 (1886): 517–532.

———, "The Freedman's Case in Equity," *Century Magazine* 29 (1885): 409–418.

———, *The Grandissimes: A Story of Creole Life* (New York: Charles Scribner's Sons, 1880).

———, "New Orleans," *St. Nicholas* 21 (1893), 40–49, 150–154.

———, "The Silent South," *Century Magazine* 30 (1885): 674–691.

———, "The Story of Bras-Coupé," in *The Cable Story Book: Selections for Reading,* eds. Mary Elizabeth Burt and Lucy Leffingwell Cable Biklé (New York: Charles Scribner's Sons, 1906), 26–65.

Richard Campanella, *Bienville's Dilemma: A Historical Geography of New Orleans* (Lafayette: Center for Louisiana Studies, University of Louisiana at Lafayette, 2008).

———, *Geographies of New Orleans: Urban Fabrics before the Storm* (New Orleans: Univ. of New Orleans Press, 2006).

Hodding Carter, *Lower Mississippi* (New York: Farrar and Rinehart, 1942).

[Henry C. Castellanos], "The Black Terror of the Bayous: A Runaway Slave Whose Death Made a Holiday in New Orleans," *Cleveland Plain Dealer* (2 July 1893), 10.

———, *New Orleans as It Was: Episodes of Louisiana Life* (New Orleans: L. Graham, 1895).

Ruby Van Allen Caulfeild, *The French Literature of Louisiana* (New York: Institute of French Studies, Columbia Univ. Press, 1929).

A. B. Chambers, ed., *Trials and Confessions of Madison Henderson, alias Blanchard, Alfred Amos Warrick, James W. Seward, and Charles Brown, Murderers of Jesse Baker and Jacob Weaver: As Given by Themselves* (St. Louis: Chambers Knapp, 1841).

Gilbert Chase, *America's Music: From the Pilgrims to the Present* (New York: McGraw-Hill, 1955).

Charles W. Chesnutt, "The Negro in Art: How Shall He Be Portrayed?" *Crisis* 31 (1926): 28–29.

John Chilton, *Sidney Bechet: The Wizard of Jazz* (New York: Oxford Univ. Press, 1987).

Marcus Bruce Christian, *I Am New Orleans: A Poem Published in Commemoration of the 250th Anniversary Celebration of the Founding of the Crescent City, 1718–1968* (New Orleans: Published by the Author, 1968).

John Ciardi, "Writing *Treat It Gentle,*" in *John Ciardi: Measure of the Man,* ed. Vince Clemente (Fayetteville: Univ. of Arkansas Press, 1987), 82–83.

Edward M. Cifelli, *John Ciardi: A Biography* (Fayetteville: Univ. of Arkansas Press, 1997).

"City Council," *New Orleans Argus* (18 March 1828), 2.

"[The City Guard]," *New Orleans Bee* (25 January 1836), 2.

"[The City Guard]," *New Orleans Mercantile Advertiser* (17 February 1834), 2.

"[The City Guard at Natchez]," *New Orleans Picayune* (16 June 1838), 2.

"The City Police," *New Orleans Picayune* (19 October 1837), 2.

Pierre Clastres, *Society against the State: Essays in Political Anthropology* (New York: Zone Books, 1987).

Le Code Noir ou Edit du Roy (Paris: Claude Girard, 1735).

H. A. Cohen and Bennet Dowler, *Cohen's New Orleans and Lafayette Directory* (New Orleans: Printed at the Office of the Picayune, 1855).

William Head Coleman, *The Historical Sketch-Book and Guide to New Orleans and Environs* (New York: W. H. Coleman, 1885).

"Communications," *Liberator* (28 April 1837), 4.

"The Congo Dance—A Glimpse of the Old Square of a Sunday Afternoon Sixty Years Ago," *New Orleans Picayune* (12 October 1879), 2.

"Council of the Third Municipality," *New Orleans Bee* (1 July 1836), 2.

James R. Creecy, *Scenes in the South and Other Miscellaneous Pieces* (Washington, D.C.: T. McGill, 1860).

Creole Tourist's Guide and Sketch Book to the City of New Orleans (New Orleans: Creole Publishing Company, 1910).

Liliane Crété, *La Vie Quotidienne en Louisiane, 1815–1830* (Paris: Hachette Litterature, 1978).

Robert M. Crunden, *Body and Soul: The Making of American Modernism* (New York: Basic Books, 2000).

Fortescue Cumming, *Sketches of a Tour to the Western Country* (Pittsburgh, Pa.: Cramer, Speer, and Eichbaum, 1810).

"[The Cypress Swamp]," *New Orleans Bee* (6 June 1836), 2.

Robert J. Damm, "Remembering Bamboula," *Percussive Notes* 53 (2015): 20–24.

"Dancing under Difficulty," *New Orleans Weekly Picayune* (15 July 1844), 2.

Shannon Lee Dawdy, *Building the Devil's Empire: French Colonial New Orleans* (Chicago: Univ. of Chicago Press, 2008).

Colin [Joan] Dayan, *Haiti, History, and the Gods* (Berkeley: Univ. of California Press, 1995).

"Death of a Brigand," *Boston Courier* (31 July 1837), 2.

"Death of Gen. DeBuys," *New Orleans Picayune* (25 May 1856), 2.

"Death of Squier," *New Orleans Bee* (20 July 1837), 2.

"Delightful Property Situated on Grand Isle," *New Orleans Picayune* (22 May 1857), 4.

Frederick Delius and Charles F. Keary, *Koanga, Opera in Three Acts,* rev. Sir Thomas Beecham and Edward Agate (1897; rev. London: Boosey and Hawkes, 1935).

Tom Dent, "Secret Messages," in *Magnolia Street* (New Orleans: Published by the Author, 1976), 61.

Nathalie Dessens, *Creole City: A Chronicle of Early American New Orleans* (Gainesville: Univ. of Florida Press, 2015).

Jeroen Dewulf, *From the Kingdom of Kongo to Congo Square: Kongo Dances and the Origins of the Mardi Gras Indians* (Lafayette: Center for Louisiana Studies, University of Louisiana at Lafayette, 2017).

Henry Didimus, "L. M. Gottschalk," *Graham's Magazine* 42 (1853): 61–69.

———, *New Orleans As I Found It* (New York: Harper Brothers, 1845).

A Digest of Ordinances, Resolutions, By-Laws and Regulations of the Corporation of New-Orleans, and a Collection of the Laws of the Legislature Relative to the Said City (New Orleans: Gaston Brusle, 1836).

Gilbert C. Din, "'Cimarrones' and the San Malo Band in Spanish Louisiana," *Louisiana History* 21 (1980): 237–262.

Gilbert C. Din, *Spaniards, Planters, and Slaves: The Spanish Regulation of Slavery in Louisiana* (College Station: Texas A&M Univ. Press, 1999).

Sylviane A. Diouf, *Slavery's Exiles: The Story of the American Maroons* (New York: New York Univ. Press, 2014).

Gary A. Donaldson, "A Window on Slave Culture: Dances at Congo Square in New Orleans, 1800–1862," *Journal of Negro History* 69 (1984): 63–72.

James H. Dormon, "The Persistent Specter: Slave Rebellion in Territorial Louisiana," *Louisiana History* 18 (1977): 389–404.

Laurent Dubois, *Avengers of the New World* (Cambridge, Mass.: Harvard Univ. Press, 2005).

Berquin Duvallon, *Travels in Louisiana and the Floridas in the Year 1802, Giving a Correct Picture of Those Countries,* trans. John Davis (New York: I. Riley, 1806).

William Earle, *Obi: or, The History of Three-Fingered Jack,* ed. Srinivas Aravamudan (Peterborough, Ontario: Broadview Press, 2005).

T. S. Eliot, "Hamlet and His Problems," in *The Sacred Wood: Essays on Poetry and Criticism* (New York: Knopf, 1921), 87–94.

Lynne Fauley Emery, *Black Dance in the United States from 1619 to 1970* (Palo Alto, Calif.: National Press Books, 1972).

David C. Estes, "Traditional Dances and Processions of Blacks in New Orleans as Witnessed by Antebellum Travelers," *Louisiana Folklore Miscellany* 6 (1990): 1–14.

Freddi Williams Evans, *Congo Square: African Roots in New Orleans* (Lafayette: Center for Louisiana Studies, Univ. of Louisiana at Lafayette Press, 2011).

Federal Writers' Project, *New Orleans City Guide* (Boston: Houghton Mifflin, 1938).

John Ferriar, *The Prince of Angola* (Manchester, UK: J. Harrop, 1788).

Rien Fertel, *Imagining the Creole City: The Rise of Literary Culture in Nineteenth-Century New Orleans* (Baton Rouge: Louisiana State Univ. Press, 2014).

Samuel A. Floyd Jr., *The Power of Black Music: Interpreting Its History from Africa to the United States* (New York: Oxford Univ. Press, 1995).

Johan Gottfried Flügel, "Pages from a Journal of a Voyage down the Mississippi to New Orleans in 1817," ed. Felix Flügel, *Louisiana Historical Quarterly* 7 (1924): 414–440.

Jeff Forret, "Before Angola: Enslaved Prisoners in the Louisiana State Penitentiary," *Louisiana History* 54 (2013): 133–171.

Albert E. Fossier, *New Orleans: The Glamour Period, 1800–1840* (Gretna, La.: Pelican, 1998).

John Hope Franklin and Loren Schweninger, *Runaway Slaves: Rebels on the Plantation* (New York: Oxford Univ. Press, 1999).

"Further Excitement in N. Orleans," *Portland Daily Evening Advertiser* (24 September 1835), 2.

Louis-Armand Garreau, "Bras Coupé," *Les Cinq Centimes Illustrés* 2 (29 March 1856): 122–126.

——, "Bras Coupé," trans. Sarah Jessica Johnson, *Transition* 117 (2015): 23–39.

——, "Bras Coupé," *Bras Coupé et Autres Récits Louisianais*, ed. Fabrice Leroy (Shreveport, La.: Centenary College of Louisiana, 2012).

——, *Louisiana*, ed. D. A. Kress (Shreveport, La.: Éditions Tintamarre, 2003).

——, "Un Nègre Marron," *Les Cinq Centimes Illustrés* 2 (2 Février 1856): 57–58.

J. Andrew Gaulden, "Tiger of the Bayous," *Negro Digest* 5 (1946): 23–27.

"General William De Buys," *Baltimore Sun* (31 May 1856), 2.

Gérard Genette, *Narrative Discourse: An Essay in Method*, trans. Jane E. Lewin (Ithaca, N.Y.: Cornell Univ. Press, 1980).

Eugene D. Genovese, *From Rebellion to Revolution: Afro-American Slave Revolts in the Making of the Modern World* (Baton Rouge: Louisiana State Univ. Press, 1979).

Gibson's Guide and Directory of the State of Louisiana and the Cities of New Orleans and Lafayette (New Orleans: J. Gibson, 1838).

Henry F. Gilbert, *The Dance in Place Congo; Symphonic Poem, after George W. Cable* (New York, H. W. Gray Company, 1922).

Ted Gioia, *The History of Jazz* (New York: Oxford Univ. Press, 1997).

Robert Goffin, *Jazz: From the Congo to the Metropolitan*, trans. Walter Schaap and Leonard Feather (Garden City, N.Y.: Doubleday, 1944).

Weston Arthur Goodspeed, *The Province and the States: A History of the Province of Louisiana under France and Spain* (Madison, Wisc.: Western Historical Association, 1904).

Karla Gottlieb, *The Mother of Us All: A History of Queen Nanny* (New York: Africa World Press, 2000).

Louis Moreau Gottschalk, *Bamboula: Danse des Nègres: Fantaisie pour Piano, Op. 2* (Paris: Au Bureau Central de Musique, 1849).

——, *Notes of a Pianist*, ed. Clara Gottschalk (Philadelphia: J. B. Lippincott, 1881).

Aram Goudsouzian, *Sidney Poitier: Man, Actor, Icon* (Chapel Hill: Univ. of North Carolina Press, 2004).

Farah Jasmine Griffin, "Children of Omar: Resistance and Resilience in the Expressive Cultures of Black New Orleans," *Journal of Urban History* 35 (2009): 656–667.

Dianne Guenin-Lelle, *The Story of French New Orleans: History of a Creole City* (Jackson: Univ. Press of Mississippi, 2016).

William Ivy Hair, *Carnival of Fury: Robert Charles and the New Orleans Race Riot of 1900* (Baton Rouge: Louisiana State Univ. Press, 1976).

Gwendolyn Midlo Hall, *Africans in Colonial Louisiana: The Development of Afro-*

Creole Culture in the Eighteenth Century (Baton Rouge: Louisiana State Univ. Press, 1992).

Kimberly S. Hanger, *Bounded Lives, Bounded Places: Free Black Society in Colonial New Orleans, 1769–1803* (Durham, N.C.: Duke Univ. Press, 1997).

M. A. Harris, Morris Levitt, Toni Morrison, Roger Furman, and Ernest Smith, *The Black Book* (New York: Random House, 1974).

Corinne Hay, *Light and Shade 'Round Gulf and Bayou* (Boston: Roxburgh, 1921).

Lafcadio Hearn, *Children of the Levee* (Lexington: Univ. of Kentucky Press, 1957).

——, "The Original Bras-Coupe," *New Orleans Daily City Item* (27 October 1880), 2.

——, "The Scenes of Cable's Romances," *Century Magazine* 27 (1883): 40–47.

Melville J. Herskovits, *The Myth of the Negro Past* (New York: Harper and Brothers, 1941).

Gad Heuman, ed., *Out of the House of Bondage: Runaways, Resistance and Marronage in Africa and the New World* (London: Frank Cass, 1986).

Jared Hickman, *Black Prometheus: Race and Radicalism in the Age of Atlantic Slavery* (New York: Oxford Univ. Press, 2016).

Arnold R. Hirsch and Joseph Logsdon, eds., *Creole New Orleans: Race and Americanization.* (Baton Rouge: Louisiana State Univ. Press, 1992).

James G. Hollandsworth Jr., *An Absolute Massacre: The New Orleans Race Riot of July 30, 1866* (Baton Rouge: Louisiana State Univ. Press, 2004).

Wim S. M. Hoogbergen, *The Boni Maroon Wars in Suriname* (New York: Brill, 1990).

Raymond Horricks, *Profiles in Jazz: From Sidney Bechet to John Coltrane* (New Brunswick, N.J.: Transaction Publishers, 1991).

"Important," *New Orleans Picayune* (28 August 1837), 2.

Thomas N. Ingersoll, *Mammon and Manon: The First Slave Society in the Deep South, 1718–1819* (Knoxville: Univ. of Tennessee Press, 1999).

Charles Tenney Jackson, *Captain Sazarac* (Indianapolis, Ind.: Bobbs-Merrill, 1922).

"Jackson Square Was the Old City's Heart," *New Orleans Picayune* (20 September 1897), 3.

C. L. R. James, *The Black Jacobins: Toussaint L'Ouverture and the San Domingo Revolution* (1938; revised ed., New York: Vintage Books, 1963).

Jerah Johnson, "New Orleans's Congo Square: An Urban Setting for Early Afro-American Culture Formation," *Louisiana History* 32 (1991): 117–157.

Rashauna Johnson, *Slavery's Metropolis: Unfree Labor in New Orleans during the Age of Revolutions* (Cambridge: Cambridge Univ. Press, 2016).

Walter Johnson, *Soul by Soul: Life Inside the Antebellum Slave Market* (Cambridge, Mass.: Harvard Univ. Press, 1999).

Georges Joyaux, ed., "Forest's Voyage aux États-Unis de l'Amérique en 1831," *Louisiana Historical Quarterly* 39 (1956): 457–472.

John Smith Kendall, *History of New Orleans* (Chicago: Lewis Publishing, 1922).

Grace Elizabeth King, *Creole Families of New Orleans* (New York: Macmillan, 1921).

——, *New Orleans: The Place and the People* (New York: Macmillan, 1895).

Samuel Kinser, *Carnival, American Style: Mardi Gras at New Orleans and Mobile* (Chicago: Univ. of Chicago Press, 1990).

Henry A. Kmen, *Music in New Orleans: The Formative Years 1791–1841* (Baton Rouge: Louisiana State Univ. Press, 1966).

——, "The Roots of Jazz in Place Congo: A Re-Appraisal," *Inter-American Musical Research Yearbook* 8 (1972): 5–17.

Felix A. Koch, *A Little Journey through the Great Southwest* (Chicago: A. Flanagan Company, 1907).

Henry Edward Krehbiel, *Afro-American Folksongs: A Study in Racial and National Music* (New York: G. Schirmer, 1914).

Barbara Ladd, "'An Atmosphere of Hints and Allusions': Bras-Coupé and the Context of Black Insurrection in *The Grandissimes*," *Southern Quarterly* 29 (1991): 63–76.

——, *Nationalism and the Color Line in George W. Cable, Mark Twain, and William Faulkner* (Baton Rouge: Louisiana State Univ. Press, 1997).

"[The Late Excitement at New Orleans]," *Baltimore American* (29 September 1835), 2.

Pierre C. de Laussat, *Mémoire Sur Ma Vie Pendant les Années 1803 et Suivantes à la Louisianne* (Pau, France: E. Vignancour, 1831).

Laws for the Government of the District of Louisiana Passed by the Governor and Judges of the Indiana Territory, 1804 (New Orleans: Jerome Bayon, 1835).

Mel Leavitt, *Great Characters of New Orleans* (San Francisco: Lexikos, 1984).

"Lecture IV," *Friend of Man* 3 (10 April 1839), 1.

Jessica M. Lepler, *The Many Panics of 1837: People, Politics, and the Creation of a Transatlantic Financial Crisis* (Cambridge: Cambridge Univ. Press, 2013).

Lawrence W. Levine, *Black Culture and Black Consciousness* (New York: Oxford Univ. Press, 1977).

James Lewicki, *The Life Treasury of American Folklore* (New York: Time Life, 1961).

George E. Lewis, "Singing Omar's Song: A (Re)construction of Great Black Music," *Lenox Avenue* 4 (1998): 69–92.

Pierce F. Lewis, *New Orleans: The Making of an Urban Landscape*, 2nd ed. (Charlottesville: Univ. of Virginia Press, 2003).

Grace Lichtenstein and Laura Dankner, *Musical Gumbo: The Music of New Orleans* (New York: Norton, 1993).

Vernon Loggins, *Where the World Ends: The Life of Louis Moreau Gottschalk* (Baton Rouge: Louisiana State Univ. Press, 1958).

Alan Lomax, *Mister Jelly Roll: The Fortunes of Jelly Roll Morton, New Orleans Creole and "Inventor of Jazz"* (New York: Duell, Sloan, and Pearce, 1950).

Henry Wadsworth Longfellow, *Poems on Slavery* (Cambridge, Mass.: John Owen, 1842).

"Look Out for Villains," *New Orleans Picayune* (9 February 1837), 2.

"Louisiana Outings: Rambles About Home," *New Orleans Picayune* (16 December 1888), 10.

Anna Maria Mackenzie, *Slavery, or the Times* (London: G. G. J. Robinson, 1792).

Henry Mackenzie, *Julia de Roubigné* (Dublin: J. Byrn and Son, 1777).

Nathaniel Mackey, *Bedouin Hornbook* (1986; reprint, Los Angeles, Sun and Moon Press, 1997).

Ted Maris-Wolf, "Hidden in Plain Sight: Maroon Life and Labor in Virginia's Dismal Swamp," *Slavery and Abolition* 34 (2013): 446–464.

Donald M. Marquis, *In Search of Buddy Bolden: First Man of Jazz* (Baton Rouge: Louisiana State Univ. Press, 2005).

Herman Melville, "Benito Cereno," *Putnam's Monthly* 6 (1855), 353–367, 459–473, 633–644.

"[Messrs. Editors]," *New Orleans Picayune* (15 February 1837), 2.

Mezz Mezzrow, *Really the Blues* (New York: Random House, 1946).

Médéric Louis Élie Moreau de Saint-Méry, *De La Danse* (Parme: Giambattista Bodoni, 1803).

——, *Description Topographique, Physique, Civile, Politique et Historique de la Partie Française de L'isle Saint-Domingue,* eds. Blanche Maurel and Étienne Taillemite (1797–1798; reprint, Paris: Société d'histoire des colonies françaises, 1958).

Leonard N. Moore, *Black Rage in New Orleans: Police Brutality and African American Activism from World War II to Hurricane Katrina* (Baton Rouge: Louisiana State Univ. Press, 2010).

"Mort du Nègre Squire," *New Orleans Bee* (20 July 1837), 3.

"Municipal Election," *True American* (1 April 1837), 2.

Jay Robert Nash, *The Great Pictorial History of World Crime* (Lanham, Md.: Scarecrow Press, 2004).

——, "The Legend of a One-Armed Murderer," in *The Almanac of World Crime* (New York: Bonanza Books, 1986).

"Necessity of Enforcing the Ordinances," *New Orleans Bee* (9 October 1839), 2.

"Negro Audacity," *New Orleans Picayune* (19 November 1840), 2.

"[The Negro Outlaw, Recently Killed in the Swamp Back of New Orleans]," *Wisconsin Territorial Gazette* (17 August 1837), 2.

"[The Negro Squier]," *New Orleans Bee* (7 April 1837), 2.

"[Negro Squire]," *Jacksonville Republican* (31 August 1837), 2.

"[Negroes in the Cypress Swamp]," *Liberator* (2 July 1836), 107.

R. Nettel, "Historical Introduction to 'La Calinda,'" *Music and Letters* 27 (1946): 59–62.

[Peter Newby], *The Wrongs of Almoona, or The African's Revenge* (Liverpool: H. Hodgson, 1788).

"New Orleans," *Baltimore Gazette* (19 September 1835), 2.

"New Orleans," *Eastern Shore Whig and People's Advocate* (26 September 1835), 2.

"New Orleans," *New York Evening Post* (4 December 1827), 2.

New-Orleans Annual and Commercial Directory for 1843, Containing the Names and Residences of All the Inhabitants of the City and Suburbs of New-Orleans (New Orleans: J. L. Sollée, 1842).

New Orleans Annual and Commercial Register of 1846: Containing the Names, Residences and Professions of All the Heads of Families and Persons in Business (New Orleans: E. A. Michel, 1845).

New Orleans as It Is: Manners and Customs, Morals, Fashionable Life, Profanation of the Sabbath, Prostitution, Licentiousness, Slave Markets and Slavery (Utica, N.Y.: DeWitt C. Grove, 1849).

The New Orleans Directory; Containing the Names, Professions and Residences of All the Heads of Families, and Persons in Business, of the City and Suburbs, with Other Useful Information (New Orleans: Stephen E. Percy, 1832).

New-Orleans Directory for 1842: Comprising the Names, Residences and Occupations of the Merchants, Business Men, Professional Gentlemen and Citizens (New Orleans: Pitts and Clarke, 1842).

The New-Orleans Guide; or, General Directory for 1837, Embracing the Three Municipalities, and Containing the Names, Professions and Residences of All the Heads of Families and Persons in Business, Together with Other Useful Information (New Orleans: Gaux and Meynier, 1837).

"Our City," *Louisiana Advertiser* (14 February 1834), 2.

"Our City," *New Orleans Bee* (15 February 1834), 2.

"Our City," *Louisiana Advertiser* (17 February 1834), 2.

"Our City," *Louisiana Advertiser* (18 February 1834), 2.

Robert L. Paquette, "'A Horde of Brigands?' The Great Louisiana Slave Revolt of 1811 Reconsidered," *Historical Reflections/Reflexions Historiques* 35 (2009): 72–96.

Stephen E. Percy and Edward Auguste Michel, *The New Orleans Directory; Containing the Names, Professions and Residences of All the Heads of Families, and Persons in Business, of the City and Suburbs* (New Orleans: Stephen E. Percy, 1832).

Clara Gottschalk Peterson, *Creole Songs from New Orleans in the Negro Dialect* (New Orleans: L. Gruenwald Company, 1902).

The Picayune's Guide to New Orleans (New Orleans: Picayune, 1900).

James Pitot, *Observations on the Colony of Louisiana, from 1796 to 1802* (Baton Rouge: Louisiana State Univ. Press, 1979).

"Police de La Ville," *New Orleans Bee* (21 July 1835), 2.

Lawrence N. Powell, *The Accidental City: Improvising New Orleans* (Cambridge, Mass.: Harvard Univ. Press, 2012).

———, ed., *The New Orleans of George Washington Cable: The 1887 Census Office Report* (Baton Rouge: Louisiana State Univ. Press, 2008).

Richard Price, ed., *Maroon Societies: Rebel Slave Communities in the Americas* (Garden City, N.Y.: Anchor Press, 1973).

Sally Price and Richard Price, *Maroon Arts: Cultural Vitality in the African Diaspora* (Boston: Beacon Press, 1999).

K. Stephen Prince, "Remembering Robert Charles: Violence and Memory in Jim Crow New Orleans," *Journal of Southern History* 83 (2017): 297–328.

Boyd Bruce Raeburn, *New Orleans Style and the Writing of American Jazz History* (Ann Arbor: Univ. of Michigan Press, 2009).

Aishah Rahman, *Anybody Seen Marie Laveau?* (1989; reprint, Alexandria, Va.: Alexander Street Press, 2002).

Frederic Ramsey Jr. and Charles E. Smith, eds., *Jazzmen* (New York: Harcourt Brace, 1939).

William Randel, "'Koanga' and Its Libretto," *Music and Letters* 52 (1971): 141–156.

Daniel Rasmussen, *American Uprising: The Untold Story of America's Largest Slave Revolt* (New York: Harper Collins, 2011).

"[Robberies Are Still Committed]," *New Orleans Picayune* (25 January 1837), 2.

John W. Roberts, *From Trickster to Badman: The Black Folk Hero from Slavery to Freedom* (Philadelphia: Univ. of Pennsylvania Press, 1989).

Neil Roberts, *Freedom as Marronage* (Chicago: Univ. of Chicago Press, 2015).

Junius P. Rodriguez, "Always 'En Garde': The Effects of Slave Insurrection upon the Louisiana Mentality, 1811–1815," *Louisiana History* 33 (1992): 399–416.

Russell Roth, "On the Instrumental Origins of Jazz," *American Quarterly* 4 (1952): 305–316.

Dennis C. Rousey, *Policing the Southern City: New Orleans, 1805–1889* (Baton Rouge: Louisiana State Univ. Press, 1996).

The Royal African: or, Memoirs of the Young Prince of Annamaboe (London: W. Reeve, G. Woodfall, and J. Barnes, 1749).

Louis D. Rubin Jr., *George W. Cable: The Life and Times of a Southern Heretic* (New York: Pegasus, 1969).

"[Runaway Negro]," *New Orleans Bee* (26 March 1830), 2.

"Runaway Negroes in the Cypress Swamp," *Liberator* (2 July 1836), 107.

Mary Ryan, *Civic Wars: Democracy and Public Life in the American City during the Nineteenth Century* (Berkeley: Univ. of California Press, 1998).

Matt Sakakeeny, "New Orleans Music as a Circulatory System," *Black Music Research Journal* 31 (2011): 291–325.

Kalamu ya Salaam, "Bras Coupe," in *The Collected Stories of Kalamu ya Salaam* (2004; reprint, Alexandria, Va.: Alexander Street Press, 2005), 19–52.

Lyle Saxon, Edward Dreyer, and Robert Tallant, eds., *Gumbo Ya-Ya: A Collection of Louisiana Folk Tales* (Boston: Houghton Mifflin, 1945).

Judith Kelleher Schafer, "The Immediate Impact of Nat Turner's Insurrection on New Orleans," *Louisiana History* 22 (1980): 361–378.

"[A Second Disturbance]," *Daily Pennsylvanian* (22 September 1835), 2.

Herman Boehm de Bachellé Seebold, *Old Louisiana Plantation Homes and Family Trees* (New Orleans: Pelican, 1941).

Victor Séjour, "Le Mulâtre," *Revue des Colonies* 3 (1837): 376–392.

Soards' New Orleans City Directory (New Orleans: Soards Company, 1875).

Eileen Southern and Josephine Wright, *Images: Iconography of Music in African American Culture, 1770s–1920s* (New York: Garland Publishing, 2000).

"[Squire and James Outlawed]," *New Orleans Bee* (30 June 1836), 2.

"[Squire, Notorious Negro Outlaw]," *Cleveland Daily Herald* (1 August 1837), 1.

"Squire, the Notorious Outlaw," *Vermont Phoenix* (18 August 1837), 1.

"Squire, the Outlaw," *Clarke County Post* (25 August 1837), 2.

"Squire, the Outlaw," *Huntsville Democrat* (15 August 1837), 2.

"Squire, the Outlaw," *Jacksonville Republican* (24 August 1837), 2.

"Squire, the Outlaw," *Liberator* (11 August 1837), 132.

"Squire, the Outlaw," *Long-Island Star* (31 July 1837), 2

"Squire, the Outlaw," *Mississippi South-Western Farmer* (18 August 1837), 2.

"Squire, the Outlaw," *Natchez Weekly Courier* (28 July 1837), 1.

"Squire, the Outlaw," *New York Spectator* (31 July 1837), 2.

"Squire, the Outlaw," *Ohio Democrat* (22 September 1837), 2.

"Squire, the Outlaw," *Philadelphia Public Ledger* (27 July 1837), 1.

"Squire, the Outlaw," *Philadelphia Public Ledger* (31 July 1837), 2.

"Squire, the Outlaw," *Wilmington Democrat and Herald* (22 September 1837), 1.

"Squire—the Outlaw!" *New Orleans Picayune* (19 July 1837), 2.

A. O. Stafford, "Folk Literature of the Negro," *Crisis* 10 (1915): 296–299.

S. Frederick Starr, *Bamboula!: The Life and Times of Louis Moreau Gottschalk* (New York: Oxford Univ. Press, 1995).

Marshall Stearns, *The Story of Jazz* (New York: Oxford Univ. Press, 1956).

John Gabriel Stedman, *Narrative of a Five Years Expedition against the Revolted Negroes of Surinam,* eds. Richard Price and Sally Price (Baltimore: Johns Hopkins Univ. Press, 1988).

Robert O. Stephens, "Cable's Bras-Coupé and Merimeé's Tamango: The Case of the Missing Arm," *Mississippi Quarterly* 35 (1982): 387–405.

Ned Sublette, *The World that Made New Orleans: From Spanish Silver to Congo Square* (Chicago: Chicago Review Press, 2008).

Wylie Sypher, *Guinea's Captive Kings: British Anti-Slavery Literature of the XVIIIth Century* (Chapel Hill: Univ. of North Carolina Press, 1942).

Jean-Pierre Tardieu, "Cimarrón-Maroon-Marron: An Epistemological Note," *Outre-Mers: Revue d'Histoire* 94 (2006): 237–247.

Albert Thrasher, *On to New Orleans: Louisiana's Heroic 1811 Slave Revolt* (New Orleans: Cypress Press, 1996).

Reuben Gold Thwaites, ed., *Early Western Travels, 1748–1846*, 32 vols. (Cleveland: A. H. Clark, 1904–1907).

Edward Larocque Tinker, *Les Écrits de Langue Française en Louisiane au XIXe Siècle: Essais Biographiques et Bibliographiques* (Paris: D'Évreux, 1923).

Roulhac Toledano and Mary Louise Christovich. *New Orleans Architecture*, vol. 6, *Faubourg Tremé and the Bayou Road: North Rampart Street to North Broad Street, Canal Street to St. Bernard Avenue* (Gretna, La.: Pelican, 1980).

Robert C. Toll, *Blacking Up: The Minstrel Show in Nineteenth-Century America* (New York: Oxford Univ. Press, 1974).

Arlin Turner, *George W. Cable: A Biography* (Durham, N.C.: Duke Univ. Press, 1956).

Frederick W. Turner III, "Badmen, Black and White" (Ph.D. diss., University of Pennsylvania, 1965).

Richard Brent Turner, *Jazz Religion, the Second Line, and Black New Orleans* (Bloomington: Indiana Univ. Press, 2009).

Barry Ulanov, *A History of Jazz in America* (New York: Viking Press, 1952).

Michael Ventura, *Shadow Dancing in the U.S.A.* (New York: St. Martin's, 1985).

Erin Elizabeth Voisin, "Saint Malo Remembered" (Master's thesis, Louisiana State University, 2008).

Bryan Wagner, *Disturbing the Peace: Black Culture and the Police Power after Slavery* (Cambridge, Mass.: Harvard Univ. Press, 2009).

Raoul Walsh, dir., *Band of Angels* (Hollywood, Calif.: Warner Brothers, 1957).

Michael Warner, Natasha Hurley, Luis Iglesias, Sonia Di Loreto, Jeffrey Scraba, and Sandra Young, "A Soliloquy 'Lately Spoken at the African Theatre': Race and the Public Sphere in New York City, 1821," *American Literature* 73 (2001): 1–46.

Robert Penn Warren, *Band of Angels* (1955; reprint, Baton Rouge: Louisiana State Univ. Press, 1983).

John Fanning Watson, "Notitia of Incidents at New Orleans in 1804 and 1805," *American Pioneer* 2 (1843): 227–237.

Barry Weller, "The Royal Slave and the Prestige of Origins," *Kenyon Review* 14 (1992): 65–78.

Ida B. Wells-Barnett, *Mob Rule in New Orleans: Robert Charles and His Fight to Death, the Story of His Life, Burning Human Beings Alive, Other Lynching Statistics* (Chicago: Published by the Author, 1900).

Espy Williams, *The Dream of Art and Other Poems* (New York: G. P. Putnam's Sons, 1892).

Martin Williams, *Jazz Masters of New Orleans* (New York: Macmillan, 1967).

Winter in New Orleans: Carnival, Racing, French Opera, the Old French Quarter (Houston: Passenger Department, Southern Pacific Railroad, 1904).

Frank Yerby, *The Foxes of Harrow* (New York: Dial Press, 1946).

James S. Zacharie, *New Orleans Guide* (New Orleans: New Orleans News Company, 1885).

INDEX

Page numbers in **bold** refer to main entries. Entries in *italics* refer to figures.

247

Boukman, 1

Bras-Coupé, 1–34; as African prince, 1–2, 18–21, 44n31, 70–75, 95, 132–134; body displayed at Place d'Armes, 1, 11, 21, 23, 51, 53, 96, 98, 101, 121, 160, 169, 173, 179; Congo Square dances and, 2, 21–28, 30, 33, 70, 89–90, 102, 176, 193–194, 196–200, 228; criminal career, 5–10, *6*, 13–14, 52–53, 60–64, 96, 98, 119–120, 159, 168, 172, 177; in cypress swamp, 37n8, 70, 82–83, 159, 168, 183–185, 194, 205–206, 219; death of, *xii*, 1, 10–11, 21, 51–54, 68, 93, 96, 98, 120–121, 155, 159–160, 168–169, 172–173, 179, 194, 226–228; escape from DeBuys, 4, 60, 160, 168, 172, 176–177, 194; escape from hospital, 5, 63, 96, 120; as hero, 1, 12–14, 33–34, 95; images of, *19*, *32–33*, 102; jazz and, 2, 25–29, 33; loss of arm, 1, 5, *6*, 18, 28, 37–38n8, 52, 62–63, 70, 94–96, 119, 167–168, 172, 177, 206; love story plot, 55, 76–93, 133–157, 198–228; manhunt for, 7–8, 21, 28, 30, 61, 63–64, 98, 120, 224–225; maroon communities and, 1, 3–5, 27–28, 30, 33, 44n31, 61, 168, 180, 205–206; names and nicknames, 1, 5, 18, 52, 63, 72, 95–96, 118–119, 176; New Orleans locations, *x–xii*; in oral tradition, 1, 13–17, 20, 27–28, 55, 97–98; outlawry proclamation, 9–10, 21, 28, 38n9; press coverage of, 11–13; rewards offered for, 7–10, 28, 40n14, 52, 54, 61, 64–65, 68–69, 98, 119, 121, 169, 178–179, 217, 224–228; supernatural powers, 1, 15, 17, 42–43n23, 85, 101, 168, 178; versions of legend, 2, 13–23, 29–31; Vieux Carré locations, *x–xi*; as villain, 1, 14–15, 52, 98; voodoo and, 79, 81–82, 87–88, 131–132, 147–153; wanted posters for, 21, 28, 65, 119, 217

"Bras Coupe" (Anonymous), **97–98**

"Bras Coupé" (Garreau), 2, 13–14, **55–69**

Brer Rabbit (Compé Lapin), 99, 193

"Brigand of the Swamp" (nickname for Bras-Coupé), 5, 52, 167, 172

Bryant, William Cullen, "The African Chief," 20

Cabildo, *xi*, 179

Cable, George Washington, *xi*, 15, 31, 43nn23–24, 118; biography, 70; "Creole Slave Songs," 16; *The Grandissimes*, 2, 16–23, *19*, 30, 34n1, 46n38, **70–93**, 94–95, 123, 161; love story plot, 55, 76–93; "The Dance in Place Congo," 22–23, 47n41, **102–116**

Calinda (dance), 113–116, 166

Cane Bayou, 37n6

Carondelet Canal, *xi–xii*, 3, 13, 15, 58–59

Carter, Hodding, 36n5

Castellanos, Henry C., 11, 14, 37n8, 40n14; biography, 117; *New Orleans As It Was*, 42n23, **117–122**

Cayetano, M., 103

Charity Hospital, *xi*, 5; escape from, 5, 63, 96, 120

Charles, Robert, 34

Charleston, armed police, 8, 39n12

Chesnutt, Charles, 43n23

children, fear of Bras-Coupé, 14, 98, 100–101, 119, 168, 172, 178

Chilton, John, 26, 48n43

Christian, Marcus, 35n3; *I Am New Orleans*, 31

Ciardi, John, 195

Circus Square. *See* Congo Square

Civil War, 30, 169, 180

Cleveland Daily Herald (newspaper), 40n14

Code Noir (Black Code), 17–18, 90–91, 122, 162–163. *See also* slavery

commerce, 4

Compé Lapin (Brer Rabbit), 99, 193

Congo Square: Bras-Coupé and, 2, 21–28, 30, 33, 70, 89–90, 102, 176, 193–194, 196–200, 228; dances in, 2, *22*, 46n40, 47n41, 48n44, 164–170; description of, 164; ethnographic studies and, 46n38, 161; location of, *xi*; "The Dance in Place Congo," **102–116**. *See also* assemblies

Counjaille (dance), 111–113, 115

Creoles, 2, 15–16, 24, 29, 44n27, 64, 82, 104, 108, 111–113, 166, 168, 192; elite, 51, 70

race relations, 159. *See also* slavery

Rahman, Aishah, *Anybody Seen Marie Laveau?*, 31

Ramsey, Frederic, Jr., 25; *Jazzmen* (with Smith), 25–26, 47n41

rape, 207–215, 217, 227–228

Rau-Ru (fictional representation of Bras-Coupé), 30–31, *31*, 180–191

Reconstruction, 30, 43–44n27, 169, 180

Revue Louisianaise (newspaper), 13

rewards, for Bras-Coupé's arrest, 7–10, 28, 40n14, 52, 54, 61, 64–65, 68–69, 98, 119, 121, 169, 178–179, 217, 224–228

rhythm-and-blues musicians, *xi*

Robin Hood, Bras-Coupé as, 1, 14, 159

Roffignac, Louis Phillipe, 164

Roth, Russell, 47n41

The Royal African (1749), 20

Rubin, Louis, 43n27

runaway slaves, 3–5, 13, 15, 53, 60–61, 64, 99, 101, 118, 217, 223; newspaper notices on, 160; punishments for, 90–91, 162. *See also* maroon communities

Saint Malo, 16, 33, 43n24

Salaam, Kalamu ya, "Bras Coupe," 31

San Domingue, 22–23, 84

Saxon, Lyle, 2, 171. *See also* Louisiana Writers' Project

"Severed Arm" (nickname for Bras-Coupé), 5, 63

slave revolts, 22–23, 40n13, 100, 159, 193; fear of, 1, 8, 17, 159–160, 162–163

slavery: African royals and, 44n31; assemblies and, 45n34, 49n43, 162–166, 176; as benevolent institution, 118, 121–122; brutality of, 106, 162, 216; jazz and, 28–29; laws on, 17–18, 45n34, 90–91, 159 (*see also* Code Noir); police violence and, 8, 159; slave narratives, 13; slave trade, 20, 71, 107–108, 159, 162. *See also* runaway slaves

Slavery, or the Times (1792), 20

Slave Songs of the United States (1967), 46n40, 110

Smith, Charles E., 25; *Jazzmen* (with Ramsey), 25–26, 47n41

Squire (owned by Monsieur Gurly), 35n3

Squire/Squier (Bras-Coupé's slave name). *See* Bras-Coupé

"Squire—the Outlaw!" *(New Orleans Picayune)*, 11–12, 51, **52–53,** 168

Starr, Frederick, 24, 46n40

St. Domingo, 100

Stearns, Jean, 47n41

Stearns, Marshall, 47n41; *The Story of Jazz*, 24–26, 46n38

Stephens, Robert O., 18

St. Louis Cathedral, *xi*, 103

supernatural powers, 1, 15, 17, 42–43n23, 85, 101, 168, 178

swamp. *See* cypress swamp

Tallant, Robert, 2, 171. *See also* Louisiana Writers' Project

Third Municipality, *9*, 10, 38n9, 54

Three-Fingered Jack, 1, 33

"Tiger of the Bayous" (Gaulden), 29–30, 42n23, **174–179**

Times-Picayune (newspaper), 51

Treat It Gentle (Bechet), 2, 26–29, 48nn43–44, **195–228**

trickster tales, 99–100

Turner, Arlin, 43n27

Twayne, 195

Ulanov, Barry, 47n41

Union Army, 30, 50n47, 169, 180

"Un Nègre Marron" (Garreau), 13–14, 55

Vaudreuil, Marquis de, 163

vengeance, 14, 61, 145, 156

Vieux Carré, map of, *x–xi*

villain, Bras-Coupé as, 1, 14–15, 52, 98

voodoo, 17, 79, 81–82, 85, 87, 166, 172; Bras-